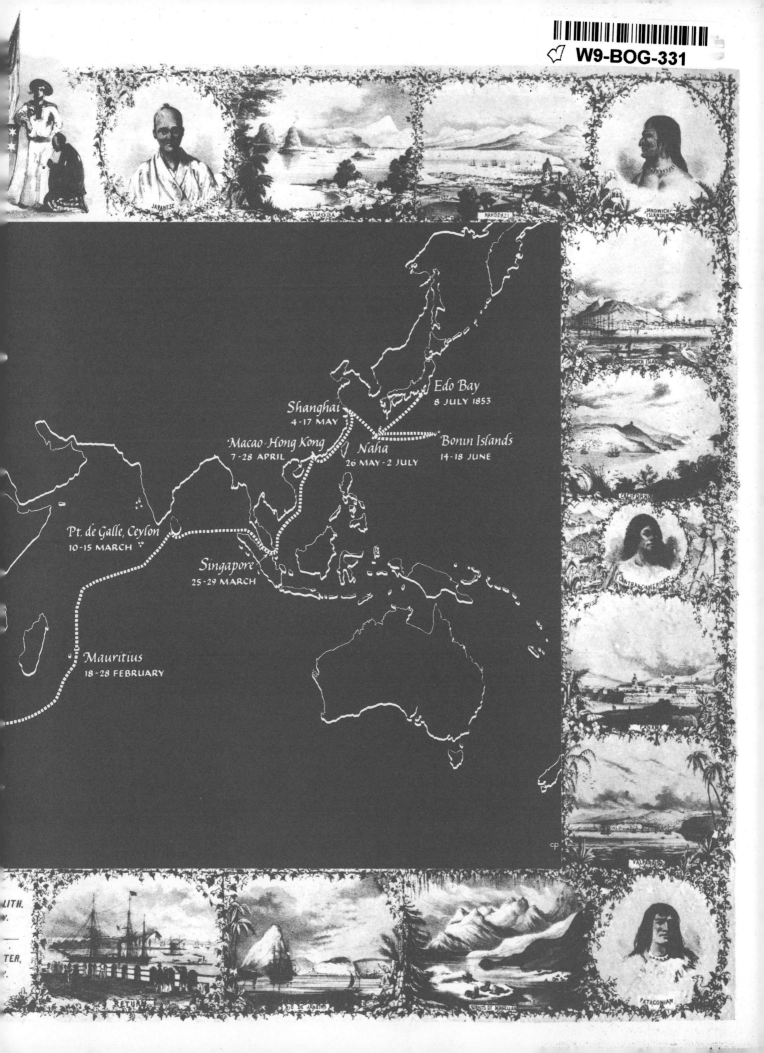

Edo Bay
8 JULY 1853

Shanghai
4-17 MAY

Macao-Hong Kong
7-28 APRIL

Naha
26 MAY-2 JULY

Bonin Islands
14-18 JUNE

Pt. de Galle, Ceylon
10-15 MARCH

Singapore
25-29 MARCH

Mauritius
18-28 FEBRUARY

THE JAPAN EXPEDITION
1852-1854

The Personal Journal
of Commodore Matthew C. Perry

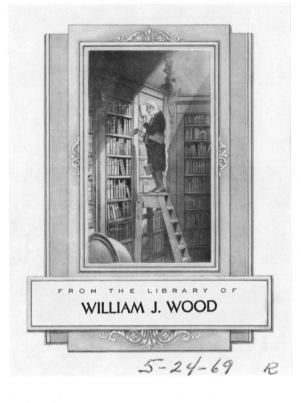

THE JAPAN EXPEDITION
1852-1854

The Personal Journal of Commodore Matthew C. Perry

Edited by ROGER PINEAU

With an Introduction by SAMUEL ELIOT MORISON

SMITHSONIAN INSTITUTION PRESS
City of Washington
1968

Dedicated to Mrs. August Belmont

In the Prefatory Note of his official *Narrative* (1856) Commodore Perry wrote that his "highest ambition" was to tell the story "in such a manner as would not only present a true picture, but also keep alive the interest of the reader." In keeping his personal journal—published now for the first time—he undoubtedly had the same "ambition," and my endeavor has been to assist in executing the Commodore's wishes. I hope that readers of this personal record will agree that the Commodore was a remarkably farsighted, perceptive, and sagacious man.

We cannot identify Commodore Perry's scrivener. The only published mention of him appears in *Harper's Weekly* for 19 March 1904, page 426, where Commodore Somerville Nicholson, USN (Retired), navigator of Commodore Perry's flagship *Powhatan* on the Japan Expedition, wrote:

Though half a century has gone by I remember the commodore as well as if I had seen him yesterday. A tall fine-looking man, he belonged to the type of old sea-dog that has passed away. Capable of using strong "cuss-words" under provocation, he was fond of his grog, and partook of the flowing bowl with a freedom that was considered becoming to a gentleman of the old school and to an officer of the old navy. At the same time, he was a man of considerable learning, with a decided taste for literary pursuits, and during the expedition to Japan he kept a very elaborate and comprehensive journal, on which he would do some work every night. Soon after dinner he would go to bed, and at about 1 A.M. he would wake up, summon young Perry, his nephew, who acted as his amanuensis, call, like Old King Cole, for his pipe and his bowl, and start in to dictate.

Unfortunately this genial and presumably eyewitness account, written half a century after the event, cannot be regarded as conclusive. "Young Perry" was the Commodore's son, Oliver Hazard Perry II, not his nephew, and he did not join the Japan Expedition until after it arrived in the Far East (see Morison, "*Old Bruin*," page 275). Yet the entire Journal is written in the same hand. Federal Bureau of Investigation experts have studied the Journal handwriting and compared it with letters written by Oliver Hazard Perry II and by scribes for Commodore Perry but found no correlation.

Perry's scrivener probably took dictation directly from the Commodore and then transcribed a fair copy on one side only of large sheets of loose paper (ten by fourteen inches) which were later bound, with the writing as verso, even-numbered pages. The recto pages were thus blank, available for watercolors, sketches, quotations, or extracts from other writings which elucidate or extend the Journal text.

It is my belief that Perry did not review this original text until 1855, when he was working with the Reverend Francis L. Hawks in preparing an official *Narrative of the Expedition of an American Squadron to the China Seas and Japan,* "compiled from the original notes and journals of Commodore Perry and his officers, at his request, under his supervision" (1856) At that time Perry read his three-volume Journal and wrote comments in it. These remarks are sparse in the first volume, more frequent in the other two. They appear usually on the otherwise blank recto pages, and sometimes on loose insert slips. Such remarks by Perry are presented in the present work as running marginal notes. In a few instances Commodore

Perry crossed out words or phrases his scriveners had written; these are indicated by a line ~~struck through~~ the type in this volume.

Footnotes from the original Journal are marked by asterisks; footnotes which I have added are numbered, with a new series for each of three parts equating to the three volumes of the original.

Dr. Hawks, as compiler of the official Narrative (and his work is referred to in my footnotes as "Hawks *Narrative*") , took the liberty of reducing some of Perry's very lengthy sentences into several short ones. I have followed his example. Various forms of representing dates in the Journal have all been presented in the logical order of day, month, and year in this work. The scrivener's Germanic practice of capitalizing the initial letter of nouns has been changed to conform to modern practice. Chance misspellings and most of the archaic spellings have been corrected, abbreviations have usually been expanded, and blank spaces filled [within brackets]. If supplying a word or words for space was speculative on my part, this is indicated in a footnote.

The Hawks *Narrative* (page 315) says: "The orthography of a language employed by a foreigner depends more or less upon his capricious estimate of the sounds that the strange words seem to his ear to possess, and accordingly different observers will necessarily employ a variety of spelling." The spelling problem was compounded on the Japan Expedition since Perry had no one who really knew the language of Japan or Okinawa. Even Chinese spellings, for which he had linguist S. Wells Williams, were not consistent because the romanization of that language was not standardized. Accordingly, I have used the device of maintaining the original Journal spelling at the first occurrence of each oriental name or word, followed by a modern rendition in brackets. Thereafter all subsequent appearances of the same word or name are in the modern form. For Chinese the Wade-Giles system of romanization is followed; for Japanese the Hepburn system. In rendering Japanese personal names I have followed the western order (given name followed by surname) rather than the Japanese practice of giving surname first.

The original Journals still exist. Volume I, owned by Mrs. August Belmont of New York City, consists of pages numbered from 6 to 336, plus 82 watercolor renderings and 9 ink or pencil drawings. The other two volumes repose in the National Archives (where they are referred to as Entry 392, Appendix D. 85½, volumes 1 and 2) , presented by the Department of the Navy, which had received them in 1946 from Commander John F. Meigs, USN (Retired) , a descendant of the Commodore. Volume II (National Archives volume 1) consists of pages numbered 8 to 372, with a dozen watercolors, a few ink or pencil drawings, and two charts. Volume III (National Archives volume 2) contains pages numbered 8 to 330, but has no illustrations. Thus the vast majority of Journal illustrations occur in Volume I, which carries the Expedition story only to late June 1853, and the first approach to the Japanese homeland. Because the original volumes lack illustrations pertaining to Japan, it has been necessary to draw on sources outside the Journal itself for depiction of Japanese events.

Foremost of these are five beautiful watercolors, one of Okinawa and four of Japan, by William Heine, the Expedition's principal artist. These are the property of Mr. and Mrs. J. William Middendorf of New York City. The Middendorfs not only lent the paintings to the Smithsonian Institution but provided financial support to permit them to be reproduced in full color. The scenes depicted in these watercolors are repeated, with some minor differences, in a set of lithographs by Heine which consists of six subjects and a cover sheet. The sixth subject is of Perry's troops drilling on the temple grounds at Shimoda, and is reproduced in this volume from a lithograph in the United States Naval Academy Museum. The cover sheet or title page has an elaborate center spread of captions for each of the six scenes, with bordering vignettes depicting various ports of call of the Expedition. That border is used in our front end papers, reproduced from a copy belonging to Mr. and Mrs. William Owens, who have one of the rare complete sets of six lithographs and cover sheet. Mr. Owens is a great-grandson of Engineer Robert Danby of flagship *Mississippi*.

Other illustrations come from a generous gift to the Smithsonian Institution by Mrs. George Tilton of Littleton, New Hampshire: twenty-five drawings of birds, by Expedition artists. Some of these are reproduced in the present volume, as are two paintings of dogs presented to Commodore Perry, which Mrs. Tilton has permitted us to reproduce.

Nine color plates depicting Okinawan and Japanese scenes of the Expedition are reproduced from Heine lithographs owned by Mr. and Mrs. W. John Kenney.

Other illustrations include photographs of Japanese art depicting various phases and views of the Expedition from the collection of Mr. Paul Blum and from the Shiryo Hensanjo (Historiographical Institute) of Tokyo University. We have also drawn on the Smithsonian Institution's Division of Naval History and the Naval Historical Foundation.

The bibliography consists of all works referred to by Commodore Perry, as well as the principal other works consulted in the editing of this volume.

The guiding star of this volume is Mrs. August Belmont, whose keen appreciation of her late husband's grandfather, the Commodore, led her to acquire this manuscript from the widow of one of his grandsons, and to allow the Smithsonian Institution Press to publish it. Since it was used as the primary source for the Hawks *Narrative*, many quotations from the journal are there given verbatim. But many other journal entries are omitted in the *Narrative*, perhaps because Perry's compiler was too timid to reveal the more tempestuous statements of his principal. Mrs. Belmont, on the contrary, has insisted that even his most outspoken statements be printed. She realizes that Commodore Perry's great prescience and integrity will be even better appreciated when it is known that these qualities were coupled with strong feelings of indignation over injustice and stupidity.

In addition to making her volume of the Journal available for publication, Mrs. Belmont and her stepgrandson Mr. August Belmont IV have financed the reproduction of 43 color plates in this volume. She has furtherx   more supplied answers to numerous questions which no amount of library research would have yielded. Her interest in and knowledge of Commodore Perry and his family is exceeded only by her appreciation and desire for all that benefits mankind.

This work is meant to be read and enjoyed. It is not intended as a scholar's source book, to serve as a letter-by-letter and comma-by-comma reproduction of the original. For that purpose the scholar may turn to the originals, or to reproductions of their pages which are on file in the Smithsonian Institution.

My assistants in this work have been too numerous for individual acknowledgment in these pages, but a few must be mentioned. Like Mrs. Belmont, Admiral Morison was willing and able to answer every question turned his way in this project, in addition to providing a gracious Introduction. It was he who instilled in me the feeling for history that makes a task such as this thoroughly enjoyable and gratifying. I also had the good fortune to accompany him and his charming wife for two months in 1966 in the wake of Commodore Perry in the Far East. That journey completed the painstaking research for his most recent publication *"Old Bruin,"* the biography of Commodore Matthew C. Perry. His able and discriminating secretary Miss Antha E. Card prepared the list of officers of the Japan Expedition which appears in Appendix C to this work. Mrs. Susan Goldsmith has contributed devotion and energy far beyond the call of duty.

Mr. Andrew Y. Kuroda of the Library of Congress gave unstintingly, as always, of his vast knowledge of the history and language of Japan. He has solved problems that other Far East experts had shrugged off as impossible. John Lyman applied his oceanographic wisdom to appreciative interpretations of Commodore Perry's work.

The British, French, Sinhalese, South African, Spanish and Thai Embassies gave prompt and willing help, as did many friends in the Library of Congress, National Archives, and Navy Departments (especially the Naval Oceanographic Office). Colleagues in the Smithsonian Institution have contributed from their widely varying stores of knowledge and otherwise encouraged this work. They and other friends have also kindly indulged my detached air or vacant stare of recent months when from time to time I have served in imagination with one of the greatest American sailors, Matthew Calbraith Perry, Commander-in-chief, United States Naval Forces, East India, China, and Japan Seas.

Roger Pineau
Bethesda, Maryland

July 1968

Contents

List of Illustrations

(SOURCE, IF OTHER THAN JOURNAL, IS INDICATED ON ILLUSTRATION.)

Commodore Matthew C. Perry after his return from Japan. Photograph by Brady
(Courtesy Library of Congress)

These Journals are a hitherto unpublished original source of the famous Japan Expedition of 1852–1855 under Commodore Matthew Calbraith Perry. The Commodore, underrating his literary powers, declined to write the official report of that Expedition himself. After an unsuccessful attempt to interest Nathaniel Hawthorne in undertaking this enterprise,[1] Perry engaged the Reverend Francis L. Hawks, Rector of Calvary Church, New York, to be the editor; and in 1855–1856 worked with him in a room at the headquarters of the American Bible Society in what was then called Astor Place, on the corner of Fourth Avenue and 8th Street, New York City. In addition to Perry's own journals, Hawks used those of flag captain Commander Henry A. Adams, Lieutenants John Contee, W. L. Maury and Silas Bent, Purser Harris, Chaplain Jones, Bayard Taylor, Perry's own secretary Oliver H. Perry II, Surgeons Green and Fahs, and others, to help him compile the report.[2] So, it is from Perry's Journal printed herewith, and the notes and diaries of his loyal officers, that the Commodore and Hawks, working together, compiled the official *Narrative*.[3] Of these important sources Perry's Journal is by far the most valuable. The original manuscript of about one third of this Journal, comprising most of the colored sketches, was inherited by Isabella Tiffany, youngest daughter of the Commodore, who left it to her son, Perry Tiffany. This manuscript was purchased from his widow by Mrs. August Belmont, whose husband was a grandson of the Commodore. Mrs. Belmont has not only graciously permitted us to print the manuscript, but she and Mr. August Belmont IV have contributed generously to the cost of the colored illustrations. The other two parts of the Journal, which contain marginal corrections and emendations in Perry's hand, are in the National Archives. We are indebted to the National Archives for permission to print, and to Miss Akiko Murakata for calling them to our attention.

The handwriting of all three manuscripts is the same; a clerical hand,

1. S. E. Morison *"Old Bruin"—Commodore Matthew C. Perry* (1967), pp. 418–21.

2. For full names, see Appendix. Other members of the Expedition, defying Perry's strict order that all notes, diaries, and journals be turned over to the Navy, retained their private journals, and several of these have subsequently been printed: S. Wells Williams, "Journal of the Perry Expedition to Japan," Asiatic Society of Japan *Transactions* XXXVII (1910); Boleslaw Szczesniak, ed., *The Opening of Japan, a Diary of Discovery in the Far East*, being the diary of Lt. George Henry Preble of *Macedonian* (1962) from the ms. in Massachusetts Historical Society; Dr. Sakanishi (Shio), ed., *A Private Journal of John Glendy Sproston*, a midshipman in *Macedonian* (1940); Henry F. Graff, ed., *Bluejackets with Perry in Japan* (1952); Allan B. Cole, ed., *With Perry in Japan: the Diary of Edward Yorke McCauley* (1942); same ed., *A Scientist With Perry in Japan: the Journal of Dr. James Morrow* (1947); Hildegarde B. Forbes, ed., *Correspondence of Dr. Charles H. Wheelwright* (1958), assistant surgeon of *Powhatan*; John S. Sewall, *Logbook of the Captain's Clerk* (1905). A few others are still in manuscript. Also, J. W. Spalding, Captain's Clerk in *Mississippi*, wrote about the Expedition in *My Voyage Around the World* (1855).

3. What I refer to as the *Narrative* is the following: *Narrative of the Expedition of an American Squadron to the China Seas and Japan, performed in the years 1852, 1853, and 1854, under the Command of Commodore M. C. Perry, United States Navy, by Order of the Government of the United States. Compiled from the Original Notes and Journals of Commodore Perry and his Officers, at his request, and under his supervision, by Francis L. Hawks, D.D., L.L.D.* Published by Order of the Congress of the United States. 3 vols. 4to. Washington: Beverley Tucker, Senate Printer, 1856. (Vols. II and III actually appeared in 1857–58). Lavishly illustrated with lithographs and woodcuts. The one-volume trade edition, published by D. Appleton Co. (1856), carries the same title but few illustrations. Abridgments: Sidney Wallach, ed., *Narrative of the Expedition*, with foreword by Rear Adm. John B. Heffernan (1954); Robert Tomes, *The Americans in Japan* (1857), and an anonymous *Japan Opened* (London: Religious Tract Soc. 1858).

xvi obviously that of Perry's flag yeoman, to use a modern term. The manuscripts are definitely not in the hand of the Commodore's son Oliver H. Perry II, who joined the Expedition at Hong Kong and acted as flag secretary.

Why have we thought it worth while to publish these original Journals of the Commodore? For several reasons. First, the Journals contain interesting personal matter discreetly omitted from the *Narrative,* such as Perry's outburst against Navy Department politics, and the shocking contrast between the China merchants' extravagant living and the penury of the sailors who protected their wealth.[4] The Journals include transcripts of Perry's correspondence with the Secretary of the Navy and others not printed in the official *Narrative,* which has become a rare and costly book. Most important, the first volume of the Journal (Mrs. Belmont's) includes many original paintings of Oriental scenes, plants, fruits and shells some of which we now reproduce for the first time. Those of the plants are the more valuable because the official floral paintings were never handed over to Perry and Hawks, and appear to have been irretrievably lost, owing to the selfish egotism of the artist, Dr. James Morrow.

This leads one to a consideration of Perry's attitude toward artists and scientists. He has been accused of entertaining an ignorant, "salt-horse sailor" prejudice against both; and it must be admitted that his statements about them in the Journal[5] lend color to this charge. The truth of the matter, I believe, is this: Perry himself was a competent amateur scientist (his special interests being botany and conchology), and he considered the Expedition an opportunity to make a comprehensive report on Japan. He wished to correct false statements by earlier writers and to bring out the true nature of Japanese society, commerce, fisheries, and agriculture. To that end he, or the department, sought an appropriation for a scientific corps to accompany the Expedition, analogous to Napoleon's which produced the remarkable 13-volume *Description de l'Egypte* (1809–1826), but was told it was no use trying to get the money. He also had the precedent of the Pacific Exploring Expedition of 1838–1843, for which Commander Wilkes was allowed to recruit civilian artists and scientists at salaries up to $2500 a year. Wilkes did enlist several specialists, but the experiment was not altogether successful; naval officers and men of science did not get along well together, and Congress was very slow to publish their scientific reports—the last did not appear until 1871. Since the Navy Department regarded the Japan Expedition primarily and essentially as a diplomatic mission, it refused to make any special provision for civilian scientists. Hence the only way Perry could obtain experts was to persuade them to accept a naval rating of acting master's mate with pay of $25 per month. As he explained to Captain Abbot, they were so rated "by special authority of the Department to give to certain scientific persons some definite position, and to make them amenable to Naval Law." Naturally he could obtain only relatively young and ad-

4. Below, pp. 59–60.
5. Below, pp. 6, 9.

venturous men on those terms. But he did select two artists, William Heine and Eliphalet Brown, Jr., from several score who applied, and it is their long-hidden paintings of scenery and plants which we reproduce for the first time here.

Peter Bernhard Wilhelm Heine, to give him his full name, was a native of Germany, twenty-five years old, who had been in the United States three years before shipping as acting master's mate with Perry. Most of the paintings we have reproduced were his. Others were by Eliphalet Brown, Jr., a pioneer photographer who gave up a lucrative business in New York to accompany Perry. He brought a daguerreotype camera and an abundance of plates with which he took many "stills" of scenery and people, and some of our illustrations, initialed W. T. Peters or H. Patterson, were undoubtedly redrawn by these two rather obscure New York artists from Brown's daguerreotypes, of which most of the originals have been lost. The other artist of the expedition, Dr. James Morrow, a 33-year-old physician who had dabbled with tropical botany on his father's plantation in South Carolina, was "wished" on Perry by the Department of State and sent out in the *Vandalia* to join him. Morrow, with the aid of S. Wells Williams and Purser Harris of *Susquehanna,* made a valuable collection of dried floral specimens which fortunately were identified by Professor Asa Gray of Harvard and (after an unseemly controversy) delivered just in time to be printed in Volume II of the *Narrative.* But Morrow withheld all his paintings of living Chinese and Japanese plants, in the hope of persuading the Department of State to publish them in a separate volume with the Asa Gray report and his private journal, over his own name. The Department refused, and Morrow's paintings have never come to light.[6] Hence the importance of those which we have recovered, by the two loyal artists.

Perry relaxed his rule against shipping civilians without a naval commission, in order to obtain necessary assistance. At Shanghai he took on board Bayard Taylor, a 28-year-old man of letters; at Macao he engaged S. Wells Williams, a leading American sinologist, as interpreter, and at Shanghai he procured a second and even more useful interpreter, Antón Portman, a subject of the Netherlands. For scientific work, however, he depended largely on his own officers such as Chaplain George Jones who doubled as geologist and astronomer, and several young men who sounded the waters adjacent to Okinawa, the Bonins and parts of Japan, and came up with excellent charts. Their reports are published in Volume II of the official *Narrative.*

One subject on which this Journal is more explicit than the *Narrative* is the description of life in the Chinese treaty ports. Here Perry shows his innate curiosity and appetite for detail. There is probably no other contemporary book where one can find such interesting data on the servants, common laborers, tailors and shopkeepers of China, the beggars, lepers and floating population of Canton River, and the peculiar amalgam of Portuguese and Chinese culture that was Macao. Astonishing are Perry's stories

6. Morison, *"Old Bruin,"* pp. 279, 421–4, 465.

of the eating capacity of the Chinese workers; it would seem that, like the American Indians, they were so often starved that when plenty of food was offered by Americans they gorged on it to fortify themselves against lean days to come.

Perry's Journals, moreover, contain more details on his efforts to protect China merchants against the Tai-Ping rebels than will be found outside the archives. His finesse is evident in that, whilst declining to take orders from the two United States ministers to China, Marshall and McLane, he managed to please the American China merchants and, without diminishing the strength of his squadron when visiting Japan, to afford ample protection to his compatriots in China.

Although Perry's account of the treaty negotiations on his second visit, in 1854, is necessarily one-sided, a comparison with the Japanese sources indicates that it is both fair and correct.[7] One Japanese chronicler does indicate that the Commodore once lost his temper when exasperated by Japanese procrastination, and threatened to come back with a bigger fleet and fight if they refused to treat; but in general he conducted himself with a firmness, dignity, and consideration that the Japanese respected and admired. The description of Perry as a boorish and bullying "imperialist" by certain leftist historians who are incapable of understanding, much less appreciating, a character such as his, is refuted by his own Journal as well as by those of the Japanese with whom he treated. And, on the other side, Perry's Journal is a convincing proof that he learned to like his unwilling hosts in the short time that he had contact with them. Moreover, in contrast to the attitude of other Westerners, who found the Japanese physiognomy strange and uncouth, Perry compares the faces of the three leading Japanese commissioners with three contemporary American statesmen— Jame Buchanan, Secretary Thomas Corwin, and Postmaster-General Cave Johnson.[8]

What we might call the key to Perry's attitude and to his success is embodied in this one sentence:

It struck me that it was better to have no treaty than one that would in the least compromise the dignity of the American character; and to agree to any arrangement that would recognize in the remotest degree the restrictions submitted to by the Dutch, could not for a moment be thought of.

Conversely, he took great care to respect the sovereignty of Japan and the dignity of individual Japanese.

Amusing details will be found of the somewhat uproarious dinners tendered by Perry to the Japanese on board *Powhatan,* and by the Japanese Commissioners to him and his aides ashore. Here is the original story, usually attributed to the wrong person, of how the chief Japanese commissioner's secretary, at the conclusion of the shipboard banquet, threw his arms about the Commodore's neck, "repeating in Japanese, as translated into English, 'Nippon and America all the same heart,' and in his drunken

7. See Morison, "*Old Bruin,*" pp. 357–82.
8. Below, p. 184.

embrace crushing my new epaulettes." And Perry includes a detailed account of his "long stroll" around Yokohama, in the course of which he was entertained by the mayor, with women and children present; a privilege accorded to no other foreigner for more than two centuries. His description of the *sumo* wrestling match is one of the highlights of the Journal. And far more detail is given of Perry's imprudent trip up Edo Bay to get a glimpse of the Shogun's capital, than is found in the official *Narrative*.[9]

At Hakodate, Hokkaido, Perry enjoyed his first opportunity to enter the homes of the better sort of Japanese, and to describe their methods of serving and eating meals. And there are documents on the negotiation at Shimoda over the rate of exchange between the dollar and the *ryo*, in which Captain Abbot asserts that the Japanese put it all over the Americans, so that the visitors could purchase souvenirs only at an exorbitant cost in their own currency.

Be that as it may, Shimoda left a very favorable impression on the squadron, and the feeling was mutual. After the lapse of over a century, Americans who visit that pretty resort and fishing town at the tip of the Izu Peninsula will find a bust of Perry facing the harbor, an Opening of Japan Monument on the heights with Perry's conciliatory words inscribed; a Perry-Harris Museum, and a complete line of souvenirs representing the "Black Ships" of the Americans, the meetings of local officials with Perry and his officers, and sundry other symbols of Japanese-American friendship.

9. Cf. S. E. Morison, *"Old Bruin,"* pp. 357–82.

Volume 1   November 1852 – June 1853

The delays and difficulties which have beset me in the equipment of the

vessels, designated to form the force to be placed under my command, for service in the East India and China seas, and especially with reference to the expedition to Japan, have been notorious, and often commented on. I shall at this time make no further allusion to the circumstances connected with those untoward disappointments, than to remark that they were not calculated to advance the reputation for science, skill, or energy of those who had the direction at the time.

It is my duty, and it certainly is a pleasure to say, that the President,[1] and every member of his cabinet evinced the liveliest interest in the expedition. They extended toward me the utmost kindness and consideration, authorized the most liberal equipment of the vessels, and invested me with extraordinary powers—diplomatic as well as naval. Yet with all these advantages and notwithstanding my frequent visits to Washington, and constant importunities and complaints, I made but little progress in accomplishing the first step in the great work assigned to me.

After waiting nine months beyond the time at which the chief of the Bureau of Construction and Equipment had promised to have the steamer *Princeton* completed, that vessel on trial was found to be utterly inefficient for service owing to the imperfection of her boilers, they having been constructed upon a new and, in this country, an untried plan. Finding that unless I sailed alone—and trusted to the chances of being joined at uncertain periods by the vessels assigned to my command and under equipment —I might be detained several months longer, I determined with the consent of the department to proceed with steamer *Mississippi* without further delay. Consequently I sailed from Norfolk on 24 November 1852, intending to touch on the outward passage for supplies of coal and refreshments at Madeira, the Cape of Good Hope, Mauritius, and Singapore.

The *Mississippi* has always been a favorite with me. As the flagship of a former squadron under my command she has rendered good service.[2] With God's Providence, I may still hope with her and other vessels of my squadron to accomplish something that may redound to the honor and credit of the country.

On 12 December we arrived at Madeira after a boisterous passage of 18

days, having made land on the previous evening. The wind for the first ten days out was strong from southward, then changed to NNE making a heavy wallowing sea. When it did haul to westward, it blew with such violence as to render the ship very uncomfortable; but she behaved, as she ever has done, most admirably, averaging during the whole passage more than seven knots. Though riding unusually deep, only eight of the twelve furnaces

1. Millard Fillmore, 13th President of the United States, 1850–1853.
2. Commodore Perry, in flagship *Mississippi*, had commanded the Mexican Gulf Squadron in 1847–1848.

4   were used, and the daily consumption was equal to about 26 tons of Cumberland coal. A southwestern current of a knot per hour[3] was experienced after crossing the gulf stream, which continued until within a thousand miles of Madeira, when it ceased altogether, nor did our observation indicate any current whatever during the remainder of the passage.

On making the northern extremity of the island, Tristram Point [Punta Tristão] the wind was blowing strongly from the WSW producing a heavy rolling sea. The ship was therefore run to the north of the island in view of finding a smoother sea, the more conveniently to bend the cables. In running along the northern and eastern shores of the island several very pretty villages were observed occupying sheltered nooks, usually at the bottom of some ravine and near to an indentation of the coast offering indifferent anchorage to small vessels employed in transporting the produce of the island to the shipping port Funchal. The rainy season had just passed and the torrents could be seen from the ship, rushing down the mountains, forming many beautiful cascades, several of which were sketched by our artist.

Knowing that the wind for the last few days had thrown into the Bay of Funchal a heavy swell, rendering the anchorage unsafe, it had been determined to run under the lee of the "Deserters,"[4] and there await a favorable moment for anchoring at Funchal. But, in rounding the southeastern point of Madeira, it was found that the wind had considerably abated, and had hauled northward of west, making it safe to proceed immediately to the anchorage. Accordingly, the ship came to anchor just at dark in 33 fathoms water; the castle back of the town just open with the Loo Rock.[5]

Mr. Robert Bayman, the United States vice consul, and several coal agents were soon alongside and arrangements were promptly made to send on board all the coal and water that might be wanted so as to permit the vessel to sail on Wednesday night. Accordingly, at daylight of the following day (Monday, 13 December) lighters containing coal and water were seen coming off. Though the weather was bad the whole of the first day, by Wednesday at four o'clock 440 tons of coal and 10,000 gallons of water, besides many other articles, had been received on board, and the ship left that evening under steam. The coal obtained here was of equal parts of Welsh and Newcastle, costing on delivery on board about $10 per ton.[6]

The coal agents were exceedingly desirous that the vessel should be anchored much closer toward the town, in about ten fathoms, so as to be sheltered from the westerly winds by the Loo Rock. But I was satisfied that it would be difficult to get safely out of the port in blowing weather from such

3. Perry's use of both "seven knots" (two lines above) and "a knot per hour" in such close proximity characterizes the 19th-century change in meaning of "knot." Earlier it had meant "a nautical mile," but it came to mean "a nautical mile per hour." Bowditch did not adopt the new meaning until 1881, but Perry had the support of good usage as to both meanings in 1852.

4. Ilhas Desertas, which lie 20 miles ESE of Funchal.

5. Forte de Nossa Senhora da Conceição at latitude 32°38'20.7" N, longitude 16°54'52.8" W. The present breakwater extends 850 yards eastward of Loo Rock.

6. This sentence appeared on a succeeding page in the manuscript.

anchorage, even with a steamer, and I positively forbade it. The anchorage
in Funchal Bay is unsafe in winter, and vessels lying in the road, when
expecting a gale from southeast round to WSW most generally put to sea,
and remain out until fine weather returns.

I abstain from entering upon any description of this place. So much has
already been written and published on the subject that it would be folly for
me to add a single remark other than to say that Funchal has lost none of its
beauties, and is still remarkable for the hospitality of its inhabitants. There
is no one of the leading men of the city more open hearted or more disposed
to entertain in the most liberal manner than our consul Mr. J. Howard
March, whose town and country houses are always open to his countrymen.
Mr. March has held the consulate for more than thirty years, has amassed a
large fortune in the wine trade, and I know of no one who spends his money
in a more gentlemanlike manner.

The crop of the last year having entirely failed, the laboring classes have
suffered considerably for want of their usual employment in plucking and
preparing the fruit for the press; but the loss of the crop has not materially
affected the prices of good wines.

Everyone knows that Funchal is a frequent resort of strangers who go
thither principally from England in search of health. The love of the
English for exercise in the open air has brought about many contrivances
for the conveyance of invalids and as the streets of the city are paved in such
manner as to forbid the use of wheel carriages, sedan chairs and hammocks
were until very recently used, not only by invalids but by all in making
formal visits.

The inconvenience of these has caused the introduction of a most novel
contrivance, which is nothing more than the common sled used for hauling
casks of wine, and other heavy weights through the paved streets. This—sur-
mounted by a sort of carriage, top gaily decorated and drawn by a yoke of
oxen—is now the fashionable conveyance.

With this equipage as the most fashionable, I made, in company with the
flag captain and my aide, all my official visits. They are kept in the streets
already yoked up—if I may use the term—as hacks or cabs are in other
places, and the price per hour is fifty cents.

I may as well remark here that the corps of artists attached to the ship will
sketch whatever they may find worthy of notice at the different places to be
visited during the cruise, a few of which will be appended to this journal.

On leaving Madeira, we shaped our course to pass to the westward of
Palma, one of the Canaries which was made at daylight of Friday the 17th
and after reaching the lee of Hierro or Ferro the southwesternmost of the
group, ten of the floats or paddle boards of the wheels on each side were
removed, the fires put out, and the ship left entirely dependent upon her
sails. At the time the floats were removed the wind was blowing moderately
from the ESE, and we had every reason to expect that it would gradually
settle into the northeast trades, but very much to our surprise it hauled more

to the south, and eventually came from the SSW. The weather was so much obscured that we saw nothing of the island of Teneriffe, though we had an indistinct view of Gomera.

I have been not a little surprised to notice since leaving Norfolk, now nearly a month past, an extraordinary swell coming from the northwest which was not intermitted for a moment until we got fairly into the trades. Even then it interposed its influence to disturb the regular sea—which is usually produced by the periodical winds—and caused a most disagreeable cross movement of the waves. It is difficult to account for this long-continued swell. Certainly we experienced no violence of wind to produce it in the region we traversed, and the winds since the 18th have been quite moderate. The presumption must therefore be that a succession of northwesterly gales in the higher latitudes has prevailed, setting in motion an ocean wave, which was not subdued until it came in contact with the steady though more quiet tropical swell.

From the time of removing the floats up to 20 December the wind continued from southward and westward, when it hauled to the north and westward, and finally into the northeast. Not until this period—about 8 P.M. of the 20th in latitude 25°44′ N, longitude 20°23′ W—should we consider this ship to have entered fairly into the trades. It is worthy of remark at a meridian unusually far south, whether the probable prevalence of strong westerly gales as before suggested may not have driven back and confined the northern boundary of the trades.

Shipboard Discipline

It is well known that I pertinaciously resisted the extraordinary influence that was brought to bear upon the government by literary and scientific persons, travelers and others from all quarters of the world to obtain employment, or to be permitted upon any terms to take part in the service entrusted to my guidance.

I was well satisfied that in the delicate duties which I should be called upon to perform, the most exact order and discipline should be maintained, and to effect which strict military control would be necessary. It could not be expected that civilians would submit patiently to the restraint of naval discipline, to the confinement of shipboard, and to the sanitary rules, necessary to the preservation of health in crowded ships.

I also knew there would be no room to spare after the proper officers of the vessels were accommodated. Scientific men, accustomed to the comfort of a shore life and abundant space for their instruments and books, would find themselves constantly annoyed by the confinement to narrow uncomfortable quarters. They would be disappointed in not being permitted to go here and there as their curiosity and desire for research might dictate. They would in all probability from inexperience or inadvertence fall into difficulties with the people on shore which might cause me much embarrassment and trouble. I therefore deemed it most prudent to decline their services altogether

Madeira Harbor scene showing U.S.S. *Mississippi* at anchor, December 1852. Sketch by H. Patterson

Hammocks were still used as a mode of travel at Madeira in 1852.

8 upon occasion of this experimental expedition to Japan, promising that if my efforts to open a friendly intercourse with this singular government were crowned with success, then those in pursuit of science might follow and be protected by our ships.

And besides I have always thought that if the same facilities were offered by the government to the officers of the Navy, that have been given to professors and students of colleges in gathering information upon scientific subjects they might not, and perhaps would not, perform the service as fully and with equal research, yet having the advantage of a good deal of practical knowledge they would be enabled to observe and write down much that would be useful, and thus furnish a fund of information to be revised and explained by scientific persons at home.

And after all, the expedition to Japan is altogether of a naval and diplomatic character, and was never intended to embrace in its operations scientific researches. Still I have determined that all shall be done under the circumstances to subserve the objects of science, and accordingly in carrying out the views and opinions already expressed, I have found it advisable to issue the following General Orders No. 1 and 2.

General Order No. 1

United States Steam Frigate *Mississippi*
At sea. 22 December 1852.[7]

In promulgating the subjoined extract from the instructions addressed to me by the Honorable Secretary of the Navy, and bearing date the 13th ultimo, I have to enjoin upon all officers and other persons attached to the vessels under my command, or in any [other][8] way connected with the squadron a most rigid adherence to all the requirements of said order.

Whatever notes or drawings may be prepared by the officers or other persons before mentioned, whether by special order or by their own volition will be endorsed by the respective parties, and transmitted through the captain of the fleet to the Commander-in-chief, who will in due time lodge them at the Navy Department, from whence they may or may not be reclaimed as it may be deemed expedient by the government [from whence they may be reclaimed as it may suit the convenience of the government].

All [arms,] curiosities and specimens of natural history are also to become the property of the United States, unless voluntarily relinquished by the Commander-in-chief.

(signed) M. C. Perry
Commander-in-chief United States Naval Forces
stationed in the East India and China Seas.

Extract

A subject of great importance to the success of the expedition will present itself to your mind in relation to communications to the prints and newspapers touching the movements of your squadron, as well as in relation to all matters connected with the discipline and internal regulations of the vessels composing it. You will therefore enjoin upon all under your command to abstain from writing to friends

7. Copy in *Mississippi* log is dated 21 December.
8. Copy in *Mississippi* log contains bracketed words.

and others upon those subjects. The journals and private notes of the officers and other persons in the expedition must be considered as belonging to the government until permission shall be received from the Navy Department to publish them.

General Order No. 2

United States Steam Frigate *Mississippi*
At sea. 23 December 1852.

Entertaining the opinion that if the talents and acquirements of the officers of the squadron are properly developed and brought into action, they will be found equal to a plain and practical examination and elucidation of the various objects pertaining to the arts and sciences that may come under their observation during the present cruise, and being aware of the limited accommodations of the vessels under my command, I have invariably objected to the employment of persons drawn from civil life to conduct those departments more immediately connected with science.

Therefore I have to request and to direct that each officer of the respective ships may employ such portions of his time as may be spared from his regular duties and proper hours of relaxation in contributing to the general mass of information which it is desirable to collect. In order to simplify and methodize these researches a paper is subjoined, particularizing the various departments in reference to which information is more especially wanted, so that each officer may select that or those departments which may seem most congenial to his tastes and inclinations.

All captains and commanders are required to render every facility consistent with the proper duties of their respective vessels to those officers who may manifest a zealous cooperation in the pursuits herein specified. It is to be plainly understood that I do not officially require the officers to perform any involuntary duty, I shall exact only that which may come legitimately within the sphere of my authority, leaving to the officers themselves to engage, as far as they may see fit in those investigations which, in an official point of view, may be considered gratuitous.

And it will always give me the greatest pleasure to identify and bring to proper notice the labors of each and every individual who may contribute to the general work.

(signed) M. C. Perry
Commanding East India Squadron

Departments for Observations
referred to in General Order No. 2

1 Hydrography.
2 Meteorology—currents at sea—etc.
3 Naval architecture and its adaptation to war and commerce.
4 Military affairs.
5 Geology and geographical observations.
6 Terrestrial magnetism.
7 Philology and ethnology.
8 Artistic matters, costumes, etc.
9 Religions of nations.
10 Diseases and sanitary laws.
11 Agricultural observations.
12 Statistics of supplies.

13 Mechanics as applied to naval purposes.
14 Infusoriae and marine algae.
15 Botany.
16 Entomology.
17 Ornithology.
18 Zoology.
19 Conchology.
20 Ichthyology.
21 Magnetic telegraph.

Atlantic Weather and Wind

During the 21st, 22nd, and 23rd the wind continued from the northward and eastward, but about noon of the 23rd, it inclined to the southward of east. In the night, however, it hauled more to the north and at noon of the 24th, when abreast of Brava and Fogo [Cape Verde Islands], it was about ENE by compass.

The haze continued to obscure the atmosphere so as to give us barely a glimpse of Fogo. This haze is common to these latitudes especially in the winter months and is caused, it is supposed, by an impalpable dust which is taken up by the wind in the interior of Africa, and carried by its influence a long distance to the westward. I have noticed it more than 500 miles west of the Cape Verde Islands. This wind is called harmattan, has been described in a series of letters, addressed by me when in command of the African Squadron to W. C. Redfield, Esquire, the distinguished and well known American meteorologist,[9] and as the observations then made may be appropriately referred to in this journal, I subjoin some extracts.

Letters from the Coast of Africa, No. 2.

African Squadron, West Coast of Africa.
January 1844.

William C. Redfield, Esquire. New York.

My dear Sir.—Having referred in my first letter to the seasons and the rains which prevail during one of those periods, I now proceed to remark upon the prevailing winds, which for better explanation may be classed under four heads; as follows:

First. The tornadoes preceding and following the rains.
Second. The southwesterly winds, blowing during the rains.
Third. The sea and land breezes, prevailing with little interruption in the dry season, except when intermitted by the harmattans.
Fourth. The harmattans.

The tornadoes take their rise in the eastern board, and invariably give timely notice of their approach.

They first appear in the distance over the land as a small light-colored irregular

9. William C. Redfield (1789–1857). His explanation of the mechanism of extended hurricanes made him a principal contributor to scientific knowledge of the earth's atmosphere. He was a founder and first president of the American Association for the Advancement of Science.

cloud which, as it approaches the sea, gradually expands and forms itself into an arc of a circle, assuming a dark grayish appearance. Within the center of the arc faint flashes of lightning* are seen and distant thunder is heard.

When the cloud has reached within a few miles of the observer, it has assumed a more threatening and terrific aspect. The arc so distinctly seen before has now changed into an extensive undefined opaque mass. The lightning has become more vivid, and the thunder more appalling. In a moment the whole surrounding space is as dark as Erebus, and the tornado strikes the ship with all its force; the rain falls in torrents, and the thunder and lightning are awful beyond expression.

This state of things is of a short duration, seldom exceeding forty minutes. The tornado passes to leeward, becoming less furious as it recedes from the land.

Prudent seamen prepare their ships for these squalls by furling all the sails excepting the fore topmast staysail, and by presenting the stern of the vessel to the point from which the gust will come so that she may be struck "en poupe."

It must not be understood that all tornadoes are as severe as described above; it is only occasionally that they blow with so much violence. Nor can any calculation be made when to expect them. As many as three have been known to occur in a day, and again, weeks have elapsed without one.

The atmosphere after a tornado becomes remarkably clear, and the sky even more brilliant than usual. The air is balmy and refreshing and remains so until the sun again exercises his influence to heat it and to destroy its elasticity.

The southwesterly winds, which prevail during the rainy season, rarely increase beyond a double-reefed topsail breeze. They frequently veer several points, and are intermitted by calms and light airs from various quarters; but they blow with sufficient constancy to be depended on in making a passage, indeed it is only during the rainy season that any correct estimate can be made as to the probable length of passages on this coast.

These winds produce a short disagreeable sea, and throw a heavy surf upon the coast, making the landing always inconvenient and sometimes with ships' boats impracticable; but the natives launch their light canoes through the surf at all seasons without difficulty and danger.

During the prevalence of the southwesterly winds, which as before observed are generally accompanied by rain, the sky is obscured and the atmosphere is frequently so thick as to prevent for days the ordinary astronomical observations; yet there is seldom a day that faint glimpses of the sun are not seen, and at these times the land may be descried at a distance of two or three leagues.

In regard to the convenience of navigating the coast, the weather of the rainy season is preferable to that produced by the harmattan, when the haze is sometimes extremely thick. The sea and land breezes are not dissimilar to those common to other tropical regions, except that they are not so regular and are lighter. The land breeze generally commences at three or four o'clock A.M. and continues until nine or ten, and the sea breeze may be expected shortly after noon, and to terminate about ten at night.

The harmattan is the most remarkable of the winds of this coast. It commences about the middle of December, and continues until the latter end of March. A thousand stories are told of its singular effects quite as miraculous as those related by Brydone[10] of the sirocco of the coast of Barbary. It is positively asserted that its dry and subtle properties will check or cure various disorders, heal up the most inveterate ulcers, destroy cabinet work, fracture window glass, stop the motion of

* The faint lightning within the arc is a certain indication of a tornado.

10. Patrick Brydone (1743–1818), *A Tour Through Sicily and Malta* (Dublin: J. Potts, 1774 and many later editions).

timepieces, and produce various phenomena hard to be credited. My own observations have satisfied me that its effects are certainly most extraordinary. In some respects it resembles the sirocco as also the levanter of the Grecian archipelago. (Euroclydon of the Bible) *

Like the sirocco, it is supposed to take its rise in the deserts of Africa, but instead of the burning and oppressive termperature of the sirocco, it is a chilly wind. Its direction is always from the land, and it sometimes increases to a strong breeze; it does not blow continually during its season, but is frequently intermitted by sea and land breezes.

At Cape Verde and the Gambia, where the northeast trades prevail, the harmattan appears to form a junction with those winds, and to blow with little interruption from January until April.

In passing over the deserts and lands of the interior the harmattan takes up an immense quantity of sand and dust, which forms a floating mass, producing an atmosphere so hazy as frequently to obscure the sun, and prevent the sight of land at a distance of two miles. Whether the haze is produced altogether by the impalpable matter just mentioned, I am unable to say. Certain it is, that this peculiar state of atmosphere is common at the season of the harmattan at the Cape de Verde Islands, lying four hundred miles from the continent, and when it is most dense the sand is constantly falling upon the rigging and decks of ships cruising among those islands. I have it from good authority that this peculiar wind and its attendant atmosphere has been met with at least seven hundred miles farther westward.

Yours with respect—"Y."[11]

The northeast trades continued with us until the 30th, the ship having reached the latitude of 6°08′ north and longitude 16°34′ west, when, in a squall from the eastward, the wind changed to the southward, and so continued though in some measure variable until 2 January 1853, in latitude 1°44′ north, and longitude 11°37′ west. At this point we met the southeast trades, bringing with them a swell which, with the wind being directly ahead, retarded our progress considerably.

Finding that the northeast trades had become light and unsteady with occasional calms, and that our progress was not such as was desirable and necessary to my plans the buckets were replaced on 29 December, and the ship again put under steam, filling and using, however, the two after boilers only, at a daily consumption of 15 tons of bituminous coal.

So long as the wind continued light and the sea smooth we could with the two boilers keep up a pressure of eight pounds and make seven knots. But

* From personal observation and experience of the winds of the Grecian archipelago, I am satisfied that the gale in which St. Paul was wrecked, was from the northeast, and not southeast as many assert, and that he was cast upon Melita of the Lybian Sea (now Malta) and not upon Meleda on the coast of Illyneum [Illyricum].[12] This I will endeavor to explain to you more fully at some future time.

11. No ready explanation has been found for this signature. It may indicate the yeoman who assisted the Commodore's son, O. H. Perry II, with secretarial duties.

12. Meleda (now Mljet or Melita, at 42°45′N, 17°30′E) had sometimes been mistaken for St. Paul's landing place, perhaps because of the mention in Acts 27:27 of Adria, which in olden days included that part of the Mediterranean between Sicily and Malta on the west and Crete on the east, not just the Adriatic of today.

when the southeast trades fairly set in, accompanied by the head sea before mentioned, not more than five knots was accomplished. Consequently the two forward boilers were filled and we continued to steam with eight fires making about seven knots, at a daily consumption of 26 tons.

I had calculated on leaving Madeira to have made the entire passage to the Cape of Good Hope without stopping, believing, with a proper use of the sails, the supply of coal on board would be sufficient. But in consequence of the northeast trades having left us at a point unusually far north at this season of the year, and the early setting in of the southeast trades, I ordered the ship to be steered so as to enable us to touch at St. Helena, if it should be found desirable so to do, though under ordinary circumstances the ship could steam direct to her destined port. It may be a measure of prudence to add to our coal at St. Helena and, hence, it is probable I may decide to. stop there for a day.

I shall say but little of the currents by which we have been influenced since leaving Norfolk. Long experience and observation at sea have satisfied me that all currents are caused by the influence of the winds upon the surface of the ocean, whether these winds be of long or short duration. Though the rule may not always hold good, it may be generally inferred that the current will be setting at a distance from the land in the direction of the prevailing winds. We certainly have found it so thus far on our cruise.

The prevailing westerly winds of the North Atlantic, as everyone knows, bend the current of the Gulf Stream from the tail of the Newfoundland Bank to the southeast. When it reaches the neighborhood of the Azores it divides, the main branch passing the vicinity of Madeira, where it receives new force from the northeast trades, and in the course of time flows into the [Caribbean] Sea,[13] and thence through the West India islands, and Yucatan passage into the Gulf of Mexico, and again returns in its regular circuit through the Honda Straits; while the lesser branch diverging at the Azores flows toward the Mediterranean, a part turning southwardly along the African coast following the sinuosities of the shores until its passing the bights of Benin and Bicifra.[14]

There are other currents in the North Atlantic. The Arctic or Greenland current and the Newfoundland current which meet that of the Gulf Stream, and aid in deflecting it to the southward and eastward, and is itself in some measure deflected to the eastward and even north of east by its [own rotation][15] and warmer stream.

This current or that part of it which does not join with and follow the course of the main stream—by way of the Azores and Madeira—flows more to the north and strikes the coast of Europe at different points from Cape Finistera to the British Channel. By the peculiar form of the coast, added to local causes, it is repulsed, and a counter stream is produced which sets from

13. Name omitted, but Caribbean seems intended.
14. Now called Biafra. These two bights are on the Atlantic in the Gulf of Guinea on the coast of west central Africa.

the Bay of Biscay toward the [southern entrance][15] of the English and Irish Channels.

The southeast trade is the principal cause of what is called the equatorial current, and that which passes round Cape St. Roque in South America. But it receives its first impulse from a current which flows out of the Indian Ocean round the Cape of Good Hope. This current is accelerated by the prevailing winds in the South Atlantic, and on reaching the equatorial latitudes arrives at its greatest velocity.

It has never yet been satisfactorily ascertained by practical seamen to what depth from the surface the currents retain their influence, or whether there may not be as many suppose, at no great depth, currents setting in contrary directions.[16]

Much has been written and published upon the winds and currents of the ocean, and one would suppose that the subject had been exhausted, but notwithstanding the plain and satisfactory accounts of distinguished navigators for the last two centuries, and the elaborate researchers and explanations of Rennel, Redfield, and Reed, we have been recently favored with discoveries innumerable in almost every branch of natural philosophy having reference to the ocean, so that we stand confounded at our former ignorance.[17]

On Monday the 3rd of January at 11:30 A.M. the ship crossed the equator, in longitude 11°01′ west. From that time up to the present date, the 7th, we have had a moderately fresh breeze directly in our teeth (south by compass) which has made the officers' apartments—especially the cabin and indeed all the after part of the vessel—exceedingly uncomfortable, as the wind has brought much of the heat and smoke from the furnaces directly upon us. Since crossing the equator, a current of about one and a half miles per hour has been experienced setting in the direction of the wind, about northwest.

In passing through the equatorial latitude we have noticed with much interest the zodiacal lights, which have been very brilliant and so remarkable that several sketches of their appearance have been taken and preserved.

St. Helena
10–11 JANUARY 1853

We arrived at Jamestown Island of St. Helena on Monday, 10 January 1853 at noon, and sailed the following day at 6 P.M. having received on board 130 tons of coal, with some water, fresh beef, and vegetables for the crew.

15. Two words supplied to fill blanks in the original.

16. Perry's curiosity was fully warranted, and it was decades before the earliest scientific answers to these questions were available. Since then the influence of surface currents has been measured at depths up to 800 meters. Subsurface contrary currents—sometimes three or four in a single location—exist in every ocean. Their elucidation and identification continue to be a major task of physical oceanography.

17. Maury had published on the Gulf Stream—including the assorted findings by various surveyors and mariners—which probably gave rise to Perry's remark about standing "confounded at our former ignorance."

During our short stay everyone made it his first object to visit Longwood and the tomb of Napoleon. In viewing the miserable building in which that extraordinary man so long resided (more than six years) ,[18] and where he breathed his last, a feeling of indignation must naturally arise in the breast of every man possessed of common humanity. The British government has, in apparent wantonness, allowed the very room in which he breathed his last to have been desecrated.

Without calling in question the necessity as a measure of state policy for the confinement of the great enemy of the peace of Europe, and in a place from whence there could be no possibility of escape, one cannot but condemn the unnecessary annoyances that were inflicted upon this fallen hero by his unfeeling jailors. Surrounded as the prescribed prison grounds of Longwood were by successive lines of sentinels, with a regiment encamped within musket shot of his dwelling and with every avenue closely guarded by numerous pickets of soldiers, and from the inaccessible character of the cliffs which bound the grounds of Longwood toward the sea, it must have been evident to the prisoner as well as to his keepers that there could not be the remotest chance of escape. Yet there was no relaxation of personal supervision even in the daytime when the island was surrounded with British cruisers and the numerous forts fully garrisoned. But the British Ministry had chosen men known by their former acts to be well qualified for the performance of the duties conferred upon them as chief jailors—[Sir George] Cockburn and [Sir Hudson] Lowe—and full well did they fulfill their task.

Many incidents in the war between the United States and England, of 1812–1814, will at once account for the selection of Cockburn for this especial duty. In that war he exhibited all the characteristics of an unprincipled freebooter, often leading in person, and always permitting and encouraging marauding parties, whose only object seemed to be to annoy and rob unprotected families even of their clothing and household furniture.[19]

But no one can hold the British government or its gallant army or navy accountable for the acts of these two men. The services of such are required in all governments and communities, but their unenviable histories are written in the memories of all who lived in their time, and will be handed down to the latest posterity.

The subjoined notes, extracted from Niles' *Weekly Register,* the most authentic publication of the country, will give some idea of the acts of this fitting person to vex and annoy a chained lion.

Extracts from Niles' Weekly Register

We learn that the assault was led on by rear-admiral *Cockburn* in person, with 18 or 20 barges and about 700 men. It commenced by terrible discharges of rockets and great guns, charged with round, canister, and grapeshot; which flew in all di-

18. Actually less than six years. As Perry says below (p. 17) , Napoleon came to St. Helena 15 October 1815 and died 5 May 1821, not quite five years and seven months. He first occupied Longwood 10 December 1815.

19. For Admiral Cockburn's depredations on the shores of the Chesapeake, see F. F. Beirne, *War of 1812,* chapter xv.

16 rections. The towns were then stormed in succession, and every house plundered; even the negroes cabbins being robbed of their supplies. What was not thought worthy of removal was wantonly destroyed; the beds were ripped open and the feathers scattered to the four winds of heaven; the looking glasses, clocks, bureaus, bedsteads, etc. broken and battered to pieces. Which being done the torch was applied and the whole presented a sheet of flame. After these brilliant achievements, the enemy spread himself on the shores, and burnt several houses. We never before heard of such wanton violence, such horrid deviations from the rules and practices of civilized war. *Such purely savage proceedings.* Deeds that I trust in God, my countrymen will despise even to retribute except on the heads of those who commanded them. *Let the infamy be wholly British.*

Cockburn and his *Winnebagoes* are in truth a band of robbers. At *Havre-de-Grace,* an officer of apparently high command, marked several articles with his name, and ordered them to be conveyed to his barge. The brave fellows had also determined to attack *Elkton,* but as a considerable body of militia were there, they thought "the better part of valor was discretion," and abandoned the beloved idea. This Cockburn is one of the veriest wretches in existence; even when a child he had all those propensities to rapine and plunder that so mark his character. So says a respectable man now in *Baltimore,* who was his school-fellow.[20]

Extract of a letter from a lady near Havre de Grace, to her brother in Philadelphia, dated 7 May 1813[21]

Since I wrote you last, Havre de Grace has been visited by a terrible bombardment. It commenced on Monday the 3d at day-light. Such a scene I never before experienced. On the report of guns we immediately jumped out of our beds; and from the top of the house could plainly see the cannon balls and hear the cries of the inhabitants. We ran down the road, and soon began to meet the distressed people, women and children, half naked children enquiring for their parents, parents for their children, and wives for their husbands. It appeared to us as if the whole of the town was on fire. I think this act, committed without any previous warning, has degraded the British flag.

The enemy robbed every house of everything valuable that could be carried away, leaving not a change of raiment to one of ten persons; and what they could not take conveniently they destroyed by cutting to pieces or breaking to atoms. The admiral himself was present at this work of destruction, and gave orders for it to his officers. Mrs. Rodgers (wife to the commodore)[22] Mrs. Pinckney and Mrs. Goldsborough, took shelter at Mr. Pringle's. When a detachment was sent up to burn that elegant building, Mrs. Goldsborough told the officer that she had an aged mother in it, and begged it might be spared. The officer replied that he acted under the admiral, and it would be necessary to obtain his consent. Mrs. G. returned with the officer and detachment, and obtained the permission that the house should be spared; but when she reached it she found it on fire, and met two men, one with a sheet, and the other with a pillow-case crammed full, coming out, which she could not then notice, but ran upstairs, and found a large wardrobe standing in the passage, all in a flame. William Pinckney, who was with her, and two of the marines, by great exertions saved the house; but some of the wretches

20. *The Weekly Register,* Baltimore, Maryland, [published by H. Niles] volume IV, number 11, 15 May 1813, pages 182–3. The motto of this paper was *Forsum et haec olim meminisse juvabit* (some day these memories, too, will bring a smile).
21. *Ibid.,* number 12, 22 May 1813, page 196.
22. Perry served under Commodore John Rodgers in the War of 1812, his daughter Sarah married the Commodore's son Robert, and his sister Anna married the Commodore's brother George W. Rodgers. Perry had often visited "Sion Hill," the Rodgers mansion at Havre de Grace, Maryland. See Morison, *"Old Bruin,"* p. 29.

after that took the cover from the sofa in the front room, and put coals in it, and it was in flames before it was discovered.

A beautiful Madona, which the commodore had been offered one thousand dollars for, they were about destroying, but the admiral ordered them to desist; at which they were so angry that they wrapped it up in the burning sofa cover, and left it as a mark of their valor.

An officer put his sword through a large elegant looking glass, attacked the windows, and cut out several sashes. They cut hogs through the back, and some partly through, and then let them run. Such wanton barbarity among civilized people I have never heard of.

The whole squadron left our waters yesterday to our unspeakable joy.

The ministry had enjoined upon these chosen jailors the safekeeping of Bonaparte. The manner of carrying out the object was left to the discretion of their faithful instruments.

Now we do nothing but justice in exempting the powers of Europe from unnecessary harshness in confining the common disturber of their realms at a place of perfect security and in the fulfillment of the object to visit upon him personal restraint and consequent inconvenience, but there can be no apology for the course pursued after the death of their imperial captive.

No one can for a moment be made to believe that the British government has been influenced by the petty annual rent of £350 to transfer the entire control of Longwood to a common farmer, and to permit him to suffer the buildings occupied by Bonaparte to fall into dilapidation, and to be occupied as a common stable. There must have been some hidden object of state policy, which we cannot comprehend. Perhaps to hurry the destruction of those silent witnesses of the cruelties committed upon a fallen enemy, but whatever may have been the motive, the perpetration of this wrong will fasten an indelible stain upon the British character, and leave a blemish upon the history of the great island chief, the "Iron Duke,"[23] who might at any time by the exercise of his powerful influence with the ministry have prevented many of the petty annoyances inflicted upon his dying rival.

St. Helena was discovered by the Portuguese in 1502, and having been abandoned, was colonized by the Dutch in 1645. Six years after, it was abandoned also by the Dutch and then occupied by the forces of the English East India Company. In 1661, the company received a charter from Charles II; from whose power it was wrested by the Dutch in 1772, but again fell into the hands of the company in the following year.

From that time up to 1834 it remained quietly in the possession of the company during which period it became the residence and place of death of Napoleon, who landed on 15 October 1815; and died 5 May 1821. His remains were embarked on board the French frigate *La Belle Poule*, commanded by the Prince de Joinville, on 15 October 1840, after the island had been transferred to the crown by act of parliament dated 25 August 1832, the transfer taking place in April of the following year.

The island is evidently volcanic, and when viewed from the sea, presents

23. Arthur Wellesley, the Duke of Wellington (1769–1852), the British general who opposed Napoleon at Waterloo.

the appearance of a series of lofty precipitous hills or mountains (the highest, Diana's Peak, is 2697 feet) separated by deep and sterile valleys. It is only after landing and passing into the interior of the island that you can see anything like cultivation, excepting a few small gardens within the town.

Jamestown, the seat of government, in fact the only town in the island, contains about two hundred and fifty houses and ships with a population probably of 2500. It is built on two sides of a wide, well-paved street which runs nearly a mile along the bottom of a valley terminating at the sea and in the rear of a strong water battery commanding the bay.

In some of the valleys, and at the sides and summits of the smaller hills, the industry of the people has brought the ground under cultivation. Barley, oats, Indian corn, potatoes, and most of the ordinary kinds of vegetables are raised in tolerable perfection. Of the varieties of fruits, the apple, peach, pear, plum, cherry, quince, apricot, and many of the tropical kinds are produced, though not of superior qualities.

Water is abundant and of excellent quality; besides the numerous springs in almost every direction about the island, there are many artificial tanks. Ships are supplied by a tank sent from the town. Fresh beef, mutton, poultry, and vegetables may at all times be procured, though at rather high prices. Fish are abundant.

The roads through the island have been constructed at enormous expense by the East India Company and are kept in excellent order by the present government. Indeed, they may be considered inclined planes adapted as well for wheel carriages and artillery as for horses and foot passengers.

In riding through the country the appearance of the cultivated fields— kept constantly green by the abundant rains falling in slight showers from the clouds which are driven by the southeast trades over the island—forms a pleasing contrast with the barren cliffs which shelter the valleys. The present is the dry season, and the midsummer here. During the winter months heavy rains are common, falling sometimes so copiously as to injure the cultivated grounds and, by their torrents, obstructing travel on the roads.

The island contains a gross population of 5500 of which about 500 are liberated Negroes. The people seem to be industrious but are certainly the most notorious extortioners in the wide world. It is said to be the practice of every householder to entertain strangers, but to charge unmercifully for their hospitality. If one of them in the excess of courtesy offers the loan of his horse, he expects not only thanks and a return of civility, but the full hire of his animal in the bargain. When there are many strangers in the island, and horses consequently in demand, the charge is from three to five dollars for a ride of a few hours.

I was most fortunate in having placed at my disposal by Mr. Solomon, a wealthy merchant, his carriage, and had only to fee the driver. But one of the lieutenants fairly fell into the hands of one of these civil gentlemen of the island.

Contemplating a visit with many others to Longwood, he had already engaged a livery horse, which he found awaiting him on his reaching the town from the ship, and was about mounting when a citizen, whom he had casually met the day before, told him that he had a much superior horse, altogether at his service, and would send for it. Consequently the livery horse was dismissed with a compensation to the disappointed attendant, and that of the polite friend accepted, which proved to be if anything inferior to the other. He was used for a few hours, however, and returned with a fee of a dollar and a quarter to the black boy who received him.

The same evening the owner visited the ship. The lieutenant was profuse of his thanks and after entertaining him made him some little presents equal in value to the fair hire of the horse. These gifts were received in such manner as to induce the officer to think there was still something more wanting. When he said, "Will you allow me to pay for the use of your horse?" and was answered, "Well I am glad you were pleased with the animal, and you need only pay me the usual charge of three dollars." Upon having received it, he coolly offered his services at any future time, and said with a knowing look, "If, when you again visit the island, you will put yourself under my guidance, I will put you through all charges at half price." Then he wished a good voyage to all on board, and passed into the boat, with the neck of a bottle protruding from one pocket, and a good supply of Havanas filling the other—the offering of his grateful friend.

The island is strongly fortified toward the north. The opposite side being exposed to the whole strength of the trades is rendered almost inaccessible on that account, but at the time these works were constructed the power of steam for ocean navigation was unknown. The batteries were placed solely to protect against sail vessels approaching the town, and are principally situated on the high bluffs commanding that approach.

From the elevated positions of the principal forts, the guns which they contain could not be so much depressed as to bear upon steamers coming from the westward, and keeping close to the shore which is quite bold. But in front of the town as before mentioned is a strong water battery, commanding the whole extent of the little bay which forms the harbor, if harbor it can be called. This battery should of course be silenced before there could be any chance of capturing the place.

Vessels under sail bound to the anchorage off Jamestown are compelled for reason of the lee currents to pass to the eastward of the island, and to haul close round Sugar Loaf Point, as soon as they luff under the lee of which they become partially becalmed and are at once exposed to the guns of a very heavy battery called "Prince Rupert's Line." From thence all the way to the anchorage is a succession of forts well provided with heavy artillery.

Since leaving St. Helena, we have had a constant trade wind, deviating very little from southeast, blowing alternately moderate and fresh, but stronger at night than in the daytime bringing with it a short head sea which has greatly retarded our progress. We were obliged to graduate our consumption of coal to that quantity (26 tons per day) which we have found the best proportion for accomplishing the greatest distance with the most economical expenditure, though a larger daily consumption would enable us to make a greater distance. Considering the difficulty of obtaining coal in these regions, its high cost, and the labor and delay incident to its shipment, I have deemed it most advisable, rather to protract our passages than to allow of extravagance in the expenditure of an article so essential to the movement of the vessel. The current has been equal to one and a quarter knots setting in the direction of the wind, and consequently against us.

I am well satisfied that the best and most expeditious route for a steamer from Madeira to the Cape of Good Hope—provided coal in sufficient quantity can be carried by her—would be to steer from the Cape Verde Islands, direct toward Cape Palmas on the coast of Africa, thence tracing the shore along to Table Bay. At St. Paul de Loango the English have a depot of coal for the supply of the African steam cruisers, and it would be a convenient point to send a coal vessel from the United States. Within recent years a depot of coal has been established by an English company at Port Grande, Island of St. Vincent of the Cape de Verde group. I was informed that a reasonable supply could always be obtained from this company by transient steamers.

If particularly desirable, steamers from the United States might proceed direct to St. Vincent without touching at Madeira, with the understanding of a positive certainty of obtaining coal at that place, from thence to take the route by Cape Palmas, via Loango. It is, however, much better that cargoes of coal should be sent ahead of steamers leaving the United States, as a security for a certain supply.

The prescribed route of mail steamers bound round the Cape of Good Hope from England, is to touch at St. Vincent, thence proceed to the Cape, via Ascension, replenishing their coal at all their stopping places. In taking this route—which they are compelled to do to leave mail at Ascension for the African squadron—they have to contend with the entire range of the southeast trades, which are directly ahead, blowing most of the time quite strong, and always producing a lee current of from one to one and a quarter knots.

By taking the route along the African coast a steamer will have the advantage of the sea and land breezes, and the favorable current usually setting to the south. It must be observed that a steamer is not so much retarded in her progress by adverse winds, as by the head sea, which such winds produce. Indeed, a steamer will sometimes go faster against a moderately fresh breeze, provided it is perfectly smooth, as the wind drawing from forward increases the draught of the furnaces.

Cape of Good Hope

24 JANUARY–3 FEBRUARY 1853

On 24 January at 9 A.M. we made the land in the vicinity of Saldanha Bay, and at 2 P.M. Table Mountain was in sight. After passing outside of Dassen Island, and through the passage between the main and Robben Island we anchored in Table Bay at half past 8 P.M. in seven fathoms of water.

The port captain on visiting the ship stated that we were too far out, and as one of the prevailing southeast gales was expected, he would return in the morning and move us farther in. He accordingly did; moving us in to five fathoms, a muddy bottom, and a position amidst the shipping corresponding with the following compass bearings: Robben Island, N by E; Mouille Point lighthouse, NW½N; Lion's Rump, W½S; Devil's Peak, SSW; Church Steeple, SW by W.[24]

This port is easy of access either by night or day, if the two lights can be distinctly seen, so that the distance from Green Point can be accurately estimated. By coming upon that point too closely there is danger of a ledge of rocks bordering the cape shore, and by keeping too far to the northward, the Whale Rock at the southern end of Robben Island may bring a vessel up. But the following notes taken from the Cape Town *Almanack* will furnish better directions than I can give.

Instructions for entering Table Bay by Night.
(*The bearings are all by compass or magnetic.*)

To enter Table Bay from the northward meaning to pass outside of Robben Island, a ship should keep the light to the eastward of south, nine degrees east, or about south and by east until she gets soundings under twenty fathoms, at a little more than a mile from the lighthouse. She may then steer east southeast, or east and by south, not to come under ten or twelve fathoms until the light bears west southwest. She may then steer for the anchorage, and may anchor in from seven to six fathoms, as soon as the lights are shutting in behind the Lion's tail.

This track leads about a mile clear of danger on Green Point, but a ship need not approach it so near if she has, by seeing Robben Island, ascertained by its bearings that she is clear of the Whale Rock. She may then round it at a greater distance from Green Point if desirable, but the soundings in that case will not alone be a sure judge.

In coming from the southwest, a ship should not get less than forty fathoms, before it bears south and by east, when the preceding directions may be followed.

From the northward, inside of Robben Island the light should be kept about southwest by south, until the ship has passed that island. In so doing she may have some casts from eight to six fathoms; and when, on that course, the water deepens to eleven or twelve fathoms, she may steer for the anchorage by the plan as before directed.

In beating round Green Point, a ship should never shoal her water under eleven or twelve fathoms, until she has brought the light to bear west southwest as before said.

In beating between Robben Island and the main, to enter Table Bay, the soundings may be taken from the island as it shoals very regularly. In standing toward the main, it appears prudent to tack at the first cast of the lead after the water shoalens.

In these directions it is taken for granted that a ship will always keep her leads going.

By day, or when the shores or surf can be seen, or indeed under any circumstances the plan ought to be a sufficient guide.

There are two lights on the lighthouse which are in one, about southwest, and by west, these appear to be of no other use than to assure the navigator which is

24. These bearings do not provide a reasonable fix according to modern charts. The log of *Mississippi* gives: Green Point Light, NW; Lion's Rump, W; Robben Island, N; Devil's Peak, SW by S; and Mouille Point Light, NW by W.

the lighthouse, if he should see other lights. The lights have been seen clearly off deck sixteen miles distant, but they will not make clear as two lights until within six or seven miles to the westward of them, and from the northward one light only will be seen.

The Cape of Good Hope is of great commercial importance to Great Britain as a convenient rendezvous for her cruisers stationed in the neighborhood, and a stopping place for vessels bound to and from the Indian Ocean. Excellent water, fresh provisions, and fruits can be obtained in any quantities, and at reasonable prices. Wood is scarce, but every description of article usually needed by vessels may be had from the numerous well-stocked stores and warehouses at Cape Town.

Bullocks and sheep in fine condition for shipping can be purchased, the former at £6 and the latter at 15 shillings per head. *Mississippi* has taken on board 12 bullocks and 18 sheep, for the consumption of the crew.

Business of every description seems to be in a most prosperous condition at Cape Town, rents are high, and there is an appearance of easy affluence amongst the government officials and the merchants and tradesmen. Numerous equipages are seen constantly in the streets, and want is unknown even to the lower classes.

Since the abolition of slavery in the British colonies the agricultural interests of those colonies have gradually fallen off, and whilst at some few of the colonial ports, Cape Town amongst the number, commerce is still thriving, there are few instances of successful planting, because of a want of laborers.

The emancipated Negroes and their descendants are very much of the character and condition of the free blacks of our own country, though by no means as intelligent or good looking. They are perfectly independent of all restraint so long as they do not violate the laws. They work when it suits them, and at their own prices, abruptly breaking off if spoken to in a manner which they consider offensive. Their ordinary charge for labor is a dollar and a quarter per day of ten hours.

Cape Town proved a dull and stupid place to us during our stay. Those who remained on shore were confined most of the time to the hotel, owing to the excessive heat and the clouds of dust which the southeast wind disturbs. Indeed these drifts of sand are sometimes piled along the sidewalks several inches deep, and men are constantly seen hauling it into heaps, to be carried away by the dust carts. To protect their eyes it is common for the men of all classes to wear veils, attached to their hats. Near to the government house is a park always kept cool and shady by the numerous magnificent oaks, which being planted in rows form various avenues of picturesque appearance.

These southeasters which make everyone so uncomfortable prevail in midsummer, and are always foretold by the appearance of a dense white fleecy cloud, which settles upon the summit of Table Mountain, and there remains until the gale subsides. They blow with great violence, sweeping across the low land east of Table Mountain, and were it not that the water in Table Bay is perfectly smooth, vessels could not hold to their anchors.

During these gales, of which we had two in seven days, business in the harbor
is entirely suspended.

The war with the Hottentots and Kaffirs which has continued so long, costing an immense amount of blood and treasure, is still prolonged by the obstinacy of the blacks. Already the whole frontier has been devastated, and, though there is now some hope of bringing about a peace, yet no one believes that any treaty that may be entered into will be longer respected by the Negroes than may suit their convenience.

In the last battle in which the English force, headed by General Cathcart himself, was victorious, it is said that the Kaffir chiefs brought into action six thousand foot and two thousand horse. These numbers are probably exaggerated but it is well known that the blacks have acquired a tolerable organization. They are well supplied with arms and ammunition, either purchased from dealers or taken from the colonists. They have hitherto had an abundance of provisions, from their own herds as well as from those stolen from the whites, but report says that, owing to the carelessness and waste always attendant upon the military movements of savages, provisions are running short with them.

The English say that the Kaffirs have been instructed in the art of war by numerous deserters from the Royal British Army and by a French missionary settled amongst them, who passed his early life in the army. This war, whilst it has enriched the merchants and tradesmen by the large expenditure of public money in the colony, has been very ruinous to the farmer. Such is the condition of many of the farms, for want of hands to work them, that in some parts of the settlement they are actually running to waste.

The description of farming is mostly of the pastoral character, vast herds of cattle, sheep, and horses are raised and mules are almost equally numerous. Their estimated prices at Cape Town are as follows: horses from 30 to 150 dollars; mules from 30 to 75 dollars.

Though the soil is capable of producing Indian corn, wheat, barley, oats, and several other descriptions of grain, for causes above mentioned, the home consumption of these products is not fully provided for. The principal articles of export are wine, hides, tallow, and wool.

I took occasion to visit in company with a party of officers, one of the celebrated vineyards of Constantia and was greatly disappointed, not only by its limited extent but by the manner in which the lands were cultivated. The proprietor, however, explained this by remarking that the laborers could not be obtained, and if it were not for the American cultivator which he had recently imported from the United States, he should be obliged to abandon the cultivation of the grape altogether. This simple plough, drawn by one horse, actually accomplished the labor of 50 men, according to their usual mode of working and cultivating the vine with the hoe.

The grape is cultivated here as in Sicily, by trimming the vine close to the ground, not permitting it to grow higher than the common gooseberry bush. The secret of the richness of the wine is in the condition of the fruit when it goes to the press. The grape begins to ripen in the early part of February but

24   it is not gathered until the middle of March. When the fruit has assumed almost the appearance of a dried raisin, in this state it is pressed. The prices of these wines on the estate are from two to six dollars per gallon, according to quality.

In our drive to and from Constantia, we passed some very pretty villas, and saw numerous beautiful avenues of trees formed by the oak and a species of fir, both of which are reared from the seed, and are extensively cultivated in the colony not only for ornament but for fuel. I also noticed very substantial hedges formed of young oaks, produced from the acorn in the short space of three years.

We particularly noticed the numerous teams of oxen, mules, and horses constantly passing to and from the city, and it was not unusual to see seven, eight, and even nine yoke of bullocks in one team, perfectly docile and in good condition. These teams are guided by two teamsters one seated in front of the wagon, which is not unlike our Pennsylvania wagons, urging the animals along by voice and a long lash, whilst the other precedes the leaders, holding a halter fastened to their horns with which he guides them.

The horse and mule teams whether two, three, or four spans are driven as with us by means of reins held by the driver sitting in front of the wagon. Our party was accommodated by a livery stable keeper with an open barouche, and four beautiful stallions driven with much skill by a colored boy. The hotels are pretty well kept. I found our accommodation at Welch's Hotel in company with the captain of the fleet, flag lieutenant, and purser having a private table at a charge of $2.50 per day, exclusive of wine.

The Cape of Good Hope, originally named Cabo Tormentoso, was first discovered and doubled in 1493 by Bartholomew Dias, a Portuguese commander, and, in 1497, was passed by Vasco da Gama of the same nation, who was the first to cross the Indian Ocean.* This southern promontory of Africa was found by the discoverers tolerably well peopled, and they were, in some respects, in far better condition than many of the tribes farther north. They possessed herds of cattle which resemble in appearance the buffalo, and sheep of the broad-tail species so highly esteemed at the present day for their excellence for the table.

The natives notwithstanding these advantages were found to be of the most savage and beastly character, utterly disgusting in their persons and habits. In this respect they have very little improved, though, poor wretches, their conquerors have given them but little opportunity of acquiring more civilized habits, pursued as they have been by a cruel wantonness. But we Americans have no right to rail at other nations for the wrongs they have inflicted upon the aborigines of countries seized upon by them. Though hardly equal to the English in the disgusting hypocrisy with which they excuse their acts, we are not far behind them in the frauds and cruelties committed upon our native tribes.

* Bartholomew Dias doubled the Cape of Good Hope in 1493; Vasco da Gama in 1497. Dutch took possession of the colony in 1652. First Dutch governor was Jan van Riebeck.

Kaffir Chief Seyolo and a wife, Capetown. By E. Brown, Jr.

Nine-team ox cart, Capetown. By Patterson under direction of Heine

26 Having taken on board from the ship *Faneuil Hall* 226 tons of anthracite coal, and from other sources 362 of bituminous, a good supply of bullocks and sheep, with our water tanks full we left Table Bay at 11 o'clock A.M. on 3 February, and on getting fairly out of the harbor, found the wind strong from the westward with a heavy swell coming from that direction.

At 8 P.M.[25] we were off the pitch of the cape from which, having Cape Hangklip[26] full in sight, we steered southeast to reach the parallel of 37 degrees of latitude to avoid the southeast gales which prevail near the cape, and cause a strong current to the north and westward, and to meet the variables which are found south of the border of those trades.

For the first three days after leaving the cape we had the wind from northwest to southwest, taking us to the latitude of 36°16′ S, and longitude 23°40′ E, when it changed to the northward and eastward rather northerly, remaining with us to latitude 35°06′ and longitude 44°03′. At this point it gradually hauled to the south enabling us to incline our course more to the north until we found ourselves in the southeast trades. But fearing that the wind might back again to the eastward, I was careful not to make too much northing, being apprehensive of falling to leeward of Mauritius, and losing the benefit of a fair wind which with steamers, as also in sail vessels, increases the rate of going and, in the latter, saves fuel.

From 11 to 14 February inclusive, the wind continued from the south and east, bringing us up at noon of the 14th to latitude 29°34′ and longitude 55°22′. From this time until our arrival at Port Louis on the 18th the wind hung to the north and east, the trades having entirely failed.

The weather during the passage was fine, the barometer ranging from 29°80′ to 29°95′. The temperature of air from 74° to 84°. The currents setting with wind about three quarters of a knot.

I fully agree with Horsburgh* that the best route for sailing ships bound from the Cape of Good Hope to Mauritius, is to make nearly the whole if not all their easting between the parallels of 35° and 38° of latitude, and to strike the southeast trades about the latitude of 27° and longitude of 55° or 57°. This will bring the ships well to windward and enable her to fetch the island without difficulty, if the trade does not haul north of E by N. In our passage it actually hauled as far as NNE. This is not unusual at this season, when northerly and northwesterly winds frequently prevail from Madagascar, toward and beyond the Bourbon and Mauritius.†

A question has been agitated whether it is advisable for steamers to make this curve in their route to Mauritius, or to steam direct from the cape to the island, passing close round Cape Aghulas, I am myself of opinion that unless

* See Horsburgh.[27]
† The name of the Island of Bourbon has been changed to Réunion.

25. Hawks *Narrative* gives this time as 6 P.M., saying, by inference, that it was seven hours after leaving Table Bay.
26. Cape Hangklip, the eastern promontory of False Bay, is at latitude 34°23′ S, longitude 18°50′ E.
27. Navigator James Horsburgh, who wrote *Memoirs: Compromising the Navigation to and from China, by the China Sea, and through the Various Straits and Channels in the India Archipelago; also, the Navigation of Bombay Harbour* (London, 1805).

Broad-tail sheep from Capetown. Commodore Perry put some of these sheep ashore on Stapleton Island in the Bonins

Yak family, Shanghai

the steamer is one of great speed, it would be unwise to take the direct route, in which she would have to contend against a strong trade, with its consequent current. The difference in the distances of the two routes is about 240 miles, which I think would hardly compensate for the loss, occasioned by head winds and currents, saying nothing of the advantages of cooler and more agreeable weather of the southern passage.

The mail steamers, and indeed all European steamers, have usually taken the last-named route, and I have heard of but one steamer, *Susquehanna,* attempting the direct course. She, though a very fast vessel, had a passage of 17 days. The *Mississippi,* of far inferior power and speed, making the run in 15 days, beat H.B.M. steamer *Styx* by two and a half days; the screw mail steamer *Bosphorus,* two days; and the screw mail steamer *Mauritius,* ten days. By doubling the Cape of Good Hope in midsummer we escaped any heavy blow, but there is rarely a week passes without a blow from some quarter. Horsburgh remarks:

In the storms off the Cape Bank and to the eastward, the sea is turbulent, and then generally accompanied with a black overcast sky, when they are about to commence and during their continuance, numbers of albatross, petrels, and other oceanic birds are seen flying about, although in moderate weather few are perceived, for at this time they rest on the surface of the sea to fish, which they cannot do in a storm.

I have observed nothing remarkable in the meteorological department. The temperature of the air and water has been similar to that in corresponding northern latitudes. The barometer has given due notice of the changes of the weather, and has proved of great utility.

There is a peculiarity in the action of the barometer in the neighborhood of the Cape of Good Hope, and in that part of the route across the Indian Ocean as far as the equator. Horsburgh says:

In the vicinity of the Cape Bank and in most parts of the southern hemisphere, the mercury rises with southerly and falls with northerly winds; those proceeding from a warmer atmosphere are much rarefied, consequently the mercury falls in the barometer, whereas southerly winds coming from the frozen regions near the pole are more dense, and cause the mercury to rise.

This ought to be kept in remembrance for when the wind is from southeast. I have several times observed the mercury to fall considerably before it changed to the north, and expected a gale, but the fall resulted only from the warmer air coming in contact with and repelling the former.

On the morning of 14 February we spoke H.B.M. steamer *Styx,* Commander Hull, thirteen days from Simons' Bay, bound to Mauritius. She was under sail, her engines having been disconnected and the wheels with all their buckets made to revolve by the movement of the vessel through the water. She made tolerable way but drifted much to leeward.

The English war steamers frequently disconnect their engines in view of saving fuel by a simple arrangement, and this process of disconnecting and reconnecting is accomplished in a few minutes. But with us it is next to impossible to disconnect our engines, and the only practicable mode of using the sails exclusively is to remove the immersed floats. This can only be done in moderate weather and the time required for taking off the floats or buckets is about two hours, and it takes double that time to replace them.

The truth is, and I am mortified to confess it, that every nation in the world having war steamers and every private steam navigation company are ahead of our navy in all that belongs to improvements in ocean steamers. This ship and the *Missouri* were the two first ocean war steamers introduced into our naval service and for a time were pronounced the first war steamers in the world. Since then we have rather retrograded than advanced in the art of constructing vessels of war, whilst most of the maritime nations of Europe, and numerous individuals and companies have put afloat vessels which ought to shame those who planned and completed the *San Jacinto, Taranac, Fulton,* and *Princeton.*

Mauritius

At 9:30 A.M., 18 February, Mauritius was in sight from the deck, bearing NNE, and at noon we were nearly abreast of Cape Brabant, having passed in sight of Grand Port, the scene of the memorable naval action in August 1810 between an English squadron under Captains Pym and Willoughby, and a French force in command of Commodore Duperré. In this action the English were worsted, losing nearly all their vessels. This extraordinary battle was fought within the coral shoals which form the harbor of Grand Port. The batteries on shore took part in the action which continued for three or four days.

Shortly after dark, being near the mouth of the harbor, we received on board a pilot who anchored and secured the ship for the night at the outer moorings, or what are called the Admiral's Moorings. The following morning the pilot again came on board bringing several launches, manned by natives of Malabar who, with the assistance of the crew, completed the mooring of the vessel, a process requiring much time and labor.

Frigates' chains, secured to mooring anchors, are brought on board, one at each bow, and one at each quarter, and in this manner all vessels entering this port are secured. The work being entirely done under the direction of the pilots, who with their launches, warps, and numerous hands are constantly mooring vessels just arrived, or unmooring others about to depart. The vessels are all moored head and stern, with their heads to the southeast, the direction from which the hurricanes usually come. As these gales generally blow directly out of the harbor there is very little sea; but such is often the violence of the wind that even the strength of the moorings with which vessels are secured give way, and scenes the most destructive ensue. Vessels are thrown against each other, and the shores are strewn with wrecks.

It is rarely that these gales blow into the harbor. When they do, a most tremendous sea is thrown into the little port, and there is scarcely a possibility of saving from disaster even the best moored and best found vessel. Every possible precaution has been taken by the government of the island to guard against the effects of these furious storms. The harbor master, Lieutenant Edward Kelly of the royal navy, a most intelligent gentleman, is indefatigable in his attentions to the wants of vessels, and seems to take under his special charge the safety of them all, giving warning of the appearances of an approaching gale, and suggesting such measures as may the better guard against accident. The whole system of port regulations is perfect, and I felt myself bound to address a note to Captain Kelly thanking him for the facilities that had been rendered to the *Mississippi.*

How many useful lessons might the members of our Lighthouse Board learn, if they were to look into these admirable regulations. But like the work of most other boards that have hitherto had their existence and death in the United States, and for the results of which no one has been found to be responsible, their labors I fear will amount to little or nothing. Even if their suggestions may be of the most praiseworthy character, the marplots of the navy—a set of parasites, swarms of whom are always to be found hanging about Washington, with access to a class of our legislators who generally prefer to legislate upon those matters upon which they are most ignorant—will be sure to prevent the carrying out of the recommendations of the board however perfect they may be.[28]

After exchanging salutes and calls with the authorities—military and civil —of the island, and making arrangements for supplying the vessel with coal, I had some little opportunity of looking about. But so much time is usually occupied in these visits of ceremony and attending dinners on arrival at an English colonial settlement that the commander of a squadron must necessarily be under engagement for several days. Unless the stay of his vessel in port extends beyond a week he is under official restraint the whole time.

The English population of Mauritius, most of them having connection with the colonial government directly or indirectly, are somewhat exclusive in their social relations. The French portion, much the more numerous and the most wealthy, are equally tenacious. Although there are no palpable dissensions amongst them, it is quite apparent to the observation of the impartial stranger, who mixes freely with the two classes, that there is very little harmony of feeling existing. However injuriously the interests of the colony might be affected by returning to the French rule, yet I think from national motives and prejudices the masses would prefer it.

As in most conquered countries the higher order of females indulge, in a greater degree than the men, in these national prejudices as they mix less in the society of (in their eyes) their interloping neighbors. So the pretty creole demoiselles keep the Saxon youths, even the red-coated ones, at a distance.

Of course during my short stay, I had very little opportunity of judging of the state of society of Mauritius. The English officials and merchants were, as I have always found them at the colonies, profuse in their open hospitality, but I was greatly pleased with what I saw of the creole population, who

28. For Perry's effort to improve American lighthouses, see Morison, *"Old Bruin,"* pp. 136–9.

evinced much intelligence and a kind and amiable bearing toward us, equally hospitable as the English, but with less ceremony.

I was particularly pleased with the Messrs. Chauvin, natives of the island, to whom the business of the *Mississippi* was entrusted. These gentlemen are quite wealthy, and in connection with commercial business are largely engaged in sugar planting.

The island of Mauritius is mountainous and of basaltic formation, having a very rich soil capable of producing various descriptions of grain and the fruits and vegetables common to tropical climates, but the planting of sugar seems to occupy the entire thoughts of the agriculturists of the island, as the more agreeable and the more profitable cultivation. Not more than three eighths of the island is under cultivation, the remainder being in its original state, though large tracts of this wild land are of excellent quality of soil.

The cane is planted in the usual manner. Before the introduction of guano as a fertilizer, the produce was from 2000 to 2500 French pounds of sugar to the French acre, but the application of the guano has brought about a most extraordinary increase of yield. The produce in ordinary seasons being from 6000 to 7000 pounds, and sometimes as high as 8000 pounds to the acre.

As evidence of the improvement in the cultivation of sugar in Mauritius I may state from official returns that in 1812 the quantity of sugar exported from the island was 969,260 French pounds, and in 1851 the quantity exported was 137,373,179 pounds, and it is estimated that the crop of the present year will reach 140,000,000 pounds. One French acre of land laid off for cane is estimated to have 2000 holes, in each of which 1/4 of a pound of guano is placed in its crude state. The cost of guano is about the same as in the United States.

The surface of the ground in its original state was found to be filled with loose rocks and stones. These have been excavated and rolled aside, forming parallel ridges about three or four feet apart, and between which the cane is planted. The cultivators are of opinion that these rocks instead of being injurious to the cane are rather advantageous as retarding the growth of weeds, shading and protecting the cane from violent winds, and as retaining moisture which is in a measure imparted to the roots of the plant.

The general abolition of slavery by the British government caused much agricultural distress in this as in all the English colonies dependent upon slave labor. But after a time the introduction of laborers from India, chiefly from Malabar, under certain regulations and restrictions, enabled the planters not only to dispense with the services of those blacks, who being freed were indisposed to work, but to obtain hired laborers on more advantageous terms. These men under the general denomination of coolies perform nearly all the labor in the island, not only on the estates, but in loading and unloading ships.

Large communities of them are to be found on all the sugar estates. Comfortable houses are provided for them and their families, and they receive, exclusive of house rent and provisions, from two to three dollars per month. On the estate of the Messrs. Chauvin about 400 working hands are employed, who with their wives and children made up a community of more than 800 souls. The municipal laws for their government are sufficiently minute, yet these people pay little regard to any bargain they may make with their employers. They go and come pretty much as they please, but with all the disadvantages of this system, the planter profits largely by their labor.

Port Louis lies according to Bowditch in latitude 20°10′ south, and longitude 57°30′ east. The island is about 40 miles in length from north to south, and 25 in breadth from east to west. Its general aspect when first discovered from the sea is mountainous and, on approaching nearer, these mountains assume a singular and grotesque appearance. The most remarkable is the one called Peter Butt, of which some traditions are related by the Mauritians. But as sketches of all the remarkable headlands seen from the ship will accompany these notes, I shall refrain from describing them with any degrees of minuteness.

The island is bound on the eastern side by coral reefs between which there are channels used by the coasters, but the only safe harbor is Port Louis and that is none of the best. Grand Port on the southeastern side is sufficiently capacious, and is more convenient for shipping the sugar—of which large quantities are grown in the neighborhood—but apart from the intricacies of the entrance it is open to the southeast, from which quarter the hurricanes blow the most furiously.

It was upon one of these coral reefs on the northeast part of the island that the French ship *St. Géran* was wrecked on the night of 18 August 1744. Out of the details of that catastrophe Bernardin de St. Pierre (who was at the time an officer of the garrison of Mauritius) based his beautiful though fabulous story of *Paul and Virginia*.

I have secured copies of the depositions* of several of the crew who were

---

* On 25 August 1744 at eight o'clock in the morning appeared at the registry; Jean Janvier, of St. Malo; pilot; and Pierre Verger, of l'Orient; artillery-man; both from the wrecked vessel, *St. Géran;* who made the following declaration.

That the *St. Géran* having sailed from l'Orient on 24 March, arrived 22 days afterward at Gorée, where they embarked 20 Negroes and 10 Negresses of the Yoloffe and Bambara "castes," one of these Negroes was strangled by the "messenger" on turning round the capstan to set up the shrouds; and one Negress died on the passage. Ten men besides died on the passage, and when they hove in sight of the Isle of France, there were more than 100 men on the sick list.

On 17 August they sighted Round Island, and at 4 o'clock in the afternoon they laid the ship to, under the main sail with the larboard tack on board, steering SSW and SW. Monsieur Longchamps de Montendre had then the watch, having under him the petty officers Ribert and Ambroise. The watch was changed at midnight, when he was relieved by Monsieur Lair who was assisted by the boatswain's mate Tessel. All the principal officers had at that time retired to their respective cabins, Monsieur Lair being alone on the quarterdeck.

At 3 o'clock in the morning the sailors in the forepart of the vessel perceived that they were about to run on the breakers, on which Monsieur Lair immediately wore ship, but it was too late, the vessel struck, and a sea striking her at the

saved from the wreck, taken before the authorities of St. Louis, and the only foundation for the tale was that on board the *St. Géran* were two young ladies, Mademoiselles Mallet and Caillon, returning as passengers from France to the colony, both of whom were lost.

The depositions state that Mademoiselle Caillon was last seen upon the topgallant forecastle of the wrecked vessel with a gentleman, Monsieur Longchamps de Montendre, who was at the time endeavoring to persuade her to trust herself to his efforts to save her. But in so doing it was necessary for her to disencumber herself of some of her clothes, this out of modesty she declined doing, and so perished with her supposed lover and the greater part of the crew. Mademoiselle Mallet was on the quarter-deck with Monsieur de Peramont who never separated from her.

---

same time on midships threw her on her beam ends on the reefs among the breakers. This brought on deck all the officers so suddenly that they had nothing on but their night clothes. On this occurrence the whole of the crew began to call out for mercy, imploring the assistance of God. The captain chanted the "Salve," and the "Ave Maria es Stella." Tassel then cast loose the spare spars to make a raft of them, but he did not succeed. It was then resolved to cut away the mainmast, and on the first stroke of the axe it fell dragging with it the mizenmast which broke in two at about 9 or 10 feet above the quarter-deck; both masts fell to leeward. They then cut away the foremast, when the wreck of all these masts and yards were thrown up by the sea with such force against the sides of the ship as to shake the vessel so as to break it in. Between 5 and 6 o'clock there being but little hope of safety in remaining in the ship, the baker was the first to jump overboard, but having on his back a bundle of his effects which prevented him from swimming, he was soon drowned in sight of all on board. A moment afterward Tassel committed himself to the sea, and as he was seen to swim to a great distance without any accident occurring to him, it gave the deponents some encouragement to follow his example. One of them, Janvier, perceiving a heavy shower coming on, and fearing that the waves might become still more rough, he threw himself into the sea with his comrade on a plank which they found at hand. At this time the cries and lamentations of Monsieur de B[   ] were most extraordinary. Mademoiselle Mallet was on the quarterdeck with Monsieur de Peramont who never separated from her. Mademoiselle Caillon was on the topgallant forecastle with Messrs. Villeormois, Gresle, Guiné, and Longchamps de Montendre. This latter lowered himself down the ship's side to throw himself into the sea, but he immediately returned to endeavor to prevail on Mademoiselle Caillon to leave the vessel with him and try to save herself.

The deponents declare that they were a long time between life and death (*entre la vie et la mort.*) although they were all good swimmers. That the waves frequently drove them among the breakers and then drew them back again with such violence that they could not resist. That at last they got through the breakers into smoother water, and ultimately succeeded in swimming to Amber Island, where the chasseurs [supplied] them with provisions, and that afterward they arrived at Port Louis by land.

Done at the northwest part of the Isle of France in the registry office the day and year aforesaid. Taken down before Antoine Nicholas Herbanet, King's counsellor in the superior council of the Isle of France, commissioner appointed to that effect.

> (signed) Jean Janvier.
> Herbault Molere.

34   The *St. Géran* had made the land before; the weather being fine and so continued up to the time of the disaster. But the vessel was lost by keeping her at night too long on the inshore tack, and at the very moment of wearing, she struck and shortly went to pieces. The account of the storm as described by St. Pierre, is altogether a fable and the description of Paul is also a fiction.

The celebrity given to the tale of St. Pierre attracted the interest of all strangers visiting the island, and the first object to be seen on arrival were the scenes of the early childhood, and the graves of these model lovers. But the illusion soon vanished when the truth was known. Still new parties were constantly arriving to be alike disappointed. At last an eccentric French gentleman having a country residence about eight miles from St. Louis, and probably near the supposed place of interment of the lovers, erected two monuments in his garden in memory of the unfortunate couple. The alleged object of the gentleman who was remarkable for his hospitality, was to attract strangers to his house and grounds, that he might have the pleasure of their society.

This singular person has been long since dead, but the tombs are still standing, though in a dilapidated state. They were of course visited by myself and many of the officers. But instead of receiving hospitable entertainment, we were required to pay for admission to the garden. But this demanding of money from visitors, who may desire to examine whatever may be curious or interesting, whether belonging to the government, or to individuals, is purely an English custom. It was the same at Longwood, and at the tomb of Napoleon, and it is the same everywhere throughout the vast possessions of the Queen.

The island of Mauritius was first discovered in 1503 by Don Pedro de Mascarenes, a Portuguese commander,[29] but it was not settled until 1644 when the Dutch took formal possession of it, the Portuguese never availing of their right of discovery. The island had, however, been previously visited by the Dutch who gave it the name of Mauritius after Prince Maurice of Orange Nassau, then stadholder of Holland.

In order to obtain servants and laborers, slaves were introduced from Madagascar. Many of these, from bad treatment, fled to the almost impenetrable forests of the island and, forming themselves into bands, harassed the Dutch to such degree as to compel them to abandon their possessions for a time and leave the island. But they subsequently returned and continued in possession until the beginning of the 18th century, when they finally withdrew altogether to the Cape of Good Hope, and from that time up to the present have had no official connection with the island.

In 1715 the French first made a lodgment upon the island, calling it the "Isle of France," and the neighboring one Bourbon, which they also settled. Roderiquez [375 miles east of Mauritius] having been subsequently peopled. From that time up to December 1810, when it fell by conquest into the hands of the English, the French held possession.

29. The discovery was made in 1505.

Of the several governors of the island during the French possession, the most distinguished were Monsieur de Labourdonnais and General Decaen. The former appears to have been governor at the time of the wreck of the *St. Géran;* his name is mentioned by St. Pierre. Decaen was in command at the time of the capitulation of the island to the English in 1810.

The population of Mauritius in 1851 was

Resident	180,823
Military	1,524
Shipping	1,159
Total	183,506

A considerable proportion of the population is composed of manumitted slaves, Chinese, and natives of India. The predominating religion is Roman Catholic.

As a place of resort for ships merely stopping for refreshments, Mauritius offers very few advantages. Every article of supply is extravagantly high, though they can be had, yet in no great abundance. Water is furnished from the government tanks and is of excellent quality. The most esteemed fruit of the island is a superior kind of mango; other tropical fruits are to be procured in their season.

Having taken on board 262 tons of anthracite coal from the American coal ship *Singapore,* and 208 of bituminous, from the town, we left St. Louis on the morning of 25 February, intending to touch for a further supply of coal, either at Point de Galle, or Singapore if it should appear possible to reach the latter named place with the coal received on board at Mauritius.

At my suggestion, Messrs. Howland and Aspinwall[30] had dispatched from New York two ships laden with coal, one to the Cape of Good Hope and the other to Mauritius, and it has turned out very fortunately that this precaution was adopted. Without these two cargos we should have had great difficulty in procuring the quantities required for the *Mississippi* and the steamers that are to follow her. These two ships arrived very opportunely only a few days before us, and after taking on board this vessel portions of their cargos, the remainder has been left for the *Powhatan* and *Allegheny.*

So much was said during our stay at Mauritius of the hurricanes (or as they are now generally called cyclones,) common to this part of the Indian Ocean and of their terrific effects that I had scarcely a hope of escaping from this region of their greatest violence without encountering one at least. The Mauritians at the season of these tempests, from December to April, seem to think and talk of nothing else. Meteorological instruments of every form and description are kept under constant observation. They have good reason for this solicitude, as these cyclones when they do come are accompanied by desolation and ruin to the merchant and planter.

---

30. Merchant shipowners William E. Howland and William H. Aspinwall. The latter, an engineer, was also a builder of the Panama Railroad, completed in 1855. The city of Aspinwall, Panama, was named for him in 1852, but was renamed Colon in 1890.

36   The theory or rather the natural laws which produce and control these storms, as first discovered and explained by Redfield and Reed, are well understood in this part of the world, and so is the direction which they usually take in sweeping across the Indian Ocean. The islands of Mauritius, Bourbon, and Roderiquez lie in their very track and if unfortunately either of them is exposed to the vortex of one of these desolating whirlwinds the consequences are terrible.

The interest created by the extraordinary discoveries of Redfield and Reed has given rise to many discussions as to the best means of avoiding them to be adopted by the commanders of vessels who may find themselves actually within their sweeping influence, or in their proximity. And though these discussions may, and doubtless will result in a better understanding of the laws which govern the winds, yet they have a tendency to confuse the simpleminded and practical sailor who at the commencement of a storm can spare little time from the cares of preparing his ship, to study out such abstruse rules. The simple instructions given by the earliest writers which the more recent publications of Piddington have further explained and simplified are now generally understood by all well informed seamen.

Of the disputants alluded to above as discussing the question of the law of storms—all residents of Mauritius—I may mention Doctor Thom whose writings are already well known; a Lieutenant Fryers of the same corps of Governor Read (the Royal Engineers) ; a Mr. Ledgwick, who has published a little work which he calls "The True Principle," subsequently reviewed by Doctor Thom; and last of all a Creole gentleman, a Mr. Bosquett, attached to the observatory at Mauritius.

This gentleman who has translated Piddington's hornbook into French, with annotations of his own, claims to be able by careful and constant meteorological observations to foretell the existence of hurricanes in the Indian Ocean and to describe the course they will take. He informed me the day before I left Mauritius that a cyclone was then blowing in a direction E by N from the island, that it would pass to the south and east.

By reference to the chart in Piddington's hornbook,[31] it will be seen that in the meridian of Mauritius these cyclones never extend to the north of 10° or 12° of south latitude; therefore vessels leaving the island in the hurricane season for any part of India, should steer to the north, passing well to the west of the Cargados,[32] a most dangerous group, thus keeping a clear sea open to the westward, that there may be nothing in the way. Should it be desirable to run to the north and west this is the true course to take, in case of encountering the southwestern or northwestern quadrants of a cyclone. A vessel from Mauritius runs this danger, in the hurricane season, until she is sufficiently far north to find herself beyond their influence. Steamers have superior means of avoiding these storms by having the power to steer the most judicious course to escape from their greatest fury.

31. Henry Piddington, *The Horn-Book of Storms for the Indian and China Seas* (London: Bishop's College Press, 1845) . 2nd ed.
32. The Cargados Carajos Shoals, about 600 miles east of Madagascar and 300 miles N by E from Mauritius (latitude 16°38′ S, longitude 59°38′ E) .

Following the advice of several experienced seamen we took the circuitous route (the distance from Mauritius to Ceylon being about 150 miles greater than by the more direct passage) passing to the west of the Cargados, and between the [island of Galega[33] and Saya de Malha Bank,] thence doubling the northern extremity of that bank, we steered to the eastward for [Addu Atoll][34] the southernmost of the Maldive group, passing which, our course was direct for Point de Galle, making the light at that port on the evening of 10 March, after a passage of 13 days.

This port is by no means a good one, open as it is to the southwest monsoons, which throw into the harbor a very heavy swell; no one should undertake the entrance without a pilot, who will generally be found a mile or two outside the harbor. In consequence of the contracted space occupied by shipping they are all moored head and stern, with their heads to seaward. Thus they always head the swell, which at certain seasons as before mentioned is very heavy. See directions for entering the harbor from an official source.*

* Port of Point de Galle.

Point de Galle lighthouse, in latitude 6°1′45″ N, longitude 80°13′05″ E, stands at the southern angle off the fort which is built on a rocky peninsula. Several rocky inlets lay off the lighthouse, one of which (named Pigeon Island) has three coconut trees on it. The harbor is to the eastward of the fort; watering point at the opposite side of the entrance bearing from the lighthouse E by S ½ S, 1 mile; it is considered safe at all seasons, but many rocks, having from 3 to 20 feet water, are scattered over the entrance and inside, rendering it necessary for vessels to take a pilot; the outermost of these rocks having 12 feet water on it, bears from the lighthouse about S by E ¾ E, ⅝ mile.

The best anchorage in the roads is to the SW of these rocks, in from 15 to 18 fathoms water, with the lighthouse on with the Haycock or the Church with Pilots' tree, or, if the marks cannot be distinguished, the lighthouse bearing from N by E to NNE about 1 mile off shore.

SW by W, 3 miles from Galle lighthouse there is a rocky bank, called Gallehoogalle Bank, nearly a mile in extent, having in one place only 16 fathoms water, the general depth on it being 18 to 22; inside this bank there is 29 fathoms and close to it outside, 30 to 35.

Bellows Rock, which always breaks, bears from Galle lighthouse S 50° E, 2½ miles, and from Danawatty Point (the extreme of the high land forming the east side of Galle harbor) SSE ¾ E a large ½ mile, there is 10 fathoms water close to the rock on the outside.

Giudura Rock which is very dangerous, lies about 2 miles directly off the mouth of the Giudura River, and bears from Galle Lighthouse W by N ¼ N, 4⅛ miles (it is called by the natives Medda Rock). There is only 9 feet water on its shoalest part 4 and 5 fathoms about a cable's length from it all round, and 15 fathoms ¼ mile outside. Oonawatty Point kept open outside the breakers of the Whale, clears on the outside, or the extreme of the land to the Northward, kept open of some rocky islets situate close to the shore, about 6 miles to the northward of Giudura Rock.

The Whale bears from Galle lighthouse W 4° N, 2½ miles, and is nearly 1½ miles from the shore; it always breaks, but in fine weather only once in 4 or 5 min-

33. The Agalega Islands (latitude 10° S, longitude 56°30′ E), and the Saya de Malha Bank (latitude 10°30′ S, longitude 61°30′ E). Bracketed words were omitted from the manuscript.

34. Latitude 39° S, longitude 73°26′ E. Bracketed words were omitted from the manuscript.

38 This port is the general rendezvous of all the English India mail steamers, as well of those passing to and from the Red Sea as of those which double the Cape of Good Hope bound to any part of India or the China seas. Large depots of coal and patent fuel[35] are brought here from England. The quantities which arrive would seem to be enormous, yet such is the consumption of the numerous steamers constantly touching at the port (about ten each month) that they are sometimes apprehensive of falling short. Hence the Oriental Steam Navigation Company has given positive orders not to supply a single ton to any foreign vessel of war, and we could obtain only a limited supply from the Bengal government.

The town of Galle is situated upon a peninsula, the inner curve of which forms the harbor. It is entirely encompassed by thick high walls, the enclosed space probably not exceeding 15 English acres. It is within these military works from which the sea breezes are almost entirely excluded, that the inhabitants are content to live suffering from intense heat. We may suppose it must be intolerable in a latitude almost under the equator, Horsburgh placing it in latitude 6° 11′ N, and longitude 80° 17′ E.

Fresh supplies of almost every description can be obtained at this port: pigs, bullocks, poultry, fruit, and vegetables. The fish are excellent and cheap. Wood is abundant and pretty good. The water is bad, but it will be supplied from the tanks in reasonable quantities.

This fortress was constructed by the Dutch when in possession of Ceylon. The inhabitants are composed of English officials and merchants, and a singular mixture of blacks of all colors, from Negro black to dingy brown.

The Sinhalese, as the natives of Ceylon are called, are not as ugly as I had been prepared to find them. Many of the men (I saw few of the women, and none of the better class) have expressive and even handsome faces, with forms of tolerable symmetry. They seem to be amiable and are remarkable for their effeminate habits and appearance; indeed as the costumes of the two sexes are somewhat similar, it is difficult to distinguish the man from the woman, the former allowing their hair to grow to great length, which they dress with care, fastening it on the top of the head with large tortoise shell combs, such as our ladies at home would not be ashamed to wear.

The common dress of the better class of Singhalese is a jacket worn next the skin and, from the waist downward, a colored petticoat wrapped in graceful folds around the limbs and falling to the feet. The head is rarely covered. Some of the common people wrap a cloth round the brow which

utes, so that a good lookout is then necessary when passing in, there are 7 fathoms water close outside, 12 fathoms 1/4 mile, and 20 fathoms 3/4 mile off.

The Little Whale, a small rock above water with 7 fathoms close to all round, lies about halfway between the Whale and Galle lighthouse on the same line of bearing.

The Haycock, a high conical mountain, conspicuous from seaward, is a good landmark for this part of the coast; it bears from Galle lighthouse N by E 1/4 E, distant about 20 miles.

(signed) T. H. Twynam,
Master Attendant.

35. Briquettes made of coal dust mixed with pitch.

they change to the body when mixing in the crowd as ordinarily they wear
nothing but a sort of petticoat.

In our short stay I had little opportunity of making any other than very
partial observations, and of course can give but an imperfect account of the
island and its resources. I doubt, however, whether it is as flourishing a
colony as Mauritius, though possessing superior geographical advantages.
Lying as it does as a sort of outpost to the principal possessions of the
English in the east, and offering in its port of Galle a point for the distribution of intelligence throughout India and China, it is much resorted to.

The stories of the fragrance of the aroma exhaled from the odoriferous
plants and trees, which abound in Ceylon, and which voyagers declare are
experienced at a distance from the land, are gross exaggerations.[36] Although
I was twice in the country I could not discover any fragrance half equal to
that which arises from magnolia of our own country or the delightful
perfume of newly mown clover, saying nothing of the delicious odor of the
heliotrope and geranium hedges of Madeira. Indeed, the cultivated flowers
that I saw both here and at Mauritius were remarkable for their want of
fragrance.

I was told that the agricultural interests of the island did not advance as
rapidly as might be expected though labor is cheap—about 12 cents per day
—and the natives are said to be industrious. Their wants are so few, living
as they do upon fish, rice, and coconuts, that it is not necessary for them to
labor much for their sustenance. In 1852 the following enumerated articles
were exported from the entire island:

Goods exported from the island of Ceylon,
for the year ended 5 January 1852.

			£	s	d
Arrack	Gals.	168,789 & 1 keg	6,269	9	7
Areca nuts	Cwt.	78,030.0.25	54,806	4	11
Cinnamon	Lbs.	508,491	50,849	2	0
Coconuts	No.	4,637,814	6,761	4	1
Coconut oil	Gals.	443,699½ & 22 jars	31,444	9	7
Coffee	Cwt.	349,957.0.10	688,156	14	9
Coir rope	"	37,512.0.12	18,285	4	1
Copperak	"	27,026.1.0	9,678	6	7
Horns	"	2,020.3.5	3,207	17	8
Plumbago	"	25,832.3.17	5,608	2	3
Precious stones		4 packages	1,205	0	0
Rum	Gals.	9,844	654	10	6
Sugar	Cwt.	1,703	1,635	4	0
Wood	Cwt.	34,740.2.14			
	Pcs.	809,558	16,993	4	4
	Bdls.	534			
All other goods			43,083	4	7
Imports re-exported	Goods		139,927	10	11
Ex the warehouses	Specie		727,311	16	3
		Total £—1,805,877		6	1

36. Perry was doubtless familiar with Bishop Heber's hymn "From Greenland's Icy Mountains" which pays tribute to the "spicy breezes" of Ceylon.

Total value of exports, £938,637 13s 10d—whilst the imports for the same year amounted to £1,998,000. The duties arising from customs for the same period were $123,842.

It would seem strange that with such superior natural advantages, this beautiful island should produce so little. In former times, before its occupation by Europeans, it was one of the richest and most productive kingdoms in the east, considering its areal extent. The natives are remarkably well skilled in the art of irrigation, and to this day numerous vestiges of extensive works for conducting water in the fields are to be seen.

The favorite occupation and perhaps the most valuable to the natives of the present day is the cultivation of the coconut tree. Everywhere, as far as the eye can reach, are seen extensive plantations of this tree. The numerous roads throughout the island are bordered with them, giving to the weary and heated traveler not only protection from the sun, but offering at all times its ever-growing fruit, the milk of which is quite as refreshing as that of the cow, and perhaps equally wholesome.

The coconut tree like the palm of Africa is valuable in many ways. The fruit in its green state is used as food; when ripe it is ground into oil of which numerous uses are made. The cake after the oil is expressed is excellent for fattening cattle and other stock, and the husk is made into coir rope, large quantities of which are annually exported. In addition to the value of the fruit, a sort of drink called toddy is made from the sap of the tree, and the leaves are put to various useful purposes. The Palmyra palm, another valuable tree, is also found on the island. Other staple products are enumerated in the list of exports.

The pearl fisheries have very much fallen off; the natives say that oysters, having the power of locomotion, have shifted their grounds which have not yet been discovered. The season of diving is in March, the interval of calm weather between the termination of the northeast and the beginning of the southwest monsoon. Diving for the oyster is a favorite occupation of the Sinhalese, as a good diver can make more than ten times the wages of a farm laborer, and the employment is not, as has been represented, unhealthy; on the contrary it gives strength and vigor to the system.

Of the wild animals of Ceylon, the elephant may be mentioned as the most remarkable, their numbers being almost incredible. They are found in all the uncultivated parts of the island, but their favorite haunts are near to cultivated farms upon the crops of which they commit great depredations, trampling down what they do not otherwise destroy. Such is the destruction which they commit that the colonial government pays a reward of 7s 6d (about $1.85) for every tail of the animal, which is brought to the authorities, and surprising as it may appear, the government agent at Galle, Mr. Talbot, told me that he had paid during the preceeding year £200 for the tails of captured elephants in the district under his jurisdiction, being compensation for the destruction of nearly 600.

What may be considered still more surprising is that a gentleman, an officer of the army, actually killed during his residence in the island no less than 1200 of these gigantic animals. Even within a few months, two officers of the garrison—one of whom, Lieutenant Lennox, I saw—destroyed forty during a six-week visit to the jungle. They are usually killed with the rifle, and are approached either in front, or as sailors would say, on the quarter. There are but two vital spots in which a rifle ball will have any effect: one directly in the forehead, the ball penetrating the brain, and the other behind the ear. The hunter, in approaching from the rear, makes some unusual noise which causes the animal to throw forward his ears, when the deadly aim is made by his ruthless enemy.

The elephants of Ceylon are smaller than those of other parts of India, and but a small proportion of them has tusks. Of serpents there are but 20 species, and, of this small number, only four are venomous of which may be mentioned the cobra, and the tu prolanga [tic polango],[37] as the most deadly. The latter, it is said, will lie in wait to attack passengers.

The stories which are told of the anaconda, boa constrictor, or python, their attacks on cattle and horses and even on horsemen are fabulous, at least so far as regards Ceylon. There is a species of boa peculiar to the island, capable of gorging a deer, and after such a meal they are easily captured; but the enormous serpent that will swallow an entire ox, horns and all, is unknown to this region.*

> * *Cure for Snake bites.*
>
> *The following mode of treatment for the bites of snakes, scorpions, centipedes, and other venomous creatures has been extracted from the Sydney* Morning Herald, *and it has been considered advisable to adopt it without alteration in justice to the subject and the writer.*
>
> *Ipecacuanha cure for venomous bites.*

You will oblige me by inserting the accompanying two cases the result of the successful application of ipecacuanha to the bites of venomous animals. One of my servants while bathing felt something run into his foot, and on putting his hand into the water to ascertain what it was received a similar injury on that member, but he succeeded in seizing the animal, which proved to be a fish about four inches long, armed with two processes of bone close to the abdominal fin. The natives call the fish singhre. I saw the man an hour after the receipt of the wounds; he then complained of severe headache, had a hot skin and general fever; the hand and arm, also the leg and foot were very much swollen, and excessively painful, the pain shooting upwards; the lids of both eyes were also very much swollen. I mixed the ipecacuanha powder with water to the consistence of mustard, and applied it to the injured parts; in two minutes the pain had ceased, and an hour after the fever had left him; and in the course of two days the swelling in all the parts had entirely subsided. I was induced to try the above remedy from having applied it with invariable success in several cases in the bite of the centipede. I was indebted to this hint to one of your correspondents some three years ago, who wrote of the success that had invariably attended the application of ipecacuanha to the bites of the centipede. The second case was that of a palkee bearer, who was bitten on the right foot by a snake, but owing to its being at night the animal es-

37. Literally "spotted snake."

42　The population of Ceylon in 1850 was estimated at 1,422,000, of which about 8,000 were whites, who were principally officers of the government and merchants with their families.

With respect to the predominant religion of the Sinhalese, most of them are Buddhists, having numerous temples in the island, and one of great antiquity, which is visited by votaries from various parts of India. At the time we were at Galle, a Siamese sloop of war was in the harbor, having brought from Siam a number of Buddhist priests on a pilgrimage to this temple.

To what extent the numerous missionaries scattered throughout the island have been successful in their endeavors to convert these people, I had no means of learning. The number of these devoted men in Ceylon may be estimated at 92, of which the Americans count 11; the English church, 14; the Baptists, 13; the Wesleyans, 20; and the Roman Catholics, 34.

The climate of Ceylon is very much influenced by the monsoons. The northeast monsoon prevails from November to February; and the southwest, from April to September; but there are local causes which modify the winds and the temperature.

The heat is not so great as on the neighboring coast of India, the thermometer ranging ordinarily at Galle from 70° to 87°. During our short stay its highest range of Fahrenheit was 85°, and its lowest, 82°; the island is comparatively healthy; indeed by reference to its bills of mortality the deaths being less than three percent, it may be considered decidedly salubrious for an eastern country.

Of the history of Ceylon I shall say very little. That it was known to Europeans at a very early period is certain. It appears from the best authorities that Onesicritus and Nearchus, the two generals despatched by Alexander to the Persian Gulf, brought the first accounts of the island to Europe,

caped. When I saw him some time after the receipt of the injury, he complained of the leg feeling heavy, and a gnawing pain throughout the whole of the limb; it was cold to the touch and swollen. The man was suffering from great depression of the vital powers and prostration of strength. I gave him a tablespoonful of sal volatile in a little water and on examining the foot discovered the two punctures where the fangs had entered. I scarified the part freely, and put the whole of the foot into hot water, but it did not bleed freely. I therefore applied the cupping glasses to the calf of the leg in two places. In a quarter of an hour I gave him another tablespoonful of sal volatile, still keeping the foot in hot water; the heaviness of the leg was less, but the gnawing sensation continued. Three quarters of an hour after I first saw him, I applied the ipecacuanha paste, in less than five minutes the man told me his foot was quite light, and then the gnawing pain had entirely left it. The man remained in my verandah two hours, and had not any return of pain, he then went to his house in the neighborhood, and the following day I heard he was free from pain but that the leg was still swollen. For three days he applied goulard water, and in ten days came and made me a salaam, perfectly well. The scarification had not quite healed, but the leg was of the natural size.

(signed)　H. I. Thornton
Assistant Surgeon

Hong Kong Gazette

and that glowing accounts were given of its herds of elephants, its precious stones, and valuable spices. From that time the Greeks and Romans, and after them the Italians carried on a valuable trade with the island.

In the early part of the 13th century, Marco Polo, and subsequently Sir John Mandeville visited the kingdom. When the Portuguese found their way to India by way of the Cape of Good Hope, they received a friendly reception from the Sinhalese. Taking advantage of the wars and dissensions which at the time prevailed in the island between the native kings, they interposed themselves as mediators and ultimately gained a foothold which they took care to maintain. In 1520 they strongly fortified themselves at Colombo and held a controlling influence over the natives, until they were dispossessed by the assistance of the Dutch, who in their turn practiced the same treachery, and became the masters of these effeminate and confiding people.

The war with the Portuguese lasted more than 20 years, and they were not finally expelled until 1656. The several fortified places erected by them —Batticolo, Point de Galle, Negombo, and Colombo—fell successively into the hands of the Dutch.

During the European wars of the latter part of the 18th century, the French got possession of Trincomalee, but it was recaptured by the Dutch in 1796. The entire island—of course as English history declares—was, at the request of the natives, taken possession of by the British crown, under whose sovereignty it still remains. It is difficult to say which of the successive masters of these poor people were the most cruel and oppressive to the rightful holders of the kingdom, though I fear little can be said in palliation of the perfidy and fraud of either of them.

On our arrival at Point de Galle we found the United States commercial agent, Mr. John Black, a native of Scotland, confined to his premises under an execution for debt, which caused me much embarrassment and not a little mortification. Various accounts of the circumstances connected with the failure of Mr. Black were communicated to me by different parties, but I studiously refrained from interfering in the least, knowing full well, that so long as the consular arrangement of the United States remains as it now is, we can have no right to expect that the consuls or commercial agents (many of whom are unfitted in every respect for their stations) will properly represent either the dignity or commercial interests of the nation.

The consular fees at many places where they are accredited will scarcely pay their tailor's bill, and of course as a measure of necessity in order to obtain a living they have to resort to some sort of trade, oftentimes not the most dignified. I am happy to say, however, that there are many exceptions to this unfortunate state of things. Some of our consuls abroad are men of high position, and exercise a powerful influence with the local governments near which they reside, but their respectability is derived more from their commercial standing than from any advantages their consular appointment may give them, though such appointment when accompanied by high social position adds very much to the influence of its possessor.

44   I have before mentioned that a Siamese sloop of war,[38] was lying at Galle during our stay at that port. For many reasons I was desirous of showing some attention to the commander of this vessel, who I found to be a young man of much intelligence, and speaking English indifferently well. I therefore sent my aide, Lieutenant Contee, to offer my services to his vessel, and to invite him on board *Mississippi*. He seemed pleased with the compliment, and came on board the following day, and was received with due honors. I also received the visits of ten of the principal Buddhist priests who had come from Siam in the sloop of war, on a pilgrimage to the ancient temple referred to before.

    On enquiry I learnt that Prince Phar-Pen-Clow-Chow-Yon-Hon [Phra Pin Klau Chau Yu Hua], who was so civil to Mr. Roberts and the officers of the *Peacock* on the occasion of their visit to Siam in 1836, is now the second in rank, or second king of Siam, as he is called. And wishing to renew the good understanding which formerly subsisted between him and our officers, which had been somewhat interrupted by the visit of Mr. Balastier, I sent him a beautiful pistol of Colt's patent, and addressed to him the following letter:

> United States Flagship *Mississippi*.
> Point de Galle, Island of Ceylon.
> 14 March 1853.

To His Royal Highness
Phra Pin Klau Chau Yu Hua
Second King of Siam

    Most exalted Prince,

    I have been most happy to meet at this port a vessel of war belonging to the kingdom of Siam, one of beautiful form and construction, and commanded by an officer of skill and merit.

    In remembrance of the kindness you extended to the late Mr. Roberts, and the officers of the United States Ship *Peacock* in 1836, I beg your acceptance of a curious pistol which has been entrusted to my charge, to be presented to some high functionary who has sufficient acquaintance with the arts to understand its mechanism and use.

    The renown which Your Highness has acquired in America for your attainments in every branch of science induces me to place at your disposal this trifling gift of Mr. Colt.

    I hope that you will send one of your ships of Siam to America, where I can promise her officers a friendly and honorable welcome.

    It will at all times give me the greatest pleasure to render to all vessels under the Siamese flag whatever aid and assistance it may be in my power to command.

> With profound respect
> I have the honor to be
> your most obedient servant.
> (signed) M. C. Perry
> Commander-in-chief of all United States Naval Forces
> in the East India, China, and Japan Seas

38. Warship *Siam Pipop* (*Favorite*) had arrived Point de Galle 18 February and departed for Siam 18 March 1853.

Ox-drawn carriage mounted on a sled as used by Perry in 1852. By Heine

Equestrienne with footman.

Longwood, St. Helena, where Napoleon died in 1821. Heine and Brown

Bumboat at Capetown, South Africa, January 1853

Coolie and Hottentot, Capetown

Fingo Chief and Fingo woman, Capetown

Kaffir crane, Capetown. Copied by Patterson

Aloes at the top of Table Mountain, Cape of Good Hope

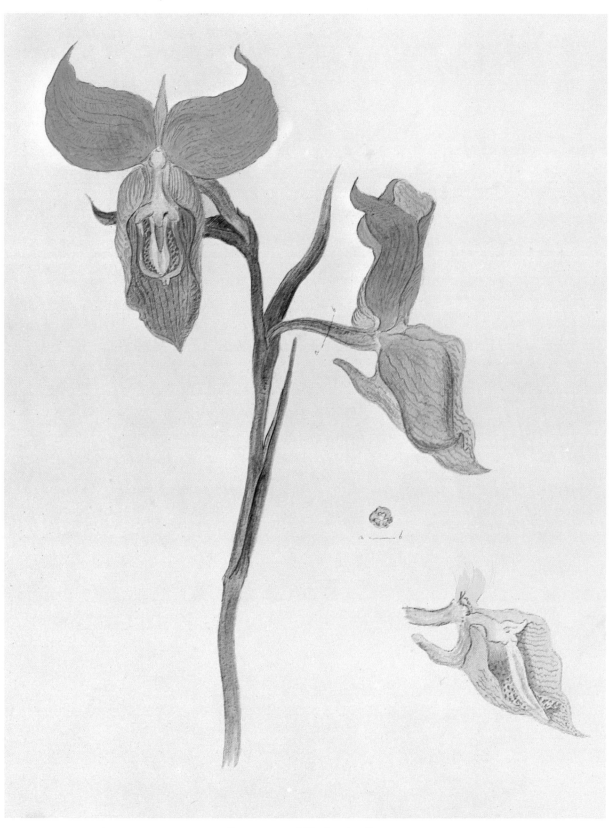

Capetown orchid, Cypripedium

Landing at Port Louis, Mauritius, 19 February 1853. Heine and Brown

Native home, Mauritius

Mauritius cathedral. Heine

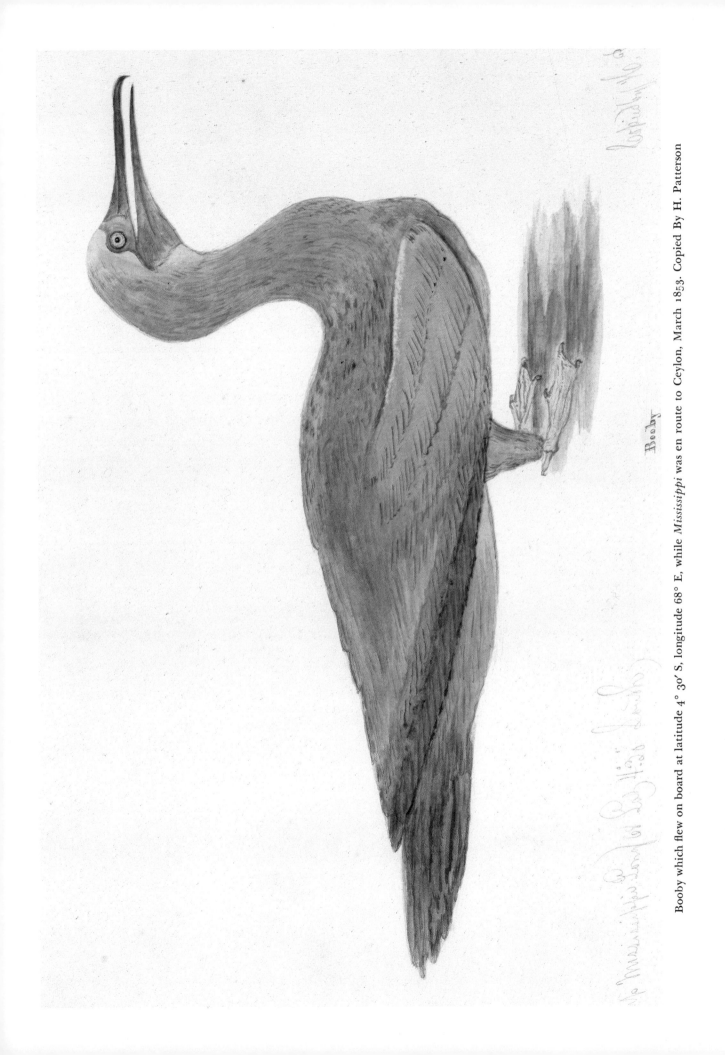

Booby

Booby which flew on board at latitude 4° 30′ S, longitude 68° E, while *Mississippi* was en route to Ceylon, March 1853. Copied By H. Patterson

Buddhist Temple, Ceylon, March 1853. By Heine.

Fishing boat, Ceylon. By Patterson

Native fishermen at Singapore, March 1853

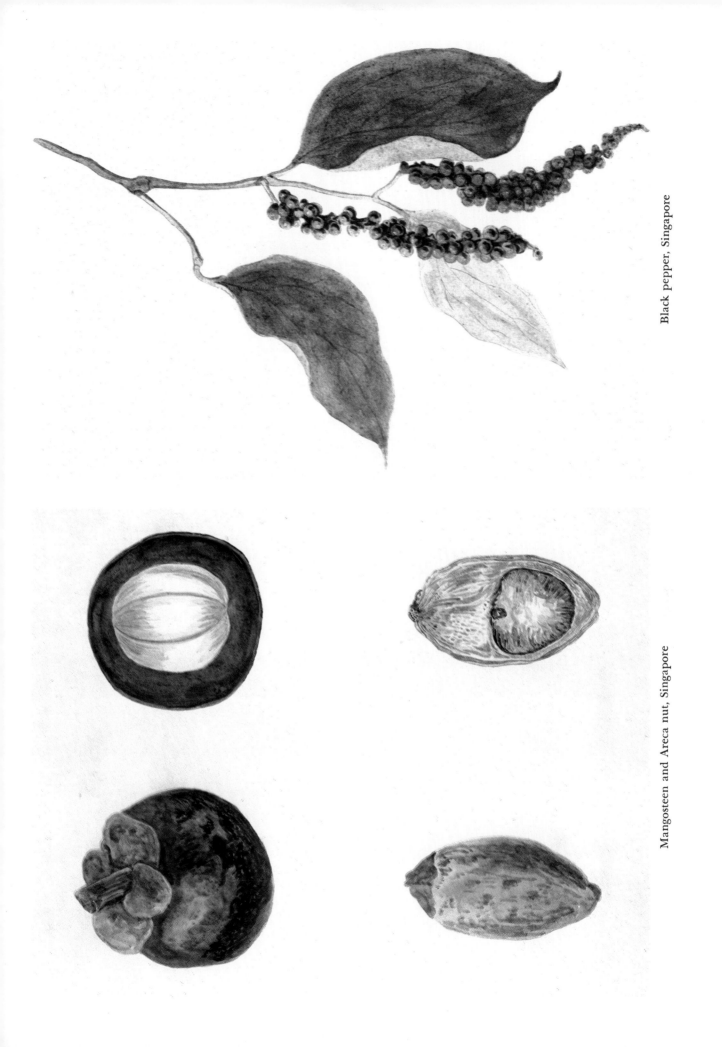

Black pepper, Singapore

Mangosteen and Areca nut, Singapore

Nutmeg from Ceylon

I also presented Captain Mun-Clow-Sar-Coun [Muen Kleau Sacora], commander of the sloop of war, with a service sword, and a copy of Bowditch's *Navigator*.

We left Galle on the morning of 15 March, and after getting clear of the harbor, shaped our course for Great Nicobar Island, the southernmost of the group of that name, intending to pass between it and Pulo Way [Pulau Weh], a small island or rock lying off the northern extremity of Sumatra. On the 20th made Great Nicobar, and passing as we had proposed, between that and Pulau Weh, we entered the straits of Malacca, steering for the Malay shore on which side of the straits the weather is represented as more settled, and the sky not so much obscured.

Fortunately the weather during our passage through the straits was favorable, and we were compelled to anchor but once. That was for the night, at the entrance of the passage between the North and South Sands, and in sight of the Aroa [Arua] Islands.[39]

On the whole the navigation of the straits is not so dangerous as might be supposed from an examination of the chart, yet it is somewhat intricate and not free from danger. A vessel can, however, always anchor, though in some parts of the channel in rather deep water.

The two most dangerous passages are what are called the East and West Channel and the narrow channel, between Formosa bank and the pyramids lying opposite, and on the northern end of the middle bank.

The first-named passage is rendered more safe by a light vessel recently anchored on "Two-and-a-half-fathom bank" and the last by the high land of Cape Formosa, the bearings and distances from which will, in clear weather, indicate the mid-channel.

Pilots for the straits may be procured at Penang when bound toward the China Seas, and at Singapore if going the other way. The *Mississippi* took no pilot, as I could not spare the time that it would require to communicate with Penang. After all—with good charts and a good lookout, added to proper precautions in anchoring when necessary—a pilot is of little further service than to identify the names of headlands and islands, and to explain the tides and currents. Indeed by trusting too much to them—as they are mostly irresponsible natives—ships may fall into dangers which experience and prudence of the captain, if left to his own judgment, would have avoided.

It is singular that the usual vertical rise and fall of the tides in the Malacca Straits is from 12 to 14 feet, and it is the more remarkable as in similar latitudes in other parts of the world there is scarcely any variation. In the depth at high and low water at Singapore the rise and fall is much the same as in the straits.

On entering from the Straits of Malacca into what is called Singapore Straits, the islands become numerous, and the passages consequently various and intricate. But in navigating this, as well as the other strait, the directions

39. North and South Sands are 20 miles east of the Arua Islands, or Cepuluan Aruah as they are known in Indonesian, which lie in latitude 2°50′ N, longitude 100°35′ E.

46 given by Horsburgh are so full and explicit that by a strict observance of them, accompanied by proper vigilance and judgment, keeping the lead in constant use, and having the anchor always ready, there is no very great danger of touching.

Singapore

25–29 MARCH 1853

On the afternoon of 25 March, being off Free Island, Mahomed, a man sent by Mr. W. W. Shaw, acting United States consul at Singapore, came on board, and at 3:50 P.M. the ship was anchored in the port.

This is a place of great resort for ships of all nations. Here you will see at anchor at the same time Chinese, Siamese, Malay, and Sumatra vessels bringing cargos, the produce of the respective countries from which they come, and taking away European and American goods. The junks from China come down the China Seas with the northeast monsoon and remain in port, retailing their cargos of teas, silks, and other products until the southwest monsoon is fairly set in, when they return to prepare for another voyage.

Singapore is a free port and commerce, being altogether unshackled, flourishes far beyond the most sanguine anticipations of those enlightened and enterprising men who but a few years ago established it as a commercial mart. At the head of these farsighted persons may be conspicuously placed the lamented Sir Stamford Raffles, a man remarkable for his sagacity and energy of purpose.

The city is built upon an island separated from the Malay Peninsula by a narrow and scarcely navigable strait. The productions of the island are similiar to those of the peninsula, the nutmeg being cultivated with considerable success.

In former times the ancient native city, upon the ruins of which the present town has been erected, was a favorite resort for pirates, the numerous islands and passages offering secure retreats from the vessels of the Dutch and English that were frequently sent in pursuit of them. Models of the various descriptions of Malay war, pirate, and sailing praus are now offered for sale by the natives, and most of them are beautiful specimens of graceful form. So much have I been struck with the beauty of a model of the sailing prau, that I propose to send one of them to the New York Yacht Club.[40]

As a commercial mart it stands preeminent, its port is always crowded with shipping, its merchants are prosperous and wealthy. Already you see scattered throughout the city, but principally along the front of the harbor and upon the quay, massive storehouses. The principal merchants occupy commodious and tasteful buildings, many of them fronting the bay. These results have grown out of the pertinacious zeal with which Raffles pursued,

40. In 1846 Commodore Perry had been elected an honorary member of the New York Yacht Club, the first person to be so honored. A *New York Herald* article of 31 March 1865 noted that the New York Yacht Club had many yacht models, and "Also as curiosities, models of Chinese war vessels, revenue boats, Singapore boats, etc., presented by the late Commodore Perry."

against the prejudices of many in superior power, his determined will in bringing his favorite project to a successful issue.

In a military as well as geographical point of view, the possession of Singapore is all important to the English. With sufficient naval force, this entrance to the China Seas may be commanded. From its advantageous position it has become an entrepôt for the produce of the neighboring kingdoms of Sumatra, Borneo, Siam, Cambodia, and Cochin China.

Singapore is a stopping and coaling place for the Peninsula and Oriental Steam Navigation Company, or as it is generally abbreviated P. & O. Company. Here that wealthy and enterprising company has erected at New Harbor, about two and a half miles from the town, a magnificent depot comprising wharves, coal sheds, storehouses, workshops, and other buildings that would do credit to any English colonial establishment, and that is giving it no faint praise.

Regular periodic mails arrive and depart this place from and to Hong Kong, Penang, and Batavia, connecting with Shanghai, Calcutta, Madras, Bengal, Bombay, Ceylon, and Mauritius by way of the Cape of Good Hope, also with the several ports of Australia, and by the Red Sea to Europe and America.

Supplies of almost every description may be obtained, and at fair prices. Water is good and is furnished in tanks by the master attendant. It is here that the famous fruit called the mangosteen is grown to perfection, but unfortunately it was not in full season at the time of our visit, but judging of it as we found it, I was greatly disappointed in my expectations of its deliciousness. Drawings of this fruit have been made by our artists, and it may be well to mention here that a series of drawings have and will be made of every object whether animal or vegetable, natural or artificial, that may be considered worthy of being noticed in this way. Already a hundred at least of these drawings have been prepared.

The domestic horse is a stumpy, fiery little creature, wonderfully strong for his size, the very best costing from $75 to $100. They are used to draw a light carriage which is in common use on the island. The driver or person in attendance runs at the head of the horse, and with a speed from six to eight miles per hour; at this rate they will traverse the crowded streets of the city. The hire of a carriage for a day is but a dollar, with a small gratuity to the driver.

The untamed animals common to the island of Singapore are generally of the same families and varieties as those of the adjoining peninsula. But the island seems to be a favorite resort for tigers, great numbers of them swimming across the narrow strait (before mentioned) from the mainland. These are of the genuine breed, making nothing of pouncing upon the unguarded traveler who may be passing through the country paths, or lying in wait for the Chinamen and natives who resort to the jungle for the purpose of cutting timber or clearing land for the planting of rice.

I have it from the best authority that a day does not pass that may not be signalized by the destruction of a human being by these ferocious beasts. At first I disbelieved the account but the acting governor, and commandant of the forces, both confirmed it by saying that so common was the occurrence that to avoid the form, trouble, and expense of a coroner's jury, which the laws require, many of these casualities were not publicly reported; but that a human life was sacrificed for every day in the year, was a fact not to be disputed. It was further remarked that a tiger who had once feasted upon human flesh would reject his accustomed food of venison and the wild boar for this more savory fare.

These accounts of the fondness of the tiger for human flesh may be somewhat exaggerated, but they claim the same authenticity as the ordinary representations of voyagers who make up their journals as well from what they hear as what passes under their actual observation. The taste of the tiger ought to be considered reasonable enough, as it is an undisputed fact, derived from the most authentic sources, that those savages who follow the practice of cannibalism are more fond of an arm or leg of a well-conditioned prisoner than are epicures at home of the favorite parts of any beast or bird.

The following quotation from the journal of Sir Stamford Raffles, an authority not to be questioned, will give confirmation to these assertions. He thus speaks of the practices of a tribe of Malays called Battas who inhabit a part of the island of Sumatra.

I have said the Battas are not a bad people, and I still think so, notwithstanding they eat one another, and relish the flesh of a man better than that of an ox or a pig. You must merely consider that I am giving you an account of a novel state of society. The Battas are not savages, for they write and read, and think full as much and more than those who are brought up at our Lancastrian and National Schools. They have also codes of laws of great antiquity, and it is from a regard for these laws and a veneration for the institutions of their ancestors that they eat each other. The law declares that for certain crimes, four in number, the criminal shall be eaten ALIVE. The same law declares also that in great wars, that is to say, one district with another, it shall be lawful to eat the prisoners, whether taken alive, dead, or in their graves.

In the four great cases of crimes the criminal is also duly tried and condemned by a competent tribunal. When the evidence is heard sentence is pronounced, when the chiefs drink a dram each, which last ceremony is equivalent to signing and sealing with us.

Two or three days then elapse to give time for assembling the people; and in cases of adultery it is not allowed to carry the sentence into effect unless the relations of the wife appear and partake of the feast. The prisoner is then brought forward on the day appointed, and fixed to a stake with his hands extended. The husband or party injured comes up and takes the first choice, generally the ears; the rest then, according to their rank, take the choice pieces, each helping himself according to his liking. After all have partaken, the chief person goes up and cuts off the head, which he carries home as a trophy. The head is hung up in front of the house, and the brains are carefully preserved in a bottle for purposes of witchcraft, etc. In devouring the flesh it is sometimes eaten raw, and sometimes grilled, but it must be eaten upon the spot. Limes, salt, and pepper are always in readiness, and they sometimes eat rice with the flesh, but never drink toddy or spirits; many carry bamboos with them, and filling them with blood drink it off. The assembly consists of men alone, as the flesh of man is prohibited to the females; it is said, however, that they get a bit by stealth now and then.

I am assured, and *really* do believe that many of the people prefer human flesh to any other, but notwithstanding this *penchant* they never indulge the appetite except on lawful occasions. The palms of the hands, and the soles of the feet, are the delicacies of epicures!

On expressing my surprise at the continuance of such extraordinary practices, I was informed that formerly it was usual for the people to eat their parents when too old to work. The old people selected the horizontal branch of a tree, and quickly suspended themselves by their hands, while their children and neighbours, forming a circle, danced round them, crying out, "When the fruit is ripe, then it will fall." This practice took place during the season of limes, when salt and pepper were plenty; and as soon as the victims became fatigued, and could hold on no longer, they fell down, when all hands cut them up, and made a hearty meal of them. This practice, however, of eating the old people has been abandoned, and, therefore, there are hopes of future improvement.

This state of society you will admit to be very peculiar. It is calculated, that certainly not less than from sixty to one hundred Battas are thus eaten in a year in times of peace.

Serpents are not very numerous, though the cobra is to be found on the island; of other animals, the deer and wild boar are common. I made inquiries respecting two remarkable inhabitants of the waters about Malacca and Sumatra, described by Raffles. These were the sailing fish the natives call *kan layer* [ikan lajar], and the *duyong* [dugong] described by Valentin,[41] and so long talked of as the mermaid, but the people told me they had become very scarce if not entirely extinct. This, however, is not probable, and it is quite certain, with the expenditure of a little time and money, specimens of both may be obtained.

Shells collected upon the adjacent coasts, and along the Straits of Malacca are brought in large quantities to Singapore for sale, and I was fortunate in obtaining many very good specimens. I also employed several of the boatmen in collecting living shells from the immediate waters; our own attempts with the trail proving unsuccessful.

I noticed a singular description of animal here called the water buffalo; it resembles in size the ox of our country, but has a different shaped head, and its skin is somewhat similar to that of the rhinoceros. Notwithstanding the thickness and apparent impenetrable character of the skin, the animal suffers much from the flies, and to avoid them immerses its body in water when not feeding. It is in common use as a draft animal, one only being harnessed in a cart with shafts. It is guided by its driver with a small rope, fastened to a ring or thong which is passed through the nostrils of the docile beast.

The chief articles of export from Singapore, most of which are brought from neighboring countries, are tin, Gambier nutmegs, sugar, tortoise shells, and some minor articles.

As has been before observed the present city has been built upon the site of the ancient capital of the Malayan kingdom or, as it was sometimes called, the kingdom of Malacca. It was erected in the early part of the

41. François Valentijn (1656–1727) who wrote *Oud en nieuw Oost-Indien,* . . . (Amsterdam, 1724–26).

twelfth century, and some hundred years after was conquered by a chief from Java, who transferred the royal residence to Malacca. From that period its population and wealth gradually diminished and, at the time it was taken possession of by the English in 1819 very few vestiges of the old city remained, it being a mere resort for pirates.

At this moment it contains a population of 80,000 composed of Europeans, Chinese, Americans, Jews, Arabs, Malays, and natives of the neighboring countries. The Europeans are the smaller, and the Chinese the greater number; of the latter it is stated there are 60,000. Amongst these industrious people are found nearly all the artisans, fishermen, laborers, and small dealers. Most of these different nations have religious temples in the city, several of which I visited, as also a mosque belonging to the Arabs.

In one of the recesses of a Chinese temple the devil is represented in human form, but of hideous countenance, and just in front of him is placed an image of the Holy Mother and Child. This was not explained, but the conjecture of myself and companion, Captain Adams, was that this additional image had its origin from some circumstance connected with the Roman Catholic religion, as introduced by the Portuguese. Whether the two images are intended to represent the Mother and Child at the mercy of the devil, or his satanic majesty awed by the presence of her gentle spirit, we could not divine.

To Sir Stamford Raffles—who ever proved himself a master spirit in every enterprise he undertook—the British government and the East India Company are indebted for this valuable appendage, and there was some degree of justice attending his usurpations, a virtue rarely practiced by the European governments, in seizing without scruple upon the finest countries of the East, and casting the thraldom of political if not servile slavery upon the inhabitants.

Sir Stamford actually purchased from the Rajah of Johore and Singapore the right of sovereignty over the island and its dependencies for a stipulated sum and an annual pension, and I believe the payments have been regularly paid. The poor Rajah doubtless made a good bargain, for his royal ancestors had been driven from their homes, and deprived of their territories without any commiseration by those people from Europe, who pride themselves upon their moral and religious qualities; first the Portuguese, then the Dutch, and more recently the English.

The various races inhabiting Sumatra, the Malayan peninsula, and the numerous islands in the adjacent seas are all of the Malay family, but widely distinguished by habits and customs. Sir Stamford remarks:

I cannot but consider the Malayan nation as one people, speaking one language, though spread over so wide a space, and preserving their character and customs in all the maritime states lying between the Sulu Sea and the southern ocean, and bounded longitudinally by Sumatra and the western side of Papua, or New Guinea.

The Malayan language may no doubt be traced to a still further extent, and particularly among the South Sea islands, but that point belongs to a dissertation on the origin of the nation and its language and need not be attended to here.

Our stay was so short that I saw but little of the European society. Exchanges of visits and salutes with the acting governor, Mr. Church, and the commandant of the forces, and some official business with Mr. Shaw, the acting United States consul, was the extent of my intercourse with the European residents at Singapore. The only person I saw, who seemed to be imbued with the true spirit of hospitality, was a Chinese merchant by the name of Whampoa, a gentleman-like and intelligent person, who spoke English very well. He has the most beautiful country residence in the island, where many of the officers visited and were hospitably entertained.

Adjoining his house which is large, commodious, and tastefully furnished —the rooms being filled with articles of curiosity and of vertu—are extensive ornamental grounds and farms upon which most of the productions of the island, useful as well as ornamental, are cultivated in great perfection. He has collected many rare birds and animals; the most remarkable of the birds are the cassowary and crowned pigeon from New Guinea; he has also a singular breed of peafowl, among them one perfectly white. In his stable he has an Arabian horse, the most beautiful animal I ever beheld, perfectly white, and as docile as a lamb. This splendid creature Whampoa keeps for his own use under the saddle. I dined and passed the night at this lovely place, and was much gratified.

I was fearful of not being able to obtain even a small supply of coal at this place. Not a pound was to be purchased, nor could I enter into an arrangement for the purchase of any from the Labuan Company. The whole produce of the mines had been engaged by the P. & O. Company under a contract to deliver 1000 tons per month. Fortunately, however, the stock of coal of that company at Hong Kong was falling short and, as it was difficult to procure vessels to transport an additional stock, the agent of the company at Singapore agreed to lend me 230 tons, provided I would return it at Hong Kong. By this arrangement I was accommodated, and the company benefited by saving the conveyance of that quantity to their principal depot in China.

Having taken on board the coal borrowed from the P. & O. Company, and a supply of water, we left Singapore on the morning of 29 March and proceeded through what is called the Middle Channel, passing near to a lighthouse, erected on a rock, called Pedra Branca, intending to run up on the Cochin China and Hainan shores.

With respect to the navigation of the China Sea I shall be very brief; so much has been published upon the subject, that any remarks of mine would be altogether superfluous. It is enough to say, that nearly the whole expanse of sea, from Borneo and Palawan across to Cochin China is rendered dangerous by numerous coral reefs, banks, and islands. Many of the reefs and banks are below the surface of the water, and however truthfully the surveys of experienced hydrographers may have marked the depth upon these banks, as allowing of sufficient water for ships to pass over them, yet, such is the rapidity with which those little architects, the coral zoophytes, build up these foundations of future islands, that the work of a few years may materially change the character and depth of the soundings.

With these obstructions in the way, it may well be supposed that the China Sea cannot be navigated without danger, and especially in thick blowing weather. Still thousands of vessels pass annually through its various channels in safety whilst now and then a disaster occurs.

The currents are influenced by the prevailing winds, but the tides here, as in other parts of the world, are governed by some mysterious laws, which the search and wisdom of man have not yet explained. The vertical rise and fall of the tides upon the coast of Cochin China vary from six to fourteen feet, and the periods and duration of the ebb and flood are by no means regular. On the same shore in latitude 12°, there is but one tide in 24 hours.

But as I am a newcomer in this part of the world, I shall not venture with my present inexperience to explain what I do not comprehend myself. Horsburgh has some general remarks upon the subject of tides, which are quoted below:

The tides in high latitudes, generally rise and fall more than in low latitudes, and it has been said that the perpendicular flux and reflux was very little within the tropics, which is not always the case. At the head of the Gulf of Cambay in Lat. 22° North, the perpendicular depth of the rise and fall of the tides is from thirty to thirty-six feet at the full and change of the moon. At the same time, it is twenty to twenty-one feet in Surat Road, and from fifteen to seventeen feet in Bombay harbor.

In the Gulf of Martaban, which is far within the tropics, the perpendicular depth of the rise and fall of the tide at the full and change of the moon is twenty-three and twenty-four feet, and off Rangoon Bar about twenty or twenty-one feet.

In Gaspar Straits, within 2½° of the equator, there is sometimes from local causes a rise and fall of 16 or 17 feet on the spring tide, but the rise and fall of the tide is seldom so great as this in places situated near the equator.

Although in most places, the tide flows twice every 24 hours, this is not universally the case within the tropics, for amongst several of the Eastern Islands the tide flows only once in 24 hours; the passage of the moon over the meridian, generally makes high water at these places; but in some parts, the tide is highest when the moon is near, or in the horizon.

In many places far beyond the tropics, the tide likewise flows only once in 24 hours, particularly on the southern coast of Van Dieman's land; but at Port Dalrymple on the north coast, the tide flows twice in 24 hours.

It will be remembered that during the last month the ship has been within the equatorial latitudes, and we again had excellent opportunities of observing the phenomena of the zodiacal light; almost every morning and evening, about the rising and setting of the sun, these brilliant radiations were beautiful beyond description. Our chaplain, Mr. Jones,[42] has given much of his time to the observance and description of these remarkable appearances, and the artists have made drawings of a few of those the most remarkable.

42. The observations of Mr. Jones were published as volume III of the Hawks *Narrative*.

Early in the morning of 6 April we descried in every direction, as far as the eye could reach, vast numbers of fishing boats. They seemed to be from ten to twenty tons measurement, and were sailing in couples about 90 fathoms apart before the wind, having a net extended between each couple, and as I have since been informed were taking a small fish similar to the sardine of the Mediterranean. Indeed the mode of taking these fish is precisely the same in both localities. No fewer than 269 of these little craft were at one time counted from the poop of the *Mississippi*. These boats were curiously rigged, having several square sails on two or three masts, exhibiting somewhat the appearance at a distance, of courses and topsails, which they hoisted or lowered to graduate their rate of sailing to keep way with their respective consorts.

The appearance of these craft gave indication of the proximity of the land, and accordingly at 10:30 A.M. it was discovered. The ship, continuing her course toward the roadstead of Macao, was anchored at dark under the Ladrones.

Hong Kong

7 APRIL 1853

The following morning we proceeded to Macao Roads, and after communicating with the shore, continued on to Hong Kong where we anchored about sunset. Here we found the sloops of war *Plymouth* and *Saratoga,* and storeship *Supply,* the *Susquehanna* having sailed about a fortnight previous for Shanghai.

On the anchoring of the *Mississippi,* the salutes prescribed by naval regulations were received from the *Plymouth* and *Saratoga,* and returned by this ship. On the following day, the customary exchanges of salutes were made with the forts, and foreign vessels of war in port, including a very agreeable interchange of civilities, official and personal, with Commodore Roquemaurel of the French Navy who had his pendant on board frigate *Capricieuse.*

It is unnecessary to note on every occasion the courtesies that American officers invariably receive from the British authorities abroad—civil, naval, and military. In no instance during a long service in foreign countries have I experienced any want of hospitable attention, though in fact the governments of all nations excepting only the United States furnish the means for public entertainments by ample allowances of "table money," and it becomes a duty with their officials to expend it. Yet the English at large are in all their social relations hospitable and they consider themselves poor indeed when they cannot occasionally have a friend to partake of a joint accompanied by a plum pudding and a bottle of wine.

On arriving at Macao I was greatly surprised and disappointed to find that the *Susquehanna*—the vessel intended by the government as my flagship—had been sent to Shanghai by Commander Kelly under his temporary authority as senior officer at one particular part of the station, and for the limited interval embraced between the departure of Commodore Aulick

54 and my arrival at Macao, though I had for some time been within the limits of my command, and was daily expected in China.

This extraordinary and injudicious exercise of a doubtful authority has greatly embarrassed me, inasmuch as it will cause serious delay in the concentration of the small force now at my disposal with which I had proposed to make an early visit to Japan. It presents a feature of questionable official conduct calculated to injure the harmony and consequent efficiency of the squadron. I shall at present, however, refrain from commenting further upon this singular course of Commander Kelly, being willing to suppose that he was acting according to the best of his judgment, and irrespectively of circumstances which had recently transpired in the squadron.[43]

This officer not only detached the *Susquehanna* on separate service, but actually left it discretionary with her commander to proceed on a mission, or as far as he could with his ship, to the city of Nanking, situated some two hundred miles up a river of very difficult navigation. Under these circumstances, I found it expedient to send an order to Commander Buchanan to remain at Shanghai until my arrival in the *Mississippi* at that port, and I despatched Commander Kelly in the *Plymouth* to convey the order.

This departure of the *Susquehanna* for Shanghai caused me a double disappointment as the commissioner to China, the Honorable Humphrey Marshall, accompanied by the secretary of legation Dr. Parker, were both passengers in her. From the latter as well as from Mr. Paul S. Forbes, United States consul at Canton, I had expected to have received much valuable information and advice with regard to my visit to Japan.

Canton

APRIL 1853

I had imagined from the description given of Canton that it was a place of great interest to strangers, that I should see myriad boats decked with gay banners and moving in all directions—the floating domiciles of a hundred thousand people moored on each side of the river—the pagodas, bungalows, and Chinese cottages as represented in books upon China and the Chinese which as a child I had studied with admiration.

But, alas, all was disappointment. The passage from Whampoa to the great city is a muddy shallow stream, with scarcely a hut upon its banks until near the city. Swarms of floating habitations are seen moored to the banks, five and six deep, and occupied by a wretched half-clad people. Through these two lines of receptacles of poverty and filth you pass until the mercantile factory, the residence of most of the foreign merchants, is seen. It is here that the stranger lands and is conducted to the house of the merchants to whom he has letters, for there are no comfortable houses of entertainment in the city.

43. Humphrey Marshall, the newly arrived envoy extraordinary and minister plenipotentiary to China, had persuaded Kelly to make this move. Perry continued to have trouble with American diplomats who wanted to use his ships.

I shall not attempt, at this my first visit, to give any account of the commercial and social condition of China. Upon those subjects volumes have been recently published by persons whose long residence in the country has qualified them to impart information upon every topic connected with this singular empire. I may refer to the *Chinese Repository;* Martin's *China; China* by Davis; *Middle Kingdom* by S. Wells Williams; *Lettres édifiantes et curieuses; A Visit to the Five Consular Ports,* by G. Smith, Lord Bishop of Victoria; *An American's Sojourn in Canton;* etc.[44]

The Chinese may be looked upon as a remarkable race of people; hardy, frugal, and industrious, and if it were not for the viciousness of the government and laws under which they live, they would become a formidable nation. In physical development they are quite equal to the mass of Europeans. The greater majority of the males are taught to read and write; of three servants in my employ all write the Chinese characters with apparent grace and ease.

Of all races they are probably the most knavish; from the highest mandarin to the lowest boatman the art of deception and trickery is practiced with consummate skill and audacity. To cheat and rob those whom they call barbarians might well be expected, considering the light in which they hold us, but they are equally prone to rob each other, both on the land and water. And there is no part of the world where piracies are at this day more open or more frequent. The Canton River swarms with piratical boats; the fishermen frequently join the marauding parties and if opportunity offers they actually rob and maltreat each other.

An instance may be adduced of this petty thievery. In proceeding with the *Mississippi* from Macao to Whampoa, one of two China boats in tow was swamped by bad steering. The other in fear of a like fate cast off, and attempted to proceed up the river under sail. Her owner who happened to be on board expressed his fears that she would be overhauled by pirates before she arrived at Whampoa, and so it happened; she was boarded and robbed a few hours after she had lost sight of the *Mississippi.*

Several piracies were committed during our stay at Hong Kong, almost under the guns of the vessels of war; and even London cannot furnish more expert thieves and pickpockets than are found in this Anglo-Chinese city. The third lieutenant of the *Mississippi* at early twilight in the evening, at the moment of stepping into a hired boat to return to his ship, was seized amidst a crowd of people, and an attempt made to pull his watch from his fob; fortunately his Pickwickian rotundity saved the watch but the chain

44. *The Chinese Repository,* 20 volumes, May 1832–December 1851, Canton, etc. R. Montgomery Martin, *China; Political, Commercial, and Social; in an Official Report to Her Majesty's Government* (London: J. Madden, 1847). Sir John Francis Davis, *China, During the War and Since the Peace* (London: Longman, Brown, Green, and Longmans, 1852). Samuel Wells Williams, *The Middle Kingdom: A Survey of the . . . Chinese Empire and Its Inhabitants* (New York & London: Wiley & Putnam, 1848). *Lettres édifiantes et curieuses concernant l'Asie, l'Afrique et l'Amérique . . .* [etc.]; published under the direction of M. L. Aimé-Martin, 4 volumes (Paris: A. Desrez [etc.], 1838–43). The Reverend George A. Smith, *Narrative of an Exploratory Visit to Each of the Consular Cities of China . . . in Behalf of the Church Missionary Society, in the years 1844, 1845, 1846* (London: Seeley, Burnside & Seeley, [etc.], 1847). Osmond Tiffany, *The Canton Chinese; or, The American's Sojourn in the Celestial Empire* (Boston and Cambridge: J. Munroe and Company, 1849).

56 was carried off in triumph. Thus the most cowardly people are frequently the most successful thieves.

On my visit to Canton, I was accompanied by several officers, most of whom were accommodated at the house of Mr. Paul S. Forbes, United States consul, and head of the firm of Russell & Company. Here we were made quite at home by Mr. Spooner, one of the firm, Mr. Forbes being absent at Shanghai. It was only necessary in purchasing articles anywhere in the city to direct the shopkeeper to send the bills to Mr. Forbes' house and he would have no hesitation in delivering the article.

Macao
APRIL 1853

On going from Canton to Macao, Mr. Spooner kindly offered me the use of the magnificent residence belonging to the same firm at that place. I accordingly with three of the officers took possession, supposing that we were to be our own providers. Consequently, our caterer, Commander Adams, who is somewhat of a gourmand, was very particular in ordering the head servant in charge of the establishment to procure this and that. It was only to express a wish, and it was promptly attended to. What was our surprise when on going on board, not a penny would be received by this prince of majordomos excepting the ordinary gratuity. He said that his employers were always happy to have their house occupied by their friends, and he hoped we would not think of going elsewhere on our next visit to Macao.

When once domiciliated in one of these hospitable mansions the guest finds himself quite at home in the enjoyment of most agreeable society. It is a custom of the merchants of the East to extend to strangers of respectability the most unreserved hospitality. Indeed, such is the freedom of the guest that he has only to order whatever he may require; nor does his host trouble himself about the matter, he is engaged with his business, and the major-domo of the establishment pays all the bills accruing from purchases and incidental expenses of the guests, though of course to be refunded.

In a word, one may imagine himself in a well organized French hotel where he has only to express a wish to have it gratified, the only difference is, in one the guest pays roundly for these conveniencies, and the other absolutely nothing beyond suitable gratuities to the servants. Afterward at Shanghai, again a guest at another splendid residence of the same firm where every want was exhausted, I was asked if I was fond of soda water. My reply was in the negative, that the only mineral water I cared for was that from the Congress Spring, Saratoga; the next morning before I was out of bed, a servant entered my room with a bottle of Congress water.

Shanghai
4–16 MAY 1853

During the stay of the ships at Shanghai, there was a constant succession of dinners and balls, and the officers were most hospitably entertained everywhere. One of the most interesting visits I made was to return that of the

Tantae [Tao t'ai] or governor and commander of the city, who called upon
me at the residence of the United States consul, Mr. Cunningham, and
afterward visited the ship.

Our party consisted of about twenty officers including the consul, all in
uniform, each being carried in sedan chairs from the consular residence to
the government house, situated in the center of the Chinese city, within the
walls. On arriving at the entrance we were received with the usual Chinese
salute of three guns, and a band of musicians. The Tao t'ai met us at the
threshold, and escorted me into the audience room. Here we were seated,
the Tao t'ai and myself, according to Chinese ceremony, upon a platform a
little raised above the floor.

In a short time refreshments consisting of teas, liquor, and cake were
handed round in succession. After a stay of an hour we returned in the same
manner we came, traversing the narrow streets of the city with our long
procession of chairs, and jostling everyone who obstructed the way.

The political condition of China at the present time is very unsettled; the
whole empire seems to be in a state of agitation auguring [45] some mighty
revolution. One half of the country is in occupation of an insurgent force
who claims to represent the old Chinese who were dispossessed a long time
since by the present ruling Tartar dynasty.

At the head of the rebel force is a very sagacious man, who from disappointment, or some imaginary wrong growing out of his examination for
literary honors (so highly prized by the Chinese) became disgusted, and at
once raised the flag of disaffection, and alternately of open rebellion. At first
he had only a few followers, but in the course of time multitudes flocked to
his standard and now, after overrunning a great many provinces, he is
quietly in possession of the great city of Nanking.

This man denounces the prevailing religion and has caused to be
destroyed numerous Buddhist temples. He professes a faith somewhat similar to that of the Mormons in America, and gives forth that he has constant
communion with God, and has been acknowledged as his Son. His ignorant
and lawless followers believe, or pretend to believe in his revelations. By
these cunning devices he has acquired immense power. He pretends to
fraternize with Christians, and argues that all Christian nations, by reason of
similar faith, should aid him in driving out of the empire the present
usurping family, and putting upon the celestial throne a true son of heaven,
a believer in the Decalogue, and a scion of the old Chinese monarchs. He
does not pretend to any claims himself to the imperial diadem, but it may
well be imagined from his professed dogmas of religion that when the time
arrives he will constitute the great celestial on earth.

It is not extravagant to suppose that these internal commotions are but
the beginning of some great change in the condition of the eastern nations,
and in connection with the extraordinary advances of the Anglo-Saxon race,
and the discoveries of new mines of wealth in countries hitherto compara-

---

45. Hawks *Narrative*, p. 148, and other sources say "arguing," but it is clearly "auguring" in
the *Journal*.

tively unknown, predict some mighty revolution which is to prostrate the despotic power which is now in the ascendant, and rear up in its place forms of government more consonant to the spirit and intelligence of the age.

All these changes are doubtless preordained and directed by an almighty hand, and the instruments which he employs to carry out his great designs are impelled by a divine power which they in their system vainly ascribe to their own superior wisdom. The fate of Japan is foreshadowed by the concurrence of so many startling events and though the catastrophe may be for a time deferred, the issue is certain.

The navigation of the coast of China, from Hong Kong to the Yang-tse-Keang [Yangtze River], is at most seasons difficult and perplexing; the frequent fogs and irregular tides and currents make it very annoying to strangers when close in with the coast. Fortunately, however, vessels are always, when near the land, on anchoring ground. Although they are sometimes obliged to bring-to in situations exposed to wind from the sea, it is better to resort to the anchor than to drift blindly amongst groups of islands and reefs.

If the weather is moderately clear, vessels may run from island to island, and thus navigate the coast with perfect safety and convenience, but the fogs which prevail at certain seasons scarcely allow of this advantage. Neither the *Susquehanna* nor *Mississippi* had a meridian observation of the sun on their passage from Hong Kong to Shanghai.

The entrance to the Yangtze River, which leads to the commercial city of Shanghai, is obstructed on either side by shoals, which make it dangerous for vessels not having pilots. On the north side is a shoal called the North Sand, extending some six leagues seaward from the mainland; and on the south side is a parallel shoal called the South Sand, projecting nearly as far from the shore on that side. The outer extremities of these shoals are beyond sight of the mainland. The channel between the two shoals may be estimated in width about two miles, and as there are no lighthouses, boats, beacons, or buoys to indicate to strangers the entrance of the channel, excepting only a small islet called Gutzlaff Island, which is to be brought to bear (if it can be seen) south by east, distant twelve miles, when the vessel is to run northwest for the channel. Although little is known of the time and set of the tide, both the flood and ebb set with a velocity of four or five knots, and vary in course an entire quadrant of the compass.

The first of the flood sets W by N, and gradually inclines to the north and west, and the last runs NW by N. The ebb first sets E by N, and changes round to SE by S and neither set directly up or down the channel until half flood or half ebb. The rise and fall in the Yangtze River averages about ten feet, and thus vessels run haphazard into the channel, or perchance upon one of the sister Sands. More than four out of every hundred foreign vessels resorting to Shanghai are lost, and still nothing has been done to remedy the evil.

On my visit to this river in the *Mississippi,* I at once saw that until proper landmarks and beacons were established to indicate the entrance to this river, it was an unfit resort for any but the smaller vessels of the squadron, and consequently an unsuitable place for a naval depot. The *Susquehanna, Plymouth,* and *Supply* all grounded on going in, and the latter remained thumping on the North Sand twenty-two hours, and was saved from total loss only by a providential change of wind. The *Mississippi* was carried by the confusion of her pilot out of the channel, but by good fortune did not stop, though she ran into nineteen feet of water (one foot less than her draft) on the South Sand. The power of her engines rescued her from danger.

In truth there is danger to all vessels entering this river. It is matter of surprise that the foreign merchants who are gathering large fortunes by the increasing trade of Shanghai are not disposed to contribute a few thousands of their earnings to render the navigation of the river less dangerous. The argument with them is, that inasmuch as they pay insurance, and the underwriters reap the premium, it is the interest of the latter, and should be their business to meet the outlay. They in reply say that as the shipowners and merchants are required to pay premiums equivalent to the risks of navigation they are satisfied. But not a thought is given to the careworn officers and crews, without whose toil and danger neither the underwriters nor the merchants would reap the profit which they so much covet. Nor do they dream of the exposure of human life by the want of these beacons which common humanity would suggest; the almighty dollar is the idol which they worship.

It is but justice to mention that Mr. Cunningham, the United States consul of the house of Russell & Co., and Mr. Beale, of the English house of Dent & Co. are ready, as I was informed, to subscribe liberally to the accomplishment of the desired object. A tugboat ordered to be built in the United States, by order of the two houses referred to, is daily expected, and will be employed in towing vessels up and down the river.

Shanghai is quite populous, containing probably 250,000 inhabitants, and like all Chinese cities is disgustingly filthy. Those who have seen much of China, say that the cities and towns throughout the empire are all similar in appearance, with narrow streets from eight to ten feet in width. These are intersected by alleys leading to the rear of the dwellings, which are still more contracted, and if anything more nasty. The filthiness of the city gives no favorable idea of the domestic cleanliness of the people; indeed, it is only necessary to see the men and women in the streets to decide at once upon their uncleanly habits.

The city proper is encompassed by walls, but the suburbs are extensive. Since the termination of the Opium War,[46] numerous splendid dwellings as residences of the foreign merchants have been erected along the margin of the river below the Chinese quarter. Here one sees wide and well-graded streets with beautiful gardens, and all the comforts and conveniencies that are to be found in any part of the world. Two handsome Gothic churches

46. Between Great Britain and China in 1840.

60   have also been erected, one belonging to the English, the other to the American Protestant Episcopal missions.

Trade has greatly increased at this place; cotton, rice, wheat, barley, beans, sweet potatoes, and other valuable products being raised. I saw no beasts of burden, everything is transported by men, the weights being suspended on the two ends of a stout piece of bamboo, which rests upon the shoulder of the carrier. In this way the heaviest weights are carried by one or more carriers. The strength of these men is truly surprising.

The singular custom of compressing the feet of female children is still very generally practiced, and women old and young are constantly seen tottering along the streets, upon deformed stumps encased in tiny shoes, scarcely large enough for an American girl of five years. This absurd, and to our taste disgusting, practice cannot be exclusively confined to the higher and richer classes, as I saw women of the lower orders, hideous in general appearance, hobbling through the streets, and some of them with burdens.

One of the peculiarities of this part of China is the general temperature of its atmosphere. Although on a parallel of latitude actually south of Charleston on the American side of the Atlantic, and of Mogador on the African side, the temperature of Shanghai corresponds better with that of Baltimore, where they experience the extremes of heat and cold. During the last winter, the thermometer stood at 14 degrees below zero. Ice, which is collected in icehouses in winter, is kept by fishermen through the summer for the preservation of their fish for market. The merchants also have their icehouses.

On the whole, Shanghai is a most delightful residence, especially to those who are accumulating fortunes to enjoy in their native land. But alas for us officers and crews of the Navy—visiting, as we do, all climes for the protection of the interests of these very merchants—we spend our lives in hard service to die in comparative penury.

On Monday evening, 16 May, the *Mississippi* moved down the river, and was followed the next day by this ship [*Susquehanna*].[47] The *Plymouth* was left behind for a short time to await the course of events in the rebel camp, her commander having orders to follow me as soon as he was of opinion he could do so consistently with the safety of American interests at Shanghai.

Storeship *Supply,* having escaped from shipwreck on the North Sand, was anchored, together with *Mississippi* and *Susquehanna,* for three days off the mouth of the river waiting for the arrival of hired storeship *Caprice,* expected from Macao. On 23 May, finding she did not make her appearance, the squadron got under way, the *Supply* in tow of the *Mississippi,* for Napa [Naha], on the island of Lew Chew.[48] Fortunately, after getting abreast of Saddle Island, we discovered the *Caprice* standing in, and I directed her to follow us to Lew Chew. It is well to mention here that a junk belonging to Russell & Co., which had been hired to convey a cargo of coal to the mouth

47. During Perry's stay of ten days in Shanghai he transferred his flag from *Mississippi* to *Susquehanna.* See Morison, "*Old Bruin,*" p. 298.
48. Now Okinawa. See Morison, "*Old Bruin,*" p. 300.

of the river to be put on board *Mississippi,* was—being at the time in charge
of the commander and officers of the *Mississippi*—lost on the north shoal.

On reaching the neighborhood of the Lew Chew group, and being in sight
of Agentin [Aguni] Island, the tow line of the *Supply* was cast off, and her
commander ordered to proceed to Naha, the *Susquehanna* and *Mississippi*
steaming toward that port, which they reached on the evening of the 26th, in
company with the *Saratoga* from Macao, having fallen in with her off the
harbor.

On 28 May the *Supply* arrived and anchored.

Everyone who has known anything of the Lew Chew Islands of late, has
heard of a Mr. Bettelheim,[49] an English missionary, who with his family has
resided seven years in the midst of the singular people inhabiting Great Lew
Chew, and in direct opposition to their wishes. Of his character or qualifi-
cations as a missionary I shall not venture an opinion, but with respect to
the impression his manner and deportment make upon a stranger, I must
confess my misgivings. He will be useful to us, however, and we must make
the best of our means.

From all the accounts received of the people of Japan and her dependencies, we have been led to believe that in chicanery and diplomatic treachery
they are unsurpassed. The character thus given them has been confirmed
by Mr. Bettelheim, and I have been prepared to interpose a little Yankee
diplomacy in opposition to their more scientific address, but, so far, very few
difficulties have occurred.

The regent, the next man in power and authority in the island to the
emperor, upon an invitation of mine, came on board to call on me, accompanied by his suite.[50] Without any circumlocution, I told him at once that I
should return his call at the palace, at the seat of government, Scheudi
[Shuri], on the following Monday, a week. This caused a little discussion
between him and his counselors who were in attendance, but I told him
that I had made up my mind to go to the palace on the day appointed, and
should expect a reception suitable to my rank and position. With this
understanding they departed, and I gave orders to make the requisite preparations.

The regent is a man calling himself 55, but looking much older. He came

49. The Reverend Bernard Jean Bettelheim, M.D., a Hungarian-born and medically trained
naturalized British subject. See Morison, *"Old Bruin,"* pp. 303–6 and 339–40.

50. The regent (*sessei* or *kokusho*) of Lew Chew throughout the time of Perry's visits was Sho
Jun, of royal blood, who occupied the position from 1852 to 1860, under close scrutiny of the
Satsuma clan, who had inspectors stationed there. To prevent his possible blundering in negotiations with foreigners, the regent's advisers (upon suggestion of the Satsuma inspectors) kept
him hidden and created a foreign affairs position entitled *tsung-li kwan* or *sorikan* (literally a
superintendent) who was presented to Perry as their highest ranking official. Thus, when Perry
speaks of the "regent" he is referring only to a *tsung-li* or *sorikan* and he never did see the real
regent. This first *tsung-li kwan* was Shang-ta-mu (Sho Taimo in Japanese), lord of Mabuni
(Mabuni *anji*).

62 on board accompanied by numerous attendants, some of them apparently of high rank, and all but the servants wearing the yellow cap, the regent alone having the red cap, a mark of distinction given only to himself, and a few other dignitaries of the kingdom. His attendants also wore a red cap, but of different fashion.

He was first received by Commanders Buchanan and Adams in their cabin, and then escorted round the ship and into the engine room. After partaking of refreshments in the captain's cabin, he was shown into my cabin, where he remained with his retinue more than an hour, and again had refreshments served to him.

It was quite apparent that he was greatly alarmed, and the concessions which he made of submitting to my propositions were entirely forced upon him by the power, which he was satisfied I possessed, of coercing civility. But I shall be careful to exercise this power with discretion, the rather to convince these misgoverned people of the lenity and humanity of our laws, than of the means by which a compulsion may be enforced.

The shore has a charming aspect from the ship; it being the season of spring in this latitude, vegetation has assumed its most pleasing dress. But I shall know more of this beautiful island before leaving it, as I intend to cause it to be thoroughly explored by competent officers of the squadron.

My determination to return the visit of the regent at the palace, and at no other place, has given occasion for that functionary and his followers to put in full practice all their talents for lying and deceitful cunning. First they begged that I would return the visit of the regent at Naha, instead of going to Shuri.* This I declined. They then endeavored to entrap me into a meeting with him, which they would have considered a return of his call upon me. In pursuance of this scheme, the mayor of Naha prepared a feast to be in readiness at two o'clock in the afternoon of Thursday, 2 June, at which it is certain the regent was to appear, and probably preside. I excused myself upon a plea of occupation in dispatching the storeship *Caprice,* to sail that day for Shanghai. The truth is, I suspected some trick, and was determined not to meet the regent again but at the palace.

Finding I did not attend, and determined to entertain me, whether or no, they dispatched two mandarins to the ship with all the good things. These were admitted on board, as a measure of necessary courtesy, and in a moment were spread out upon the quarterdeck various preparations of poultry, fish, vegetables, fruit, and cakes. I did not myself witness the display, as I thought it politic to remain in my cabin.

I had, amongst other reasonable demands, made requisition upon the local authorities of Naha to furnish me with a house for the accommodation of the officers when on shore, and for which rent would be paid. This, after the usual equivocation, was granted, and a sort of audience hall designated for our occupation.

* According to Mr. Bettelheim, Shui is the correct mode of spelling the name of that city. [Now generally spelled Shuri, but Perry also used Sheudi and Scheudi.]

Thereupon an officer was directed to take and hold possession of it, but scarcely was the building fairly occupied, than a request was made that it should be vacated, for reason of its being a place of public meeting of the authorities. I replied that I was willing to remove to any other suitable place; when they assigned an unoccupied temple, in the same part of the town, which they call Shung hein [Sheng hsien ssŭ], the "Holy Presence Temple," or "the temple protecting the anchorage."

After the failure to draw me into an informal interview with the regent at Naha, and being convinced that I should persist in going to the palace, yet with a pertinacity peculiar to them, they adopted another plan of diverting me from my purpose. They endeavored to work on my humanity as well as credulity, and begged that I would go to the palace of the prince instead of that of the royal residence, and for the reason that the queen dowager was sick, and would be made worse by our visit. The letter stated that on the occasion of a visit more than a year ago, of an English naval captain,[51] bearing a letter from Lord Palmerston to the Lew Chewan government, the said captain insisted on presenting it at the palace, which after a controversy of a week, was at last acceded to. The queen dowager was so much shocked at this desecration of her royal abode, that she took sick, and has remained so ever since, taking by advice of her physicians broth and medicine. So says the letter, and if I were also to go there she would be made worse.

Though I was satisfied that the story of the illness of the prince was untrue, I at once consented to postpone my visit to him. At the interview on board ship, nothing was said of the sickness of the queen, or any positive objection made to my visiting the palace if I insisted on it. I am perfectly satisfied—and in this Messrs. Williams and Bettelheim concur with me— that the illness of the queen, and that of the prince also, have been set forth as a part of their system of falsehoods.

A translation of the letter, or as he terms it, petition, of the regent, *tsung-li,* is subjoined, together with my reply.

A prepared petition.

Shang-ta-mu, regent of the kingdom of Lew Chew, and high officer, hereby petitions upon business with the sincerest feelings.

On the 21st of this month I personally received Your Excellency's commands, that on the 30th at 10 o'clock, you intend to go to the capital and present your thanks. Also on the 26th it appears that Naha mayor Chang-Ching-lich [Cheng Chang-lieh] reported clearly, as was properly his duty, that he had received a reply from your excellency's officer to this effect, that you had decided to go to the palace in Shuri on the 30th at 10 o'clock to return the visit of the regent.

It is well known that the capital city of our little kingdom is greatly unlike the provincial capitals of China, for we have only a palace for the king and neither hall, nor market, nor stores besides, and heretofore the men and officers of other countries have never entered the palace. In February last year a general from England came with a public letter which he wished to deliver in the palace to the high officers; but with earnest feelings we begged him to deliver it in another place, for we could not hear of his forcing his way into the palace. At that time,

51. This was Captain Shadwell of H.M.S. *Sphynx.*

all from the mother of the young prince down to the officers and people, were filled with apprehensions and dread, and we could not quiet the queen dowager, who has ever since been greatly afflicted with sickness and pain, and has lately grown worse, and the physicians have prescribed broths and medicines for her, but she is not yet well, so that all the officers are in great anxiety of heart respecting her. Having heard it said that the ruler of your honorable country is of boundless consideration and commiseration, and fully appreciates the virtues of humanity and compassion, we earnestly beg your excellency will likewise exhibit the same great humanity and compassion that he does and having regard to the serious illness of the dowager, will stop entering the palace to pay your respects. But if you must come to pay your respects, then we can only request you to go to the palace of the heir apparent, there to have a personal interview for returning thanks.

It is learned from the mayor, who has reported respecting renting a house to live in, that on the 24th he had stated the reasons why he requested it to be vacated, and that on the 26th he had received the document from your excellency's officer, stating as follows: "When officers go ashore from the ships to walk about, they have no place to go to, and as there are no inns in your country, if they meet rain or wind, or cannot return on board at night, they have no place to stop, without obtruding into the people's houses; and as we do not understand your country's language, if one should wish a glass of water, he could not get it." It is clear that the house which is now occupied, is a place where the official employees assemble to deliberate on public matters, as you wish a house to remain in, there is a temple called the "Holy Presence Temple" (*Sheng hsien ssŭ*) which protects the anchorage; in which you can reside, and we pray you to give orders to remove to that temple where you can stay for the time, and by so doing all ranks of officers, and even the prince will alike be obliged by your great humanity for them.

An urgent petition.
Hsien-feng 3d year, 4th moon, 27th day (3 June 1853)

The commander-in-chief of the naval forces of the United States, in the Indian Ocean, China, and Japan Seas has had the honor of receiving the communication of his highness, the regent of the kingdom of Lew Chew, and expresses his deep sorrow at the illness of her majesty, the queen dowager.

The commander-in-chief conceives it his duty to go to the palace, the place where high functionaries are usually received, and where an officer of the Queen of England recently had an audience.

He disclaims all intention of intruding upon her majesty the queen dowager, and is quite certain that so far from disturbing her, should she not deem it desirable to remove to the palace of her son on the occasion of his visit to the royal palace, his peaceful escort will amuse her, and the learned physicians who accompany him will be most happy to attend upon her majesty, and with their well known skill, assist in restoring her majesty to health.

The commander-in-chief will be most happy to order a removal of the officers to another building, provided on examination it is found to be of suitable accommodations.

Naha, June 1853.

Before he could receive my reply, however, he came on board quietly, I might almost say clandestinely, and without giving any previous notice, indeed no one knew of his coming until he was fairly alongside. The pretended object of his visit was to urge in a second communication the miserable condition of the queen, and to say, that if I were admitted to the palace, her life would be endangered.

As I had previously said I would meet him only at the palace at Shuri, I declined receiving him in my cabin, and he was entertained by Commanders Buchanan and Adams.

On reflecting upon this pertinacious system of crooked diplomacy, I am led to believe that all the falsehood, tricking, and deception which they practice—the details of which they keep full record—is done to satisfy the spies that are kept about them by the Japanese government, and to show that every means has been resorted to, to avert consequences which ultimately become inevitable, notwithstanding their duplicity.

Monday, 6 June 1853. According to my fixed purpose, the cavalcade appointed to accompany me to the palace at Shuri, was paraded in due order precisely at the hour of 10 A.M. and took up its line of march immediately after being formed.

It was composed of two companies of Marines, preceded by two pieces of artillery, with the bands and field music of the *Susquehanna* and *Mississippi*, the cortege being increased by some forty officers. As the procession moved through the winding road, lined on both sides by trees and flowering shrubs, I cannot conceive of a more beautiful pageant.

The cavalcade was preceded by two mandarins in yellow caps, who conducted the procession to the gates of the city, and there we found the regent, *tsung-li*, and three other high functionaries, *Poo-Chings* [pe-chings] with red caps ready to receive us.

Another attempt was evidently made to divert us from visiting the royal palace, and to draw us to that of the regent; but we had our guides with us who had been requested to lead the procession directly to the palace. The regent finding that I merely returned his salutations and proceeded on, hurried to the palace, and was there in readiness to receive us.

After entering the outer portals of the palace, which were enclosed with high massive walls, we passed through several gates until we came in front of the royal residence, opening into which were three gates. The mandarins who again resumed their station in front of us, directed our course toward the left entrance, but the interpreters pointed to the center portal, through which I passed, followed of course by the officers, the escort being left outside. I mention this to show how desirous these foolish people were of denying to me the honor, as they might deem it, of the principal entrance to the palace.

At last, however, they seemed to quietly acquiesce in all our movements. They exhibited alarm only when they supposed the sailors and Marines, with all their arms and equipments, were to enter within the palace walls. When they were assured that none but the officers would enter they evinced signs of great relief.

We entered the audience room, and were very politely received by the regent, *tsung-li,* and the three treasurers, *pe-chings,* of the kingdom, one being designated for [each of] the three several districts of the island. These

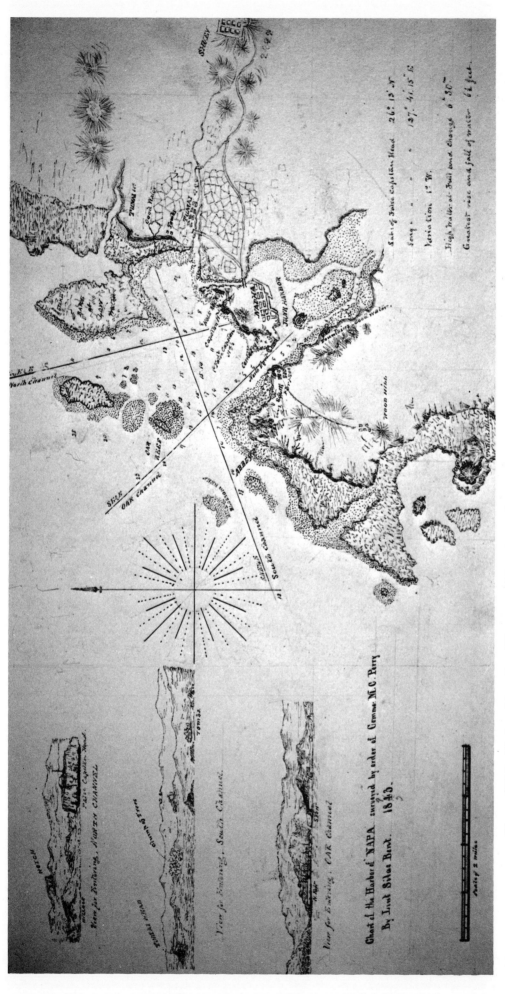

Chart of Naha Harbor, May 1853. The route of Perry's parade to Shuri Castle started at Tumai where their small boats landed. (Note that date "1843" has, quite properly, been questioned.)

yellow.

We remained here about half an hour, having had slight refreshments offered to us. After a few complimentary flourishes, the regent apologized for the scantiness of the refreshments, and expressed a hope that I would call upon him at the vice regal hall. To this I consented and, adjacent to the entrance gate of the city, at the place where we had been first received by the regent, we found him again ready to welcome us. Walking a few yards we were ushered into a splendid building and room, the state apartment of the regent, and in a short time a most interesting entertainment was set out, consisting of some dozen courses.

The dishes were preparations of flesh, fish, vegetables, and fruits, chiefly served in form of broth or soup in little bowls with accompaniment of Sackee [saké] in minute cups, and tea in the ordinary size tea cups without saucers. The tea was quite weak, and without sugar or milk.

The preparations were really very good, much more savory we thought than Chinese cookery. The etiquette was that the host and his brother mandarins bowed to the guest (the same as taking wine in our country) at every successive dish.

After laboring through all the courses, and drinking many complimentary healths in saké from little cups holding scarcely a spoonful, I made a move. The tsung-li and the three pe-chings escorted me to the gate of the city where I took formal leave and, the military array having formed, we returned in the same manner we came. It may be mentioned here that horses* and kagos† [palanquins] and kago bearers had been provided for myself and some of the officers. But I had the precaution to have a comfortable sedan chair made on board ship, and was conveyed in it to and from Shuri by eight of the coolies taken from the ship. It would have been very undignified for me to have walked. The officers, who might have availed of the conveyances provided, preferred rather to walk, than to be cramped in those most uncomfortable of all conveyances, the kago, which I presume are the same as the cages described by Americans who were imprisoned in Japan.[52]

We reached the boats at about three o'clock, having been absent five hours, and everything going off as I could have wished. The Marines—under Major Zeilin and Captain Slack, accompanied by the two fine bands of the squadron—and the officers and sailors were all well dressed, and together made a splendid turnout.

According to eastern custom, I had prepared presents for the four higher functionaries of the kingdom: the prince, the regent, the chief treasurer, and the mayor of Naha. These were carried in great state in the procession by

* The horses are very small, but seem well formed and spirited.
† Kago is a sort of sedan chair, but so low that the occupant must sit cross legged in a most uncomfortable manner.

52. Survivors who reached Japan from shipwrecked New England whalers in the North Pacific complained bitterly about their maltreatment at being transported in these undersize—for Americans—palanquins.

68 Chinese coolies, under an escort of two Marines, and were left in the royal palace, whence we resorted to the palace of the regent. Subsequently, I sent presents to the queen, and to the two other treasurers. Amongst the presents to the queen was a mirror with some French perfumery.

On the whole I was pleased with the suavity of manner and apparent sincerity of their hospitality, giving them the credit at least of being good actors if they were not sincere; and in the very palace into which they solemnly declared, if I were to enter, the life of the regent, *tsung-li,* would be endangered, and the queen would die outright.

I was well satisfied, however, that the whole story of the sickness of her majesty was a fiction. I could imagine whilst sitting in the audience room that the queen and her ladies of honor—for I suppose she has such attendants—were peeping at us through some crevice, greatly amused at what they saw.

The road from the landing place to Shuri, a distance of about four miles, was elaborately paved with coral rock, very neatly fitted together, and the upper surface rendered smooth, either by artificial means, or by frequent travel over it. On both sides within the outskirts of the village of Tumai [Tomari], through which we passed, as also those of Shuri, the houses were enclosed within high walls, the same as in Naha.

During the whole way to Shuri, the eye was constantly attracted by the most charming landscapes, every spot of ground was cultivated to the highest degree of perfection, the fields of rice were magnificent, and crowds of husbandmen attracted by our pageant, were seen running toward the highway to gratify their curiosity. The whole road was thronged by persons who seemed to have little or no employment; but, singular as it may appear, not a female was seen. Judging, therefore, from the great number of males which crowded the way, an inference may be fairly drawn of the populousness of the island.

Shuri is situated upon an elevation, probably 150 feet above the level of the sea, and as the road is ascending, it is somewhat zigzag. Never have I seen a city or town exhibiting a greater degree of cleanliness, not a particle of dirt or even dust could be seen, so different from the filthiness of all Chinese cities.

The entrance from Naha has two gates, one about 200 yards within the other. Through the first we passed with only the ordinary salaam of the authorities, but at the second and interior gate, the regent and other functionaries of the kingdom drawn up in line gave the grand salaam, bowing their heads almost to the ground.

The numerous people met on the road, most of whom were of the lower orders, exhibited a miserable, squalid appearance, many of them naked, excepting a small piece of cloth round the loins. These I suppose compose the laboring class, receiving for their toil scanty food and harsh treatment. The idlers are the priests and the army of spies and policemen who throng the highways, and whose eyes are constantly upon everybody and everything going on, whether by night or day.

On the occasion of my visiting a Japanese junk in the inner harbor, I had scarcely been five minutes on board, before five or six spies were at my heels. They are quite respectful. One or more of these people accompany everyone who goes far into the country whether for a walk or to shoot, and they are very civil and obliging, pointing out the best places for game, and actually carrying the game of the sportsman.

The markets of Naha are well supplied with fresh pork, poultry, fish, vegetables, and a few descriptions of fruit. The stalls are usually kept by women, who on the approach of strangers run off leaving their truck to look after itself. Those whom I got glimpses of were of the most filthy and hideous appearance, from whom I should be as ready to fly were I to suppose there was danger of coming in contact with them.

There can be little doubt of the dependency of the Lew Chewans upon Japan, and that all the islands between Lew Chew and Japan, as well as those between the former and Formosa, are also Japanese dependencies. These islands are embraced within the sovereignty of the prince of Satzuma [Satsuma], who is also lord of Kiusiu [Kyushu], of which Nagasaki is the principal port. This powerful prince owes fealty to the emperor, but in some respects is independent of his sway, though it is questionable whether under the extraordinary system of espionage, which has been brought to such perfection throughout the empire, he could move in any act of opposition to the imperial power, without its being discovered, and immediately made known at Edo.

There are no means of knowing whether a prince as powerful as the lord of Satsuma, could be ordered at a moment's notice to the imperial court, there to answer the accusations of some secret spy, who has been placed about him, or whether if he should undertake to put such a mandate at defiance, his own subjects would dare to support him in rebellion. With our present imperfect knowledge of the political and social condition of Japan, all is speculation, but we may hope ere long to obtain intelligence which will enable us to know more of this singular government.

If they are as deceitful and unscrupulous of truth as the Lew Chewans, who have been represented by a notorious romancer as the most innocent people on earth, they will be bad enough, but we have reason to believe that they are infinitely more cunning and more treacherous. Having the power of resisting by force the approaches of foreigners, which the Lew Chewans have not, they may for a long time succeed in maintaining their system of exclusiveness. But the time will come when they will be obliged to give way to the march of civilization and human rights, and it may be hoped that the Americans will have the honor of opening the first avenues to a prosperous and happy intercourse with them.

It being necessary to await the return of the *Caprice* from Shanghai with a suitable interpreter—the person brought by Mr. Williams being utterly useless and in a dying state—and as I had contemplated a visit to the Bonin Islands sometime during the summer, I thought it advisable to avail of the period of absence of the *Caprice*, that would otherwise be comparatively

Port Lloyd chart, Chichijima, Bonin Islands, June 1853

lost. Consequently, taking *Saratoga* in tow of this ship, and leaving Com- 71
mander Lee with *Mississippi* and *Supply* at Naha, we left the harbor at seven
A.M. of 9 June.

My instrùctions to Commander Lee strongly enjoined him to exercise
every possible kindness and forbearance in his intercourse with the authorities and people on shore, and to be careful not to allow any but the most
orderly persons to go on shore for fear of some difficulty with the natives,
which might mar the favorable state of things subsisting when I left. Already they have agreed to furnish the ships with whatever they may need,
and the island can spare, and to receive payment for the same. As yet,
however, they have not consented to open their markets to us; every article
that has hitherto been supplied has been sent on board by purveyors,
appointed probably by the authorities.

I was fearful that the consumption of bullocks by the crews of the several
ships might inconvenience the farmers, who use them chiefly for ploughing.
I have forbidden their being asked for oftener than once a week and have,
moreover, requested the authorities not to furnish them at all if they could
not do so with perfect convenience.

I had purchased at the Cape of Good Hope some sheep and pigs, and at
Shanghai an additional number, together with some bulls and cows, in view
of presenting a part of them to the Lew Chewans, that their stock of bullocks
might be improved. Of sheep they have none, but the time has not yet
arrived when they can be made to accept and take care of them.

Half the stock I have is intended to be put on shore at the Bonin Islands.

11 June 1853. We have up to this time, 8 A.M., run about 350 miles, the
Saratoga being still in tow. The southwest monsoons or a southerly wind
(for it is doubtful whether the monsoons extend as far north as this parallel)
continue to blow steadily.

At one o'clock this morning the old Chinaman, who had been employed
by Mr. Williams as interpreter, breathed his last, aged as he said 55 years.
He was an educated man, and had been employed in teaching the Chinese
language to foreigners, among others to Mr. Williams. He had for many
years of his life been an inveterate opium smoker, and his frame had become
so weak and attenuated in consequence, that when he came on board this
ship, everyone predicted that he could not long survive. Thus we are left
without a Chinese interpreter, for though Mr. Williams can convey the
meaning of English words into the Mandarin dialect, and thus dictate, he
cannot himself write the Mandarin language.

After a pleasant passage we made the Bonins at daylight on Tuesday, 14
June, and the tow lines of the *Saratoga* having been previously cast off,
Commander Walker was directed to lead in toward Port Lloyd, where we
anchored about 10 A.M., pilots having come out to both ships. In running
for the harbor, we saw two whaling ships cruising amongst the islands, one

The Bonin Islands
14–18 JUNE 1853

showing American, the other English colors. This it seems is a favorite cruising ground. Doubtless there were other vessels in the vicinity, indeed, we saw a third sail from the masthead.

The Bonin Islands extend in a direction nearly north and south, between the latitudes of 26°30′ and 27°45′ north, the center line of the group being in longitude about 142°15′ east. The principal islands and indeed all of them, have been named by Captain Beechey of H.M.S. *Blossom,* with the proverbial modesty and justice of all English surveyors. The northern cluster he called Parry's Group; to the middle cluster, consisting of three larger islands, he gave the names respectively of Peel [now Chichi Jima], Buckland [Ani Jima], and Stapleton [Ototo Jima]; and the southern cluster he called Bailey's Islands, utterly regardless of the fact which he mentions himself in these words.*

The southern cluster is evidently that on which a whale ship, commanded by a Mr. Coffin anchored in 1823, who was the first to communicate its position to this country, and who bestowed his name upon the port. As the cluster was, however, left without any distinguishing appellation, I named it after Francis Bailey, Esquire, late president of the Astronomical Society.

To the principal port of Chichi Jima he gave the name of Lloyd, a pretty liberal distribution of honors by this accidental visitor in 1827 to a group of islands that had been known, and of which we have authentic accounts as early as the 17th century.

The islands are evidently volcanic, the internal fires being still at work. Mr. Nathaniel Savory,[53] the oldest surviving settler in the island informed me that they experienced two or three tremblings of the earth every year. The islands, headlands, and detached rocks present the most grotesque forms, exhibiting the appearance of castles, towers, animals, and almost every hideous thing conceivable to the imagination. These geological formations must be of great antiquity, as we noticed numerous canal-like passages in the cliffs, as one might suppose hewn out by the work of the chisel. They have evidently been dikes produced by the overflowing and cooling of the lava, and then smoothed by the abrasion or attrition of the torrents, which are precipitated in the rainy season down the sides of the mountains toward the sea.

These dikes in many parts of the island—where the action of the water courses assisted by the atmosphere has not produced any material change— still retain their peculiar steplike formation. The observer might imagine that he was gazing upon a series of steps cut in the solid rock by the hand of man to facilitate his descent and ascent to and from the summits of the mountains.

* I quote from Findlay's *Directory of the Pacific Ocean,* not having Beechey's work before me.

53. Mr. Savory, born 31 July 1794 in Bradford, Massachusetts, arrived Chichi Jima 26 June 1830, died there 10 April 1874. On a visit to Chichi Jima in 1966 with Admiral S. E. Morison, I met Nathaniel's grandson Wilson (born 1887, son of Horace Perry Savory) and great-grandson Nathaniel (born 1908). R.P.

Indeed I know of no part of the world which can offer greater interest to the research of the geologist than these islands present. They are of course of trappean formation,[54] as naturally connected with their volcanic origin, but I am not sufficiently acquainted with mineralogy to distinguish the several varieties of which the masses are composed, though specimens have been procured for the examination of scientists.

Port Lloyd is situated on the western side, and nearly in the center of Peel Island. It is easy of ingress and egress, and may be considered a safe and commodious harbor, though of deep anchorage, ships usually anchoring in from 18 to 22 fathoms.

The port is laid down on Beechey's chart to be in latitude 27°5′35″ north, and longitude 142°11′30″ east. This position is, I conceive, erroneous, as by two sets of observations made by the master of the *Susquehanna*, the longitude was found to be 142°16′30″ east; five miles more to the east than Beechey makes it.[55]

According to Ruschenberger [p. 440], Captain Beechey remained in the *Blossom* from 8 to 15 June, and yet he has given a survey of the port and the entire group of islands. Now it would seem to be impossible that in that short time anything more than a hasty examination of so large an extent of ocean could be made, though the harbor chart of Port Lloyd is in most respects correct.

The safest anchorage is to be found as high up the harbor as a ship can conveniently go, having regard to depth, and room for swinging and veering cable. Strangers can easily discover by examination the proper position, to which they can warp their ships.

Beechey's directions for entering the port are sufficiently correct. Castle Island which he speaks of is easily distinguished, and furnishes a good mark. The starboard shore or Southern Head, should be kept [close] aboard, clearing it one or two cables to avoid a small rock lying about 150 or 200 yards from the bluff, and having upon it only eight feet at low water. I have caused the letter S in a circle to be painted upon the bluff of Southern Head, to mark the bearing off the rock due north from said mark Ⓢ.

Wood and water can be obtained in abundance, though the former must be cut by the crew, and of course taken on board green. The water is obtained from running streams and is of good quality.

The few settlers still remaining on Peel Island—the other islands being uninhabited—raise considerable quantities of sweet potatoes, Indian corn, onions, taro, and a few fruits the most abundant of which are watermelons, bananas, and pineapples; a few pigs and some poultry are also raised. For these they find ready sale to the whale ships, constantly touching at the port for water and other supplies. During the four days we were at anchor at Port Lloyd three whalers—two American and one English—communicated by means of their boats with the settlement, and carried away many supplies,

54. Meaning trap or trap rock.
55. But Beechey is more accurate according to the United States Naval Oceanographic Office which gives latitude 27°5′ N, longitude 142°11′ E for Port Lloyd (now Futami Ko).

74 procured generally in exchange for articles, of which ardent spirits are the most acceptable to many of the settlers.

Were it not for the scarcity of working hands, a much greater extent of land would be cultivated. At present there cannot be more than 150 acres under cultivation in the whole island. This is in detached spots, generally at the seaward termination of ravines furnishing fresh water, or upon plateaux of land near the harbor.

The soil is of excellent quality for cultivation, very much resembling that of Madeira and the Canary Islands (the latter being in the same parallel of latitude), and consequently is admirably adapted for the cultivation of the vine, and of wheat, tobacco, sugar cane, and many other valuable plants. Of sugar and tobacco the settlers already cultivate enough for their own consumption.

Timber for building purposes is rather scarce, and would soon be exhausted if any increase of population were to call for the erection of many buildings. The best kinds are the jamana and wild mulberry. The former is similar to the redwood of Brazil and Mexico, and is very enduring.

I caused the island to be thoroughly explored by two parties of officers, and their reports will be duly filed with other similar papers.[56] The masters of this ship and *Saratoga* also surveyed the harbor.

The scarcity of sea and land birds has been noticed by everyone as singular; not more than five or six varieties of land birds have been seen. Of these the common crow and the pigeon are the largest, the others are of small size. Of gulls or other sea birds we saw very few, the booby being the most numerous. I noticed before reaching the islands a few petrels, these were of unusually large size, and of singularly brilliant plumage.

Of quadrupeds, we may enumerate hogs, goats, deer, bullocks, sheep, and any number of cats and dogs. Many of the cats and hogs having strayed to the jungle are honored with the appellation of wild cats and wild hogs and are hunted accordingly with dogs. A few deer and goats were some years ago placed upon North, or Stapleton Island by the settlers, and the goats have multiplied prodigiously.

Bulls, cows, sheep, and a few goats were landed from the *Susquehanna,* in view of their increase. Two bulls and two cows were put on shore at Sand Bay, on the north side of Peel Island, and two rams, five Shanghai broad-tail sheep, and six goats on North Island. On Buckland Island, there are a good number of hogs. The settlers have recently stocked two others of the smaller islands with goats, so that in the course of time they will increase to many thousands.

The harbor of Port Lloyd and the neighboring waters, abound with excellent fish, which may be taken by the hook or seine. The places for hauling the seine are few, however, owing to the coral, which in many parts lines the shore. The best place for hauling the seine in Port Lloyd is upon a sandy beach in Ten-Fathom Hole, where there is a small clear spot. The varieties of fish are not very numerous; of those taken in the seine of the

56. These reports are summarized in Hawks *Narrative*.

Susquehanna, I noticed but five, the mullet (the most numerous), two   75
varieties of perch, the gar, and the common ray. Sharks are very numerous
and, when quite small, they frequent the shallow places amongst the coral
rocks near the shore. There they are pursued by the dogs, seized upon, and
dragged on shore.

Of edible shell fish there are none that I could learn excepting the Chama
gigas (Tridacna) which must be very tough and indigestible. Of other
varieties of the testacea, there are many but none of any rarity. The family
of crustacea is, however, more extensive, but the kinds are chiefly confined to
the land crab, which are of every variety of size, form, and color. A most
numerous kind is what is generally called the pirate. These are seen in every
direction near the shore, traveling about with their ridiculous domicile
upon their backs, which they seem to have selected more by chance than
choice. The favorite tenements of these artful dodgers are the Buccinum,
Murex, and Bulla, of about an inch and a half in length, but, for want of
better lodging, they are fain to take up with any sort of habitation. It seems
to be necessary that the tail part of the animal, which is soft, be under
shelter, the head and claws, being always protruded when moving. It is not
known whether these animals attack the live inhabitant of a shell and
destroy it, and then seize upon its domicile, or whether they are content with
the occupancy of a shell, of which its natural inmate has previously been
dispossessed, either by accident or death.

I was greatly amused on landing, at what Captain Beechey calls "Walk-
ers" Bay, to see these helmeted little animals marching about in all directions in search of food. Our party dined at this place, and the remains of our
dinner doubtless furnished high feasting to the pirates. One of the dishes
was a roasted pig; someone had picked pretty clean the hock of a foreleg,
and thrown it behind him. A few minutes later Commander Adams in
looking about saw this identical bone moving along in a mysterious manner.
On examination he found that it had been seized upon by a pirate, who was
marching rapidly off with it, notwithstanding the weight of a heavy shell,
which he carried on his back. When caught he still held pertinaciously to
the bone.

The waters of the Bonin Islands furnish an abundance of fine crawfish, as
also green turtle of which we obtained a good supply.

According to Kaempfer these islands were known to the Japanese as early
as 1675 and they described them under the name of Bune Shima [Bonin
Shima], and as abounding with fish and crabs, some of which were from four
to six feet long. From this description of the crabs, I am led to believe that
they mistook the enormous green turtles, which are so common here, for
crabs. Other accounts give a much earlier date for the discovery of these
islands by the Japanese. At all events the English have not a particle of
claim to their discovery.

Extract from Kaempfer [page 69]

About the year 1675 the Japanese accidentally discovered a very large island; one
of their barks having been forced there in a storm, from the island Fatseyo

76 [Hachijojima], from which they computed it to be 300 miles distant toward the East. They met with no inhabitants, but found it to be a very pleasant and fruitful country, well supplied with fresh water, and furnished with plenty of plants and trees particularly the arrack tree, which however might give room to conjecture that the island lay rather to the south of Japan than to the east; these trees growing only in hot countries. They called it Bonin Shima, and because they found no inhabitants upon it, they marked it with the character of an uninhabited island; on the shores they found an incredible quantity of fish and crabs, some of which were from four to six feet long.*

Extract from Klaproth's translation of San Kokf Tsou Ran to Sets [Sankoku Tsuran to Setsu, A Survey of Three Countries, pages 256–62]

The original name of these islands is Ogasawara Shima, but they are commonly called Munin Shima (in Chinese, Wu-jen tao) or "islands without people," and this is the name which I have adopted in my work. That of Ogasawara Shima, or the Ogasawara Islands was given to them after the navigator who first visited them, and who prepared a map of them. In the same manner has the southern part of the New World been called Magellania, (Magellan) who discovered it some two hundred years since.

The Bonin Islands are found 270 ri to the southwest of the province of Izu. From Shimoda in that principality, it is 13 ri to the island of Myake [Miyakejima]; from thence to Sin Sima [Niijima] or new island, 7 ri; from Shin Shima to Mikoura [Mikurajima], 5 ri; from thence to Hachijojima, 41 ri; and lastly from this to the most northern of the uninhabited islands, it is reckoned to be 180 ri; and to the most southerly, 200 ri.

In the sea between Hachijojima and the Bonin Islands, are five other islands of which one is a bare rock. Between the island of Mikura and Hachijojima there is a very rapid current, called Kouro se gawa [Kuroshio], or the "black gulf current." It runs so rapidly that seamen regard it as the most difficult passage in these seas to get over. It is to be seen on the map.

The large and small islands and the rocks composing this group are eighty-nine in number; those of the greatest size among them are two large ones, four of medium size, and four smaller ones. These ten islands are spacious, and covered with shrubs and trees, and their plateaux offer a pleasant residence to man. The remainder seventy steep rocks, have not yet been sufficiently examined to ascertain whether they could be inhabited.

This archipelago lies in the 27th degree of north latitude, the climate is warm and makes the valleys, lying between the high mountains, watered by rivulets, to be very fertile, so that they produce beans, wheat, millet, grain of all kinds, and sugar cane. The tree called Nankin-fase [hase], or tallow tree (*Stillingia sebifera*) grows there, and likewise the wax tree. The fishery is good, and might be made very productive.

Many plants and trees grow in these islands, but there are very few quadrupeds. There are trees so large that a man cannot embrace them with his arms, and which are frequently thirty Chinese fathoms (or 240 feet) in height, their wood is hard and beautiful. There are also some very high trees, resembling the Siou-ro-Tsoung-liu [*shuro* or hemp palm], or *Chamaerops excelsa;* cocoanuts, areca palms, that tree whose nuts are called Pe-Couan-tsy in Chinese; the Katsurau, the red sandalwood, the Tou-mou, the camphor, tub-figs of the mountains; a high tree whose leaves resemble those of the ground ivy, the cinnamon tree, mulberry, and some others.

* Doubtless mistaking turtle for crabs. M.C.P.

Among the plants, the *Smilax china* (or China root) called San-ke-rei; the To-ke; a medicinal herb called Assa-ghion-keva; and others are to be reckoned.

Among birds there are different species of parakeets, cormorants, partridges, and some resembling white sea-mews, but more than three feet long; all these birds have so little wildness, that they can be taken with the hand.

The chief productions of the mineral kingdom in this archipelago are alum, green vitriol, stones of different colors, and petrifactions.

Whales are found in the sea, also huge crawfish,* enormous shells, and echinee which are called "gall of the sea." The ocean here is unusually rich in various products.

In the third year of the reign Ghen-fō [Empō 1673–1680] (1675), Sinaye Saghemon [Saemon Shimae], Biso Saghemon [Saemon Biso], and Simaye dairo Saghemon [Tairozaemon Shimae], three inhabitants of Nagasaki, took a sea voyage to the principality of Izu. They were embarked in a large junk, built by a skillful Chinese carpenter. These three men were well acquainted with astronomy and geography, and accompanied by Fatobe [Hachibe] the chief ships-carpenter of the port of Edo, who dwelt in the lane of nets. The vessel was managed by thirty sailors. Having obtained a passport from the imperial marine, they left the harbor of Shimoda the fifth day of the fourth month [6 May] and steered for Hachijo Jima. From thence they sailed toward the southeast and discovered a group of eighty islands. They drew up a map, and an exact account of them, in which are some curious details respecting the situation, climate, and productions of this archipelago.

They returned the twentieth day of the sixth month [11 August], in the same year to Shimoda, where they published an account of their voyage.

It is singular that this writer makes no mention of the swift current Kuroshio, which is experienced between Mikura and Hachijo Jima. Its breadth exceeds 20 *cho* (about half a *ri*) and it flows with a great swiftness from east to west about 100 ri. This omission would be inexplicable if this current was not much less rapid in summer and autumn than it is in winter and spring. Shimae, in his passage to the Bonin Islands, passed it in the first part of the intercalary month, which succeeds the fourth month; on his return in the latter part of the sixth month, he should have found the current less rapid, and thus his attention was not called to this dangerous passage.

The largest of the eighty islands is 15 *ri* in circuit, and thus is a little less than Iki Island in size; another is 10 *ri,* in circumference, and about the size of Amakusa Island. Besides these two, there are eight others which are from two to seven *ri* around. These ten islands have flat plateaux which could be made habitable, and where grain would grow very well. The climate is warm and favorable to cultivation, as one might infer from their geographical position. They afford various valuable productions. The remaining seventy islets are only mere steep rocks, and produce nothing.

A colony of condemned criminals has been sent to these islands, there to labor; they have tilled the earth, and planted some patches. They are collected in villages and have brought together the same things found in other provinces of the empire. One can visit these islands and bring back its products in the same year. In this way a trade would easily spring up, and the benefit to be drawn from it would be considerable. This must be plain to all.

In the era of An Yei [Anei] (from 1771 to 1780) I was sent on a commission into the province of Fisen [Hizen], where I became acquainted with a Dutchman

---

* In Chinese *ta-hai-lau* or the old man of the sea; in Japanese, *oho yebi; yebi* means crawfish, and is the synonym of the Chinese *hai hai,* the name given to the great sea crawfish, commonly called *lung hia* (or dragon crab). Kaempfer relates, Vol. 1, also that great crawfish, some of them 4 or 5 feet long, are found in the Munin Shima.   Klaproth's Note.

78 named Aarend Werle Veit, who showed me a geography, in which mention was made of some islands lying 200 ri to the southeast of Japan, called Woest Eiland by the author, the word *woest* means desert and *eiland* (or Yeirand, as the original reads) island. He remarks that these islands are not inhabited, but that many sorts of herbs and trees are found there. The Japanese might establish a colony on one of these islands on which grain and other productions would thrive. In spite of the length of the voyage thither, the establishment would be useful to them for these purposes. The Dutch company would derive very little advantage from the possession of these islands, they being too small and too remote for their use.

I have thought proper to repeat these words which deserve to be borne in mind, and with them I bring to a conclusion all that I have to say respecting the Bonin Islands.

Upon the subject of the early discovery of these islands I shall have more to say. It is only necessary now to remark that the descriptions given in the two preceding extracts correspond exactly with the present appearance of the islands. The arrack, or areca tree, is found upon Peel Island, as well as many other tropical trees and plants.

And in further confirmation of the accounts given by Kaempfer of the accidental visit of a Japanese junk in 1675, I was informed by Mr. Savory that about 13 years ago a small Japanese vessel of about 40 tons came into Port Lloyd, having been driven by stress of weather from the coast of Japan. She had on board nothing but dried fish. Remaining during the winter she sailed on her return home in the spring, being provided gratuitously by the settlers with provisions.

Again about five years ago a French whaling ship cruising off Stapleton Island discovered smoke on shore and, sending a boat to the spot, there discovered the wreck of a Japanese junk and five of her crew—the only survivors—in a most helpless condition. They were taken on board and conveyed to Port Lloyd, and they were subsequently taken away by the humane Frenchman with the intention, as he avowed, of landing them upon one of the Japanese islands.

A party of officers from the *Susquehanna* on a visit to Stapleton Island accidentally saw the wreck of this vessel, and the following is the account given by one of them, Mr. Heine.

In the little bay where we landed, we found the wreck of a junk, kept together with large copper nails, and having nailed on it several pieces of sheet copper. From these materials, I concluded that it was a Japanese junk. The wreck could not be very old as the edges of the boards were but little rubbed or damaged.

Of the settlers who came from the Sandwich Islands in 1830, accompanied by several natives of those islands, male and female, there are but few left. The names of the whites, who were the leaders in this adventure, were as follows: Matteo Mazarro, a Genoese; Nathaniel Savory and Aldin B. Chapin, of Massachusetts; John Millinchamp,[57] of England; and Charles Johnson, of Denmark.

Of these Nathaniel Savory is the only one at present on the island.

57. The Journal gives his name as Richard Mildechamp and Mildchamp, but see L. B. Cholmondeley, *The History of the Bonin Islands* (London, 1915), p. 17.

Mazarro is dead, and Savory has married his widow, a pretty native of   79
Guam, one of the Ladrone Islands, and still quite young, only 25. Millinchamp is alive and residing at Guam.

Having long been satisfied of the importance of these islands to commerce, my present visit has been induced by a desire to examine them
myself, in view of recommending Peel Island as a stopping place for the
line of steamers, which sooner or later must be established between California and China. To this end I have caused, as before mentioned, the island to
be explored, [the harbor to be surveyed][58] and a few animals placed upon
two of the group as a commencement of a provision for future wants. I have
also distributed garden seeds of every description to the present settlers, and
have held out hopes to them that I may furnish them with implements of
husbandry and a greater number of animals. Indeed I have gone so far as to
secure a suitable spot for the erection of offices, wharves, and coal sheds.

I very much regretted that I could not remain longer at these interesting
islands, and extend my explorations to the southern group, but the necessity
of returning to Lew Chew was so paramount that I reluctantly got under
way with the two ships, the *Saratoga* in tow, on the morning of Saturday, 18
June; and, after clearing the harbor, directed the vessels to be steered
toward Disappointment Island. On our passage from Lew Chew, I was
desirous of sighting and determining the position of this islet, about which
so much has been written. Fortunately we had made it in the afternoon of
the 13th, the day previous to our arrival at Port Lloyd, and though we stood
toward it, there was not time then before the intervention of darkness, to
ascertain except by computation its exact position.

For this reason I was the more particular to see it again, and shortly after
noon we again made it ahead, and passing it at a distance of three or four
miles, its exact position was accurately determined by data derived from our
noonday observations. Several sketches were also made by the artists of its
appearance at different bearings; it is a low island with two detached rocks,
extending a cable or two from its extreme points. It lies in latitude 27°15'
north and longitude 140°56'30" east from Greenwich. It may be presumed
that Disappointment and Rosario are one and the same island.[59]

Having established the position of Disappointment or Rosario Island, I
was desirous of sighting the Borodinos on our return passage to Lew Chew,
and consequently ordered the ships to be steered directly for them, according to their ascribed position on the charts.

On 22 June we made them directly ahead and, on a near approach, found
them to be two in number, situated about five miles apart and lying in a
direction NNE and SSW. They seem to be of coral formation but of great
antiquity, as trees of considerable size crowned the uplands. The most
elevated parts of the islands may have been forty feet above the level of the
sea. The sea about them appears to be clear of dangers, but we could
discover no indentations in the shores which might afford safe anchoring
places.

58. Bracketed phrase inserted by Commodore Perry.
59. Now called Nishino Jima, the Naval Oceanographic Office lists the longitude as 140°53' E.

80   No signs of people were to be seen, and the presumption is they are uninhabited. The position of the south extremity of the southern island was estimated to be in latitude 25°47' north and longitude 131°19' east.[60]

During our return passage from Peel Island to Lew Chew, we had moderate breezes from the SSW to SW with warm weather, indeed the wind continued from the south and west ever since we left Naha, by which we may infer that the southwest monsoon extends as far north as this parallel.

60. Now called Minami Daito Jima; Naval Oceanographic Office gives southern extremity as latitude 25°48'45" N, longitude 131°14'20" E.

Volume 2   June 1853 – February 1854

On our return to Naha we found the *Plymouth* at anchor, Commander Kelly having upon due consideration exercised the discretion with which he had been empowered, to leave Shanghai (believing as he did, that there was no longer any necessity for his remaining) and to join me at Naha, as under certain reservations he had been ordered to do.

On anchoring at Naha I recommenced my efforts to conciliate the authorities and people of the island, and renewed an invitation to the regent (*tsung-li*) and treasurer (*pe-ching*) to dine on board *Susquehanna* on Tuesday, 28 June, offering to send boats for them. This invitation was accepted and they moreover expressed a willingness to receive the cattle, sheep, and seeds I had brought as presents for them. Indeed they not only received them but sent the interpreter on board to return thanks and to say to me that as my presents had been so liberal it was not right that charge should be made for the supplies furnished the ships. My reply was that it was a rule of our government to receive nothing in the form of supplies for our army and navy without payment being made for it; that unless the people of Lew Chew did receive such remuneration I should be reluctantly compelled to decline any further supplies. To this they seemed willingly to acquiesce. The presents which I gave them they were told were mere trifles, intended to show the good will of the President toward them, who was desirous that the agricultural condition of their beautiful island might be improved, and that several implements of husbandry would probably be sent from the United States for the benefit of their farmers. They were told that it is a matter of general interest with the civilized world to improve the means of tilling the ground, as well to save human labor as to relieve involuntary toil of dumb animals and also to obtain the greatest yield from the land—thus benefiting the poor as well as the rich.

About the time of my return from the Bonin Islands I was credibly informed that the regent Shang-ta-mu[1] had either resigned or been deposed. A story was in circulation in the squadron that he had committed suicide, and for reason that he had given offence to the spies who had been placed about the old man in visiting the *Susquehanna* and receiving me at the palace. The truth is, so far as I can ascertain, he resigned in favor of another of the same family, Shang-Hung-Hiun [Shang Hung-hsün], a much younger man who not only did not hesitate to accept my invitation to dinner but went even further in courtesy than did his predecessor.

It would be an act not only of humanity but of justice to relieve these oppressed people of the burdens which are now grinding them to the dust. It appears from what I can learn that the soil is held in right by the government, which employs its myrmidons to collect and consume its produce.

---

1. During Perry's two-week absence from Naha the first *sorikan* (*tsung-li kwan* in Chinese) Shang-ta-mu or Mabuni Anji (lord of Mabuni) was "retired" because of his failure to keep Perry from entering the royal castle. He was replaced by Shang Hung-hsün (Japanese Sho Ko-kun), also of royal blood. Shang Hung-hsün continued as *sorikan* through the remainder of Perry's visits to Okinawa. In signing the treaty he indicated his official position as *sori daijin*, a title that had not existed before Perry's visits and it is not seen again in the history of the Ryukyus. Shang Hung-hsün, who negotiated with Perry, actually succeeded to the regency in 1861.

84 According to the best accounts we have, the actual cultivator receives not more than one fifth of the produce, three fifths go to the lord of the soil, and one fifth for the expenses of supervision of the land and collection.

The art of producing the most out of small parcels of land of whatever character and condition, and however topographically placed, is carried to great perfection in this island, and, as I read, in all the neighboring groups actually under cultivation. Irrigation is understood and practiced, though not to the extent known in some other countries particularly the Canary Islands. But the poor naked creatures toil from morn till night, not knowing the relaxation belonging to the Sabbath or to holidays, a rest generally recognized by the most cruel task masters.

The wage of a field laborer is from three to eight cents per day and the mechanic may receive ten cents. Out of this he has to find shelter, food, and clothing for a family, with which most of the common people are burdened. It is surprising to see how soon the boys—for we see nothing of the girls—are made to labor. In looking into a blacksmith's shop at Naha, I noticed a father and two sons engaged in making nails. The eldest son, probably ten years old, used the hammer, whilst the younger, not more than five, was blowing the bellows, or was rather moving a piston of a sort of air pump. When we entered the shop neither of the three took the slightest notice of us but went on with their labor. Even the little boy scarcely looked at us, and this was the case with laborers and all others whom we met when they supposed they were watched by spies that infest every corner and threshold.

In many instances I directed the attendants who hastened to disperse these spies, but they soon reappeared.

As we passed along the streets these fellows could be seen preceding us, directing all the doors to be shut and the women to conceal themselves. The people themselves, whenever they were sure of not being seen, accepted little gratuities, but they were like hungry hounds who, whilst snatching a morsel from a strange hand, trembled in fear of being seen by their master.

God pity these poor creatures who have been represented by Captain Basil Hall[2] as so innocent and so happy. I have seen much of the world, have witnessed savage life in many of its conditions, but never, unless I may except the miserable peons in Mexico, have I looked upon such an amount of apparent wretchedness as these squalid slaves would seem to suffer.

The people according to my observation are divided into four·classes. First are the high officers of state, second the priesthood and literary men, third the under officers and spies, and fourth the laboring classes, by whose labor all the others live. No one could discover that any individual of the three first classes seemed at any time to have the least employment, excepting indeed the spies who were met at every corner.

We have already made considerable progress in conciliating the people of the higher classes, those of the lower and degraded class dare not even by a look evince the slightest emotion. Their stolid and impassive features express nothing but toil and care, a sufficient index of their abject condition.

In the accomplishment of a friendly intercourse with Japan, which of

2. Who wrote *Voyage of Discovery* . . . after his visit to Lew Chew in 1816 in sloop *Lyra* with *Alceste* (Captain Murray Maxwell) on a British mission to the Far East.

Lew Chew woman selling bean curd

琉球婦人賣豆腐　Lewchewan woman selling bean curd.

Wise men in council. Len Chen. 琉球長老 } Lewchewan Elders

Lew Chew wise men in council. Two of Perry's ships at anchor in Naha Harbor.

course must be a work of time, the possession of Lew Chew and the Bonin Islands will be all important. So far as it rests with me, I will continue to hold a controlling influence over them. With respect to Lew Chew, I can conceive of no greater act of humanity than to protect these miserable people against the oppressions of their tyrannical rulers. Inhabiting an island beautiful beyond description, they are trodden to the earth. Indeed, it will be nothing more than strict justice to protect the authorities from the tyranny of their Japanese rulers, since by their acts of stealthy kindness to us they have compromised themselves with their vindictive masters. By protecting the higher classes and dispersing the spies, the lower orders will be allowed to hold up their heads. Hence it will be politic and just to continue to these people the protection which I shall give them so long as I have the power and the countenance of American authority.

Every day points out the importance and the positive necessity of bringing the government of Japan to some sort of reason, and the least objectionable course will be to establish an influence which they cannot prevent, here at the very door of the empire.

It will be well to modify my remarks as to the presumed influence which the Japanese authorities exercise over the Lew Chewans. On my second visit to Japan I was led to believe that the imperial government maintained very slight authority over the government and people of Lew Chew. This power belonged more to the Prince Satsuma, but not to the extent I at first imagined and have represented in my journal.

True.

To be enlarged upon. See Klaproth and other writers.

ORIGIN AND HISTORY OF LEW CHEW

The origin of the people of the Lew Chew and doubtless the other inhabited islands between Formosa and Japan is wrapt in uncertainty. Like the Chinese they claim to have had their origin from some divine power, according to Chow-Hwang [Chou Huang], a Chinese writer who was sent to Lew Chew in 1757, as envoy from China, and who on his return published an account of the island.*

The islanders declare that the original progenitors of Lew Chew were two, a man and a woman. They had five children; the oldest was a son named Tíen-Sun (offspring of Heaven) who was the first master or ruler of the nation; the second son acted the part of his minister, and the third constituted the people. The oldest daughter, for the protection of the country, took the place of the God of Heaven, and the youngest personified the god of the sea. Tíen-Sun and his descendants having maintained the government for 17,802 years were at length succeeded by Shunteen, a branch of the then ruling family of Japan. This occurred about A.D. 1200, when the Ming dynasty arose in China. Three kings ruled in Lew Chew; one was styled king of the Central Hills; the second, king of the Southern Hills; and the third, king of the Northern Hills, all were tributary and reigned by permission of the "Son of Heaven." At length the first became master of the whole country which has ever since remained under one king, always acknowledging himself a tributary of the Chinese Empire.†

These remarks may be brought in in connection with a description of the ruins discovered on the island.

Klaproth agrees in his account of Lew Chew (as derived by him from Chinese and Japanese writers) pretty well with the foregoing description

* See *The Chinese Repository*. July 1837. Volume 6. [Chou Huang went to Lew Chew in 1756 with an embassy to accord recognition to the new ruler. He returned to China in 1757 and presented a history of the islands to the throne. Hummel, vol. 2, p. 841.]

† It will be recollected this account is by a Chinese writer who claims for the Celestial Majesty, sovereignty over the island. See what Klaproth says.

given by Chou Huang, and says that the race of kings reigning in Lew Chew are related to the imperial family of Japan, that both China and Japan claim the sovereignty, and that the islanders pay tribute to both.

Note.

It is difficult to arrive at any correct data by which the origin, early history or form of government of the people of the Lew Chew Islands can be traced. There have been a thousand speculations upon the subject; pages have been written by learned men who have derived their information almost entirely from books, and from the accounts of the few Europeans who have visited the principal island.

The description of Captain Basil Hall is a mere romance; the production of the prolific brain of a writer nowise scrupulous of historical truth. The account of Doctor McLeod of the *Alceste* is not much nearer to accuracy. Subsequently Captains Beechey and Belcher [1827], surveying officers of the British Navy have visited the island, and their accounts may be considered more reliable. But, after all, they had no better means of acquiring a knowledge of the history, laws, and civil institutions of this singular race than were possessed by those who preceded them.

The exploring party from the squadron found the ruins of two very extensive buildings which are said to be, and doubtless are the remains of the palaces of the two other kings—of the northern and southern hills.

The palace at Shuri,[3] the ancient residence of the King of the Central Hills, is the only one remaining entire, and is now the regal residence of the present reigning family. This is the palace in which I was received, into which it was declared if I entered the queen dowager would be sure to die.

The prince, heir apparent, occupies another palace, as does also the regent, *tsung-li*.

My own opinion is that Lew Chew and the other islands (those which are inhabited) were originally peopled by accident. The original inhabitants may have been thrown on shore by shipwreck; and as there has been from the earliest times commercial intercourse between China, Japan, and Formosa, the crews of many of the very unsafe vessels—which even to this day navigate these seas—were from time to time adding to the number. Having found the islands worthy of possession, they settled and enticed men and women to join them from the several regions from which they originally came. Thus the Lew Chew race, as well as the people of the other islands, may have been made up of Chinese, Japanese, and the people of Formosa, with a probable small admixture of the Malay race.

The Lew Chewans are not a handsome people and yet they cannot be considered an ugly race. In color they correspond with the complexion of the Chinese. They have black hair and eyes. The hair is dressed with great care, the whole gathered in a knot at the top of the head.

On 2 July 1853, after many unforeseen delays, I got away from Naha with only four of the thirteen vessels which had been so repeatedly promised me.

To Japan
7 JULY 1853

---

3. This palace was totally destroyed in 1945 in one of the most bitterly contested Pacific land battles of World War II.

88 Not one of the rest of the squadron had arrived, nor could I calculate upon any day, week, or month when to expect them.

On getting clear of the harbor and stretching beyond the shelter of the southeastern extremity of the island—*Saratoga* being in tow of *Susquehanna,* and *Plymouth* of *Mississippi*—we encountered a strong wind from the east. Because the steamers were deep I thought it advisable to stand off on the port tack in order to get well clear of the land, the vessels in tow dragged them to leeward notwithstanding the power of their engines.

Sailors scrubbing hammocks on board *Mississippi*. Pencil sketch by W. Heine.
(Courtesy Naval Academy Museum)

At 1 P.M. we were pretty sure of weathering the eastern part of the island and consequently got on the other tack, thus making our way in the direction of Japan, however slow our progress.

The track taken by the squadron east of the chain of islands which stretch from Formosa to Lew Chew and from thence to Japan—very properly called by Blunt, the Southern, Middle, and Northern Groups—has rarely been traversed by the ships of modern nations, and the islands on the east side of the Chain are unknown to our present navigators.

The French Admiral Cecille, in 1846, employed one or more of his squadron in the exploration of the islands about Lew Chew and along the western side of the Northern Group. But according to the best authorities (Von Siebold among others) these islands of the Northern Group have never been visited, certainly not on the eastern side, by modern navigators.

The principal island of the Northern Group is called by the Japanese Oho-Sima [O Shima],[4]—by the Chinese "Ta-tao"—meaning in both languages great island. It is about the size or nearly so (including one or two islands adjoining) as Great Lew Chew, and is probably governed by similar laws. It has one chief city and several towns, and is doubtless highly cultivated.

This island contains, according to Von Siebold, several good harbors, and it is my purpose either to examine it myself or cause it to be examined by one or more vessels of my command. The *Susquehanna* and the other ships in company were probably the first European or American ships that ever passed along the entire extent of this Northern Group. Von Siebold says that

4. Known today as Amami O Shima in the Nansei Shoto. Approximate latitude 28°20′ N, longitude 129°20′ E.

Broughton saw the northeast point, and Captain Guerin, commander of the French corvette *Sabine*, traced the western shore in 1848.

It was this island that Commander Glynn saw in 1848 and which he supposed to be a new discovery. The islets which he mentions to have seen, bearing NNW, were the Cleopatra Islands, examined two years before by one of the vessels of Admiral Cecille's squadron. I have in my possession pretty accurate charts of these islands, which have been compiled by Von Siebold, and may be found appended to his great work on Japan.

In taking the bearings of the principal headlands of O Shima, we found their positions as laid down by Von Siebold to agree tolerably well with our observations; but, as I shall have more to say on the subject of these islands, I shall at present make no further remarks until I have made myself better acquainted with their condition. Their position upon the globe is already tolerably well determined. It is too often the case that navigators as well as travelers jump to conclusions upon very imperfect data. I wish to avoid as far as possible this error.

It is said that a current setting to the north and east is continually in motion throughout the year. An expression of the islanders is that it always goes toward Japan and never comes back. We found it of no great strength, though it is difficult in a steamer to estimate the rate and direction of currents, as they are generally overlogged, because of the backward movement of the water given by the revolution of the wheels.

On Thursday, 7 July,[5] the squadron at sunset, was according to our observations about 40 miles from Cape Nagatsuo [Nagatsuro], otherwise called Cape Idzu [Izu]. Consequently, at midnight the heads of the ships were put offshore until 4 A.M. At daylight not only the cape was seen from the masthead, but also several of the islands to the east, and called by Von Siebold *Goebroken Eilander* (Broken Islands), and the two largest of the group, bearing the Japanese names of Tosi-Sima [Toshi Shima] and Sikine-Sima [Shikine Shima]. Steering directly for the entrance of the bay we passed within a mile and a half of a small islet called Rock Island, about three fourths of a mile in length.

Edo Bay
8 JULY 1853

The weather was fine, but the atmosphere so hazy that we could see but a short distance. This was very much to be regretted as it prevented our getting an outline of the coast. It was not till we had reached our anchorage off the city of Uraga* that we could distinctly see the tracery of the shore.

The land on both sides of the bay of Jeddo [Edo] is precipitous toward the shore and gradually rising into abrupt eminences inland. Here and there small bays are formed at the bottom of ravines, furnishing small tracts of level land on which villages have been reared, protected by batteries erected upon the projecting headlands. Indeed the shores on both sides appear to be

* Sometimes spelt Oragawa.

5. The original manuscript (Volume II, p. 36) mistakenly gives the date as the 9th.

occupied by these villages, or rather towns, wherever the formation of the land will permit.

Uraga is composed of two of these towns which are separated by a bluff point; through the largest a river passes and empties into the bay. This river is sufficiently deep to admit junks of 70 or 80 tons, perhaps larger, and the town seems to be a sort of entrepôt, as most of the junks passing up the bay stop here, probably to pay their custom dues.

Just before the squadron anchored off Uraga, the atmosphere became more clear, when we could distinctly see Mount Fuzi or Fusi [Fuji], and some high mountains farther inland. Mount Fuji is conical in shape, and comparing it with other similar eminences I should judge it to be 8,000 or 10,000 feet in height. It lies about W ½ N from Uraga, distant fifty or sixty miles.[6]

Long before we anchored we noticed many of the Japanese guard boats in pursuit of us, some of them coming from a town which we had passed about eight or ten miles below Uraga. I had, however, given orders, verbally and by signal, forbidding the admission of anyone on board any of the ships, excepting the flagship, and with respect to her only those who had business with me. It had been the practice heretofore for ships of war to admit these people indiscriminately on board ship, and at one time many hundreds were on board the *Columbus*. These made no hesitation in partaking of the hospitality of the officers—and made themselves quite at home—but when they spoke of going on shore, answered by signs that that was impossible.

I had therefore determined to exercise an equal degree of exclusiveness, and to permit only the Japanese functionaries to communicate directly with *Susquehanna,* and with her alone. Some of the leaders in the boats signified by signs some dissatisfaction at not being permitted on board, but my orders were fully obeyed.

A short time after the squadron had anchored in a line ahead—the ships commanding with their guns the entire range of batteries and two considerable towns—a large number of these guard boats came from all directions, evidently prepared to assume their stations around the ships, as the crews had every apparent preparation of water, clothing, sleeping mats, and other provisions for a long stay.

About this time a boat with an officer from the shore came alongside, one of the party having a scroll of paper in his hand which he did not exhibit, though one was held up to read alongside the *Mississippi*. The written words were in French, and were in the form of an order for the ships to go away and not to anchor at their peril.

The functionary, who was alongside *Susquehanna,* was accompanied by an interpreter who spoke Dutch very well. He asked to see me, and was told that I would see no one but a mandarin of the highest rank and that he might return on shore. He asked a great many questions which were not replied to, yet he was very pertinacious in urging to come on board. He stated that he was the vice governor of Uraga. He was then asked why the

6. Mount Fuji stands 12,385 feet in height, bears 279° (W 1/2 N) from Uraga, and is distant 49 miles.

governor did not come off, and he replied that he was prevented by the laws from going on board of ships in the road, and proposed that I would appoint an officer of corresponding rank to himself to confer with him, being desirous of communicating to the government the object of my visit. I consented to this, and consequently my aide, Lieutenant Contee, was appointed to receive him. He was by my directions told that I had brought a letter from the President of the United States, addressed to his emperor,[7] and that I wished that a suitable officer might be sent on board to receive a copy of the same, in order that a day might be appointed for me to deliver the original.

He replied that neither himself nor any person with him could receive any such communication, but he would go on shore and report to the governor, and asked permission to return the following morning. This was granted, and he was told that I would not submit to have the ships watched by guard boats, and if they did not at once disperse, I would compel them to do so, and if they remained it would be at their own peril. After some hesitation he said he would order them away, and most of them upon his order dispersed.

In the latter part of the night of Friday, the day of our casting anchor upon the coast of Japan, a most remarkable meteor was seen by Lieutenant Duer in command of the watch, who describes it as follows:

During the watch from midnight to 4 A.M. a very remarkable meteor was seen. It made its appearance in the south and west and illuminated the whole atmosphere. The spars, sails and hulls of the ships in company as well as our own reflected its glare as distinctly as though a blue light were burning from each at the same time. From the south and west about 15 degrees above the horizon it pursued a north-easterly course in a direct line for a long distance, when it fell gradually toward the sea and disappeared. Its shape was that of a large blue sphere with a red wedge-shaped tail, which it could be easily observed was formed of ignited particles, and resembled the sparks of a rocket as they appear upon its explosion.

The ancients would have construed this remarkable appearance of the heavens as an omen promising a favorable issue to an enterprise undertaken by them, and we may pray God that our present attempt to bring a singular and half barbarous people into the family of civilized nations, may succeed without resort to bloodshed.

But I will discontinue for a time these daily remarks and substitute a copy of the notes forwarded by me to the Navy Department, giving an account of my visit to Edo Bay.

> *Notes referring to events which transpired pending the preliminary negotiations of Commodore M. C. Perry, with the authorities of Japan in July 1853.*

The squadron consisting of the steamers *Susquehanna* and *Mississippi,* and the sloops of war *Plymouth* and *Saratoga,* commanded respectively by Com-

7. Unknown to Commodore Perry and the rest of the outside world, Japan was being governed by the Tokugawa shogunate in Edo (Tokyo) as it had been since 1615 when Shogun Ieyasu established his family's supremacy. Shogun Ieyoshi, fourth son of Ienari (1773–1841), had succeeded his father in 1837. Shogun Ieyoshi died 27 July 1853, just ten days after Perry's first visit ended, and was succeeded by his fourth son, Iesada, who was invested on 22 November 1853. Thus, while Perry refers to the emperor throughout the Japanese negotiations, he was actually dealing with representatives of the shogun. Emperor Komei, who had succeeded Ninko in 1846, was living in Kyoto as the sovereign, but without real power or administrative function.

manders Buchanan, Lee, Kelly, and Walker, left Naha Port, island of Lew Chew, on Saturday, 2 July, and anchored off the city of Uraga, Bay of Edo, Japan, on the afternoon of Friday, 8 July.

I had, before reaching the coast, fully considered and determined upon the course I should pertinaciously pursue in conducting the delicate and responsible duties which had been entrusted to my charge. It was to adopt an entirely contrary plan of proceedings from that of all others who had hitherto visited Japan on the same errand: to demand as a right and not to solicit as a favor those acts of courtesy which are due from one civilized nation to another; to allow none of those petty annoyances which have been unsparingly visited upon those who had preceded me, and to disregard the acts as well as the threats of the authorities if they in the least conflicted with my own sense of what was due to the dignity of the American flag. The question of landing by force was left to be decided by the development of succeeding events. In pursuance of these intentions I caused the crews to be thoroughly drilled and the ships kept in perfect readiness as in time of active war.

Being thus prepared for any contingency, I determined to practice upon them a little of their own diplomacy, by forbidding the admission of a single individual on board any of the ships, excepting those officers who might have business with me. The visits of these were to be confined to the flagship, on board of which they were not allowed to enter until they had declared their rank and the business upon which they came.

I had also made up my mind to confer personally with no one but a functionary of the highest rank in the empire, and consequently refused to see the lieutenant governor and governor of Uraga, referring them to Commanders Buchanan and Adams and Lieutenant Contee who had orders from me to receive them, and to reply under my instructions to their enquiries and verbal communications.

I was well aware that the more exclusive I should make myself and the more exacting I might be, the more respect these people of forms and ceremonies would be disposed to award me, hence my object, and the sequel will show the correctness of these conclusions.

Preliminary Encounters

9 JULY 1853

On anchoring off the city of Uraga, a commercial place, distant 27 miles from Edo—the place of anchorage of the *Columbus* and *Vincennes*,[8] and the British sloop of war *Mariner*[9]—the ships were immediately surrounded by numerous boats filled with men, many of whom attempted to get on board, but were in obedience to my previous instructions repulsed. One of the most conspicuous of these boats having on board a personage of distinction was permitted alongside the flagship and the officer being asked his rank and

8. Commodore James Biddle's ships on his unsuccessful visit in July 1846.
9. This surveying ship (Commander Matheson) came to Uraga in June 1849, and afterward visited Shimoda Bay.

Unnamed fruit from Macao

Singapore fish: Needlefish (top) and Carongid

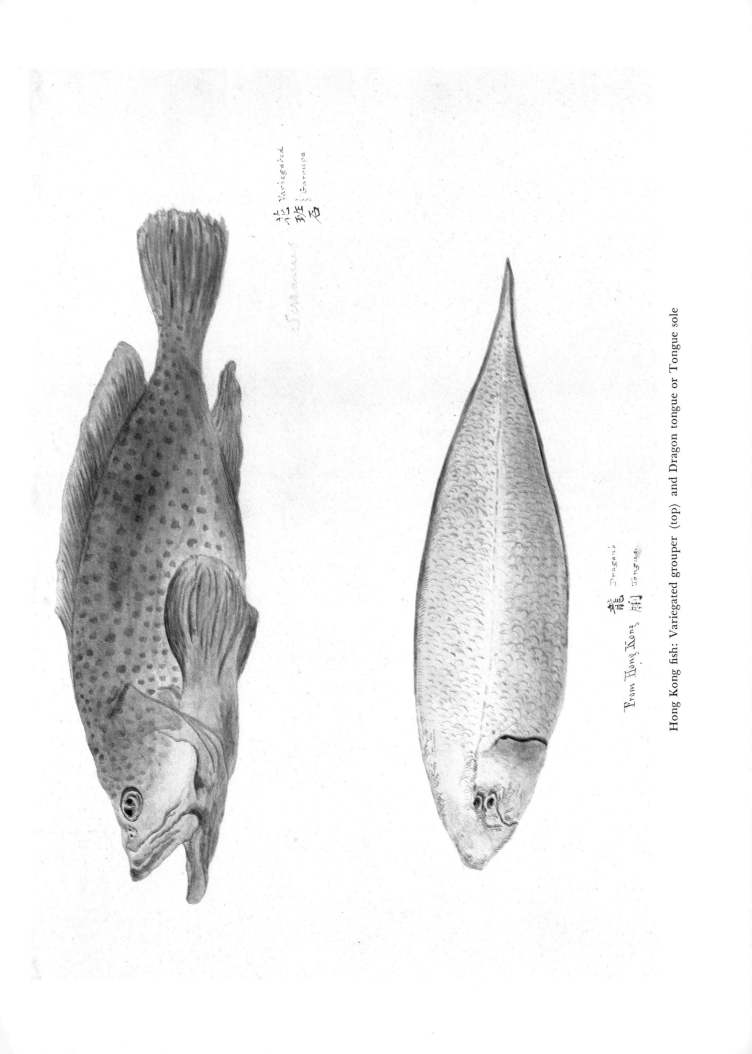

Variegated Grouper
花 Variegated
斑 { Garoupa
石

Serranus

龍 Dragons
脷 Tongue

From Hong Kong

Hong Kong fish: Variegated grouper (top) and Dragon tongue or Tongue sole

Tanka woman poling her boat, Macao

女
人 China Woman from Macao

Chinese woman with bound feet, Macao

Chinese junks on the Canton River, April 1853

American Consulate, Shanghai, May 1853

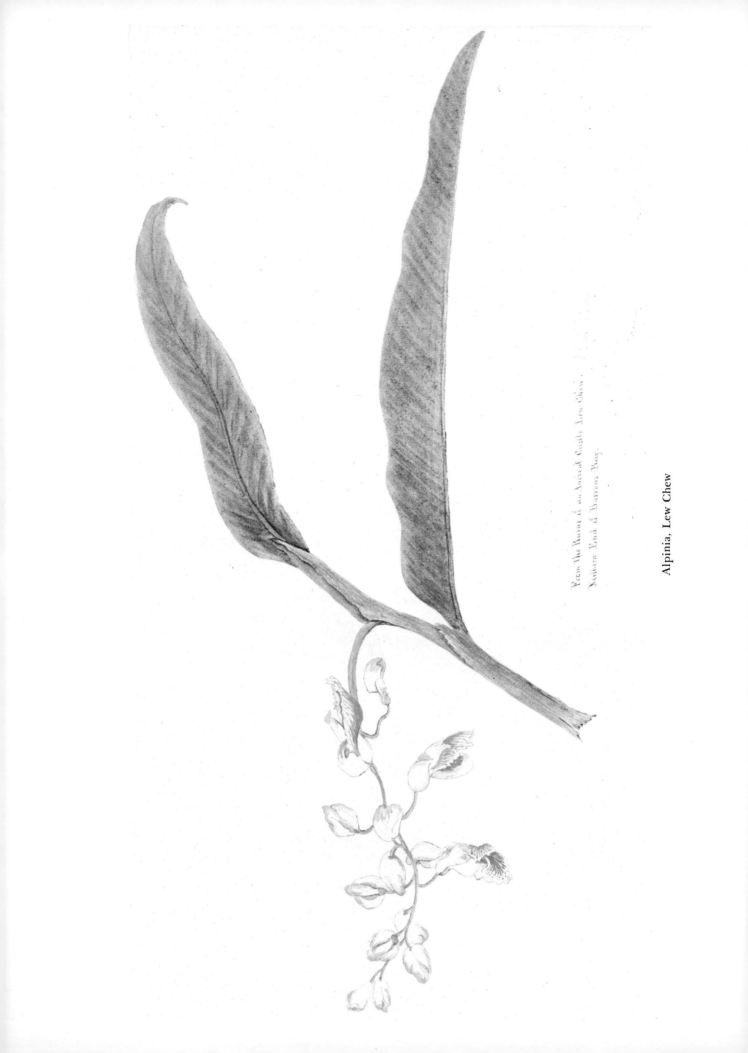

From the Ruins of an Ancient Castle Lew Chew.
Western End of Barrow Bay.

Alpinia, Lew Chew

Chinese rose in a Shanghai garden

Azalea from a Shanghai garden. "Said to be nondescript. If so, to be called Perryana in honor of Commodore M. C. Perry."

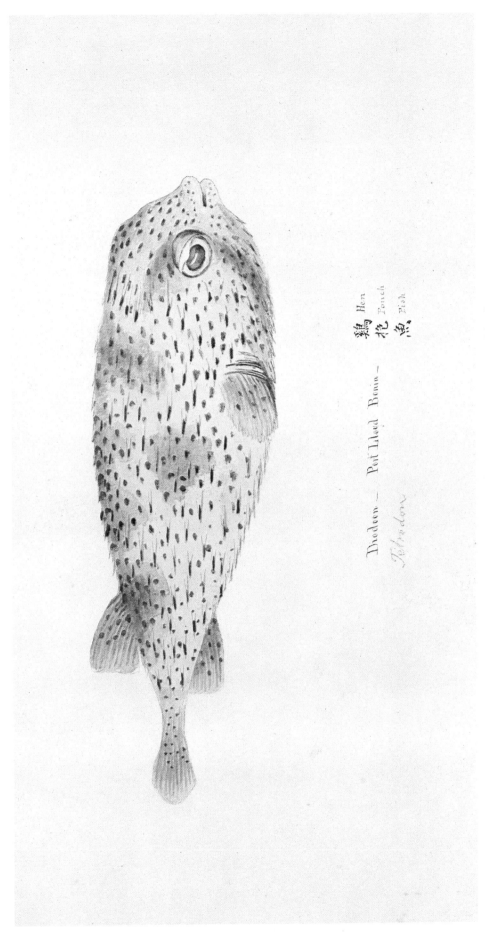

Diodon — Port Lloyd Bonin —
Tetrodon

鶏 Hen
花 Flower
魚 Fish

"Hen-Pouch Fish," Diodon Hystrix, Port Lloyd, Bonin Islands

Chinese barber at Hong Kong, April 1853. Heine

Chinese Soldier　唐人兵丁帶牌　Chinese soldier carrying Shield

Chinese soldier at Shanghai

From nature by W. Heine Shipping by Lieut.F.Walke

J.Queen del.

P.S.Duval & Co.Phil.

American ships, Naha Harbor, Great Lew Chew, May 1853. Duval lithograph from Heine and Walke (Courtesy Mr. and Mrs. W. John Kenney)

Commodore Perry at "Gate of Courtesy," Shuri Castle, Great Lew Chew, 6 June 1853. Sarony lithograph from Heine (Courtesy Mr. and Mrs. W. John Kenney)

Commodore Perry and troops returning from visit to Shuri Castle, 6 June 1853. Note Commodore's sedan chair just left of center. Heine watercolor. (Courtesy Mr. and Mrs. J. William Middendorf II)

business answered that he was vice governor of Uraga* and wished to see the officer commanding the squadron in view of learning his object in coming to Japan. He was told that I would confer with no one but a functionary of the highest rank.

He still urged the necessity of his coming on board to make some enquiries, stating that he held the highest rank in the city, and was the proper person to visit the ship. On being peremptorily refused admission he suggested as an alternative that he might be allowed to confer with an officer of rank corresponding with his own. To this proposition I consented after some intentional delay, and my aide, Lieutenant Contee, was appointed to receive him, assisted by the interpreters, Messrs. Williams and Portman, one speaking Chinese, and the other Dutch. The vice governor had an interpreter with him who conversed fluently in the Dutch language.

A conference followed in which the vice governor propounded numerous questions very few of which were answered. He was merely told, under instructions from me, that I had been sent on a friendly mission to Japan with a letter from the President of the United States for the Emperor, and it was my desire to have a personal interview with a dignitary of the highest rank in order to make arrangements for the delivery of copies and translation of the documents with which I had been charged preparatory to the formal presentation of the originals.

He replied that Nangasaki [Nagasaki] was the only place according to the laws of Japan for negotiating foreign business, and it would be necessary for the squadron to go there. To which he was told that I had come purposely to Uraga, it being near to Edo, and should not go to Nagasaki; that I expected the letter to be duly and properly received where I then was, that my intentions were perfectly friendly, but I would allow of no indignity. Nor would I permit the guard boats which were collecting about the ships to remain where they then were, and if they were not immediately removed I would disperse them by force. On having this interpreted to him he suddenly left his seat, went to the gangway and gave an order which caused most of the boats to return to the shore, but a few of them remained in clusters. An armed boat from the ship was sent to motion them away, at the same time showing their arms, which had the desired effect. All of them disappeared and we saw nothing more of them near the ships during the remainder of our stay. Here was the first important point gained.

The vice governor shortly after took his leave, saying that he had no authority to promise anything respecting the reception of the President's letter, but in the morning an officer of higher rank would come from the city who might probably furnish some further information.

* His name was subsequently ascertained to be N. Saboroski [Saburosuke Nakajima].[10]

10. In the *Journal*—which usually gives the names of Japanese in the native order of family name first—this name was rendered simply, "N. Saboroski." Names of Japanese in this work are given in occidental order.

Nakajima was not the vice governor of Uraga, but merely one of his *yoriki* or minor functionaries.

On the following morning, the 9th, the governor of Uraga, Kayamon Yezaimon [Eizaemon Kayama],[11] came on board thus giving the lie to the vice governor who declared himself of the highest authority in the city. As this officer was of superior rank to the visitor of the day before, I directed that he should be received by Commanders Buchanan and Adams and Lieutenant Contee, still refusing to receive myself anyone but a counselor of the empire (cabinet minister).

The governor after a long discussion in which he more than once declared that the Japanese laws made it impossible that the letter should be received at Uraga, that the squadron must go to Nagasaki, and even if the letter of the President were to be received at this place, a reply would be sent to Nagasaki. In answer to this he was told that I would never consent to such arrangements and would persist in delivering it where I then was, that if the Japanese government did not appoint a suitable person to receive the documents addressed to the emperor, I would go on shore with a sufficient force and deliver them, whatever the consequences might be.

On this being communicated to him he said he would return to the city and send a communication to Edo asking for further instructions; that it would require four days to obtain a reply. He was told that I would wait until Tuesday, the 12th—three days—when I should certainly expect a definite answer; accordingly he left the ship with the understanding that there would be no necessity for any further discussion until the time appointed for the delivery of the answer from court should arrive.

At this interview the original letter of the President together with my letter of credence were shown to the governor, encased as they were in the magnificent boxes which had been prepared at Washington, the exquisite workmanship and costliness of which evidently surprised his excellency. On leaving the ship he made an offer for the first time of supplies of water and refreshments, but was told that we did not stand in need of anything.

Surveys and Soundings

9–13 JULY 1853

I had directed that a surveying boat, well manned and armed, from each ship of the squadron should commence at daylight this morning, the 9th, the survey of the harbor and bay of Uraga, and thinking it quite possible they might meet with some resistance, I instructed Lieutenant Silas Bent in command of the surveying party not to go beyond the range of our guns, and caused a lookout to be kept upon them that assistance might be sent should they be attacked. Although they were followed by numbers of Japanese boats they did not, on seeing our men well armed, venture to molest them.

The governor enquired what these boats were doing, and on being told they were surveying the harbor, he said it was against the Japanese laws to allow of such examinations. He was replied to that though the Japanese laws forbade such surveys, the American laws command them, and that we

11. Actually, Kayama was only another *yoriki*, or functionary of the governor, but a shade higher in rank than Nakajima.

were as much bound to obey the American as he was the Japanese laws.
Here was a second, and a most important point gained.

The following day, the 10th, was Sunday and no communication was had with the Japanese authorities. A boat with some mandarins accompanied by an interpreter came alongside and requested to be admitted on board. On being asked if they had any business with the Commodore, and they replying that they had no special business, but merely wished to have a talk, they were told by order that they could not be received.

Monday, 11 July. The surveying boats were despatched early this morning higher up the bay, and Commander Lee in *Mississippi* was directed to get his ship under way to protect them. The governor on seeing *Mississippi* going higher up than any foreign vessel had ever before ventured, came on board as I expected he would, though he was told on Saturday that there would be no necessity for further discussion until the reply from Edo was received.

I had purposely sent *Mississippi* and the boats on this service, being satisfied that the very circumstance of approaching nearer to Edo with a powerful ship would alarm the authorities and induce them to give a more favorable answer to my demands, and so it happened. The governor pretended that his visit to the ship was to bring information that it was very probable the letters (meaning, as I then supposed, the translations of the originals) would be received on the following day and forwarded to Edo. But he evidently came to ascertain for what purpose *Mississippi* and the surveying boats had ascended the bay, and soon put the question.

Anticipating such an enquiry, I directed that he should be informed that unless the business which brought the squadron to these waters was arranged at this time, I should return in the ensuing spring with a larger force. As the anchorage in front of Uraga was not convenient or safe, I was desirous of seeking a more favorable situation nearer to Edo which would make our communications with that city more convenient.[12]

Tuesday, 12 July. This being the day on which a reply was to be received from Edo, the governor was on board by 10 A.M., accompanied by the interpreters.

But previously to his arrival I had written the following letter to the Emperor, not supposing he would so readily accede to my demands and appoint a cabinet minister to meet me, as will be seen by the events of the day, that he had already done.

United States Steam Frigate *Susquehanna*
Uraga, 12 July 1853

The Commander-in-chief of the United States naval forces in these seas, being invested with full powers to negotiate treaties, is desirous of conferring with one of

I deem it desirable that some of the most important of my letters and those addressed to me should be inserted in the finished narrative. M.C.P.

12. Curiously, Perry makes no mention of tense moments in the morning of 11 July when some thousand Japanese soldiers embarked in thirty to forty guard boats and headed for the surveying party. Lieutenant Bent called for *Mississippi*—then two miles southward—to approach, and this had the desired effect of discouraging the armed Japanese. The guard boats withdrew and the survey work continued. Thus was resolved one of the most tense and critical moments of the entire Perry Expedition to the Far East. The scene is recorded in William Heine's painting "Crossing the Rubicon."

the highest officers of the empire of Japan, in view of making arrangements for the presentation of the original of his letter of credence, as also the original of a letter with which he is charged, addressed to His Imperial Majesty, by the President of the United States.

It is hoped that an early day will be appointed for the proposed interview.

To his Imperial Majesty
the Emperor of Japan

The governor then went on to say that there had been a misapprehension as to the delivery of the translations of the papers before the originals had been received. Although I was certain there had been no such misunderstanding, nevertheless I consented, after much discussion, to deliver the translations and originals, as also a letter from me to the Emperor at the same time, provided the Emperor should appoint a suitable officer to receive them at my hands. I repeated that I would consent to deliver them to no other than a dignitary of the highest rank. The governor then said that a building would be erected on shore for the reception of myself and suite, and a high official personage especially appointed by the Emperor would be in attendance to receive the letters; that no answer would be given here, but it would be transmitted to Nagasaki through the Dutch or Chinese superintendents. This being reported to me, I wrote the following memorandum and directed it to be translated into Dutch and fully explained to the governor.

The Commander-in-chief will not go to Nagasaki, and will receive no communication through the Dutch or Chinese.

He has a letter from the President of the United States to deliver to the Emperor of Japan or to his secretary of foreign affairs, and he will deliver the originals to none other. If this friendly letter of the President to the Emperor is not received and duly replied to, he shall consider his country insulted and will not hold himself accountable for the consequences.

He expects a reply of some sort in a few days, and he will receive such a reply nowhere but in this neighborhood.

Upon receipt of this he went on shore, probably to consult some higher authority, as doubtless there were more than one high officer of the court at Uraga secretly directing the negotiations. He returned in the afternoon to the ship with the assurance that a very distinguished personage properly accredited by the Emperor would be appointed to receive me on shore the day after tomorrow. Being asked what proof I should have of his rank and the validity of his credentials, he said that he would bring on board certified copies of the original documents in order that I should be fully satisfied.

He was then asked where the reception was to take place, to which he replied at a small village (Gori-Hama) [Kurihama] situated at the head of the bay, since named Reception Bay in our chart; about a Japanese mile from Uraga.[13] The enquiry was then made why the meeting could not take place in one of the houses or forts opposite the ships. He replied that he would ascertain if such arrangements could be made, and would give an

13. The Japanese mile or *ri* is the equivalent of 2.44 English statute miles.

answer in the morning, saying he would be on board early to bring the promised papers and to announce the arrival of the dignitary who had been appointed to receive me.

The surveying boats were actively engaged all this day.

Wednesday, 13 July. The governor came on board in the afternoon of this day apologizing for not being earlier, by saying that the high officer from Edo had only just arrived. He brought with him the original order of the Emperor addressed to the functionary who had to receive me, as also a copy and translation of the same in Dutch, and a certificate of his own, verifying the authenticity of the appointment. He also said that the person appointed by the Emperor had no power to enter into discussion with me but was empowered merely to receive the papers and carry them to his sovereign.

Here follows translations of the papers referred to.

Translation of letter of credence given by the Emperor of Japan to his highness, Toda, Prince of Izu.[14]

I send you to Uraga to receive the letter of the President of the United States to me, which letter has recently been brought to Uraga by the Admiral; upon receiving which you will proceed to Edo, and take the same to me.

5th month in
1853.[15]

Here is the Emperor's Seal.

Translation of certificate of Eizaemon Kayama, governor of Uraga, verifying the authenticity of the Emperor's letter and seal.

You can rest assured that the high officer who has been accredited by the Emperor of Japan himself, and who consequently comes here to Uraga from Edo for the purpose of receiving the original and translated letters, is of very high rank, equal to that of the Lord Admiral. I do assure that.

(signed) Eizaemon Kayama

These letters should be included in the Narrative.

The governor remarked that he had made enquiry as to the practicability of changing the place of meeting, and said that a suitable building had already been constructed, and it would be inconvenient to make a change. This reply I had expected and was prepared for, and not knowing whether any treachery was intended had ordered the surveying party to examine the little bay at the head of which the building had been erected for my reception. They promptly performed the service and reported that the ships could be brought within gunshot of the position, where they observed great numbers of people employed in the completion of the building, transporting furniture, and other preparations. Accordingly, I directed the squadron to be removed in the morning to an anchorage in line covering the whole bay, being determined to be prepared against the well known duplicity of the people with whom I had to deal, the object of selecting this place of meeting not being clearly explained to my mind.

14. Toda was one of the two governors of Uraga. In that position he rated the "princely" suffix *no kami* added to his clan name of Izu. Thus he was called Toda Izu *no kami* or prince of Izu.

15. According to Japan's lunar calendar, but it was July by western reckoning. The western calendar was adopted in Japan on 1 January 1873, which by the lunar calendar was the third day and twelfth month of the fifth year of the Emperor Meiji.

Thursday, 14 July. This being the day appointed for my reception on shore, and every preparation having been made for landing a formidable escort of officers, seamen, and Marines from the respective ships. They were about 400 in number, all well armed and equipped, and, being ready for disembarkation, the two steamers moved to a position commanding the proposed landing place (the sloops of war not being able to move for want of wind). Shortly after, the detachments forming the escort were in their boats and on their way to the shore where they landed and formed, and were immediately followed by me.

The whole shore of the bay extending more than a mile was crowded with Japanese troops, from five to seven thousand drawn up under arms. These troops were composed of cavalry, artillery, infantry, and archers; some of the infantry with flint muskets, others with matchlocks.

On landing I proceeded at once to the building erected for the purpose, and was there received by the prince of Izu, first counselor of the emperor, and his coadjutor the prince of Iwami.[16] To the former of these I presented the President's letter, my letter of credence, and three communications from myself together with transcripts of the same in the English, Dutch, and Chinese languages, for which the prince of Izu gave me a receipt.

The princes were attended by the governor of Uraga, the chief interpreter, and a secretary. As it was understood that there was to be no discussion at this meeting, I remained but a short time, taking my departure and embarking with the same ceremony with which I had landed.

The letter of the President to the Emperor, as also my letter of credence, were each contained in magnificent rosewood boxes, about twelve inches long, with locks, hinges, and other mountings, all in solid gold.

The letters were of folio form, and not folded but were bound in blue silk velvet, with the seal of the United States attached to each by cords made of gold and silken thread, at the end of which were large gold tassels. The seals themselves were encased in circular boxes, made of pure gold, and were about six inches in diameter, and three deep, costing as I was informed a thousand dollars each.

These splendid specimens of American workmanship, were covered with scarlet cloth and carried into the audience room by two of the best looking boys of the squadron, selected for the purpose, who were guarded by a couple of tall jet-black Negroes, completely armed.

Translation of receipt given by the
princes of Izu and Iwami to Commodore Perry.

The letter of the President of the United States of North America, and copy are hereby received and delivered to the Emperor. Many times it has been communicated that business relating to foreign countries cannot be transacted here in Uraga, but in Nagasaki. Now it has been observed that the Admiral, in his quality of ambassador of the President would be insulted by it; the justice of this has been acknowledged; consequently, the afore-mentioned letter is hereby received, in opposition to the Japanese law.

16. Ido, Iwami *no kami,* the other governor of Uraga.

Japanese painting of Commodore Perry's first landing in Japan, 14 July 1853. Americans filing from landing boats into meeting house.
Note positions of Daimyo defense forces (Courtesy Shiryo Hensanjo)

Because this place is not designed to treat of anything from foreigners, so neither can conference nor entertainment take place. The letter being received you will leave here."

The 9th day of the 5th month.[17]

Facsimile of signature.

The above is a literal translation from the Dutch, in which language the conferences were held, and into which the receipt of the chief counselors, the princes of Izu and Iwami, were doubtless badly translated from the Japanese by their interpreter.

The following would probably be the correct translation from the Japanese.

This should be included.

The letter of the President of the United States of North America, and copy, are hereby received, and will be delivered to the Emperor.

It has been many times intimated that business relating to foreign countries cannot be transacted here in Uraga, but at Nagasaki. Nevertheless, as it has been observed that the Admiral, in his quality of ambassador of the President, would feel himself insulted by a refusal to receive the letter at this place, the justice of which has been acknowledged, the above-mentioned letter is hereby received in opposition to the Japanese law.

As this is not a place wherein to negotiate with foreigners, so neither can conferences nor entertainment be held.

Therefore as the letter has been received, you can depart. Facsimile of signature.

Parthian Surveys

15–16 JULY 1853

To show these princes how little I regarded their order for me to depart, on getting on board I immediately ordered the whole squadron underway, not to leave the bay, as they doubtless expected, but to go higher up. Having determined to examine the channel toward Edo, being satisfied that the employment of so large a force in surveying service, and so near to the capital, and in waters hitherto unknown to foreigners, would produce a decided influence upon the pride and conceit of the government, and cause a more favorable consideration of the President's letter.

The four ships stood off in a line abreast, running lines of soundings across the bay until they passed out of sight of Uraga, and at night anchored at a place I have called American Anchorage,[18] ten miles higher than any foreign vessel had ever before ascended.

The following morning, the 15th, the surveying boats were early at work sounding still farther up the bay, and in the afternoon I ascended in the *Mississippi* ten miles higher, taking the ship within seven miles of Edo, and twenty miles higher than the usual anchorage at Uraga. We could distinctly see the port or shipping place of Edo filled with innumerable junks, but the city containing, like those of China, nothing but low buildings, was hidden behind a projecting point.

17. Japanese lunar calendar equivalent of 14 July.
18. Just outside the present-day port of Yokosuka.

I might have gone still higher but was apprehensive of causing too much alarm, and thus throwing some obstacle in the way of a favorable reception at court of the President's letter, which I had delivered only the day before, and which was probably then under consideration. Thinking that I had done enough to work up the fears of the Emperor without going too far in my experiment, I caused the ship to rejoin the squadron at the American Anchorage.

In my absence the Eizaemon Kayama came alongside *Susquehanna* apparently very much annoyed at the motions of *Mississippi* and said, probably as an excuse for coming so far from his city, that the letter of the President had been received at court and would doubtless have a favorable consideration, and he begged the acceptance of a few presents. As I had previously given orders that no one should be admitted on board the ship without my especial permission, neither he nor the presents were received and he went on shore with the expressed intention of returning the following morning.[19]

During the day all the boats that could be spared from the ships, twelve in number, were busily engaged in surveying the western shore of the bay above Uraga.

The next morning being Saturday the 16th, the ships were at daylight moved to a bay about five miles above Uraga, which I have called Susquehanna Bay,[20] in the survey of which the boats were now employed. The governor was alongside before we had anchored, with his presents and with a renewal of his prediction of the favorable reception of the President's letter. Nothing was said now of sending the answer to Nagasaki, and it seemed that the nearer we approached the imperial city the more polite and friendly they became.

He was told by my orders that the presents which he brought alongside could not be received if others from me were not accepted in return, to this he at first demurred by interposing the invariable plea that the Japanese law forbade it, upon which he was answered that *our* laws enjoined a reciprocity of courtesy, and his presents would not be received. Finding me resolute upon this as upon all other points of ceremony, he consented to receive in return whatever (excepting arms) I might be disposed to present. Consequently some few articles of more value than those he brought were sent on deck. When he saw them he declared they were of too much value, and he dared not take on shore anything but what his interpreter and himself could conceal about their persons. When he was informed that if he could not receive the articles openly and without concealment, I would send those

19. This is at variance with the Hawks *Narrative* which says that Kayama came on board to ask why the ships were moving up the bay. Informed that they sought a better anchorage for the occasion of their return next year, he and his companions accepted an invitation "to share in the hospitalities of the cabin. A convivial scene ensued in which abundant supplies of ham, ship's biscuit, and other stores—washed down by plentiful draughts of whiskey—quickly disappeared. The cheer seemed to be much relished, . . . not satisfied with well-filled paunches, they carried off in their capacious sleeves pieces of the bread and ham, wherewith to refresh their memories and their future appetites." Hawks *Narrative*, pp. 266–267.

20. Otsu Wan, the bay just south of Yokosuka naval base, in which lies Saru Shima (Monkey Island) or Perry Island as it was named by the expedition.

which he had brought on board back into his boat. Upon this he left the ship carrying with him all my gifts excepting three swords which he was permitted to leave.

In the afternoon he came on board with a trifling present of poultry and eggs. Determining to be under no obligation to these people I sent in return presents of greater value to the wives of the governor and his interpreters. Here was another point gained in the unprecedented circumstance of their consenting to exchange presents.

Having completed the survey of the west side of this magnificent bay from Uraga to a point about 14 miles below Edo, and sounded with *Mississippi* and boats six miles nearer to that city, and acquiring a sufficient knowledge of the bay to conduct *Vermont* to the American Anchorage,[21] and higher if necessary, I thought it advisable to return to Lew Chew, intending to despatch *Saratoga*, after we cleared the coast of Japan, to Shanghai, and employ the other vessels on the way in the further examination of O Shima. Unfortunately, before reaching that island we encountered a severe gale which in part defeated the object.

It has already been observed that in adherence to my previous determination I had no personal communication with the governor of Uraga, the officer employed by the Japanese government to visit the ship and conduct the preliminary arrangements for my reception. The only persons with whom I had an interview were the princes of Izu and Iwami. The conferences with the governor were conducted on my part by Commanders Buchanan and Adams and Lieutenant Contee assisted by the Chinese interpreter Mr. A. Wells Williams, and by the Dutch interpreter Mr. Portman. Although these officers acted under my immediate instructions and were in constant communication with me, much credit is due to them for managing the discussion with great judgment and skill. I take pleasure also in commending the coolness and industry with which the surveying officers under Lieutenant Silas Bent conducted their laborious duties.

It is proper that I should add in conclusion that the governor in the several conferences on board ship evinced great anxiety to learn how long I intended to remain upon the coast, remarking repeatedly that it was the custom of the Japanese government to be very slow in deciding upon matters having reference to foreign countries. Upon these representations and knowing that the propositions contained in the President's letter were of such importance as to require time for deliberation, overturning as they would if acceded to many of the fundamental laws of the empire, I deemed it advisable not to wait for a reply and for the following reasons:

I had not provisions or water sufficient to allow of my remaining on the coast more than a month longer. I well knew that they could easily and very reasonably defer for a long time any satisfactory reply for reason of the alleged necessity of calling together and consulting the princes of the empire, as also to consult the *dairi* or ecclesiastical emperor. Thus I should be

My reason for leaving Japan at this time with the intention of returning and in view of giving the Japanese government full time to consider my propositions should be fully set forth as a stroke of policy which had the happiest effect—though in truth the condition of the squadron and other circumstances as set forth in the Journal made it indispensably necessary that I should do so.

21. Perry expected that ship-of-the-line *Vermont* would be bringing the gifts for presentation on the next visit.

put off from day to day and utlimately be obliged to sail without any satisfaction whatever. This would be construed into a triumph by them, and cause a serious injury to the success of my mission.

Taking into view also the present disturbed state of China, and the need of one or more ships of the squadron in that quarter, and considering that not a single vessel—which had been promised by the department should immediately follow me—had yet joined my force, and being without the presents sent from the United States and expected in the *Vermont,* I was glad to have a good excuse for consenting to wait until the ensuing spring for the final answer from the Japanese government.

In the spring I shall have concentrated my whole force and be prepared with store and coal vessels and all other conveniencies for remaining, if it be necessary, an indefinite time to secure such concessions as I believe they will be constrained to make. The exhibition of so large a force and a continuation of the policy so far successfully pursued, and having given them full time for the consideration of the propositions of the President, I shall be prepared to act very decidedly and I trust with continued success; provided there shall be no curtailment of the force promised me by the government before my departure from home.

Under these considerations I determined to make a credit of necessity, and accordingly prepared a letter to be delivered with other documents on the occasion of my reception on shore, but which of course would have been withheld if an unfriendly course had been adopted by the Japanese government.

The following is a copy of the letter just referred to, which accompanied the other papers.

United States Steam Frigate Susquehanna
Uraga, Edo Bay, 14 July 1853

It having been represented to the undersigned that the propositions submitted through him to the government of Japan, are of so much importance and involve so many momentous questions, that much time will be required to deliberate and decide upon their several bearings:

The undersigned, in consideration thereof, declares himself willing to await a reply to these propositions until his return to Edo Bay in the ensuing spring, when he may confidently hope that all matters will be amicably arranged, and to the satisfaction of the two nations.

With profound respect,
(signed) M. C. Perry
Commander-in-chief United States Naval Forces
in the East India, China, and Japan Seas

To His Imperial Majesty
the Emperor of Japan

It will be perceived by a perusal of the foregoing notes, that in the eight days the squadron remained in Edo Bay I was successful in gaining several important advantages hitherto denied to all other nations excepting in a very limited degree to the Dutch and Chinese, and awarded even to them at the expense on their part of the most degrading concessions.

First. Guard boats which have up to this time surrounded foreign ships by hundreds were immediately dispersed by my orders.

Second. Extensive surveys were made of waters hitherto unknown to foreigners, within a few miles of Edo and under the guns of numerous batteries.

Third. The accomplishment of my predetermined intention to confer with no one but a dignitary of the highest rank in the empire, and of being received in a manner honorable to my government and myself, and without the slightest deviation on my part from those simple rules of diplomatic courtesy recognized by our institutions. Whilst the governor of Uraga prostrated himself on every occasion of addressing the prince of Izu, myself and staff were quietly seated opposite the princes of Izu and Iwami and their secretary with no more ceremony than was due to a similar conference with any other commissioner duly accredited.

Fourth. I required that in the receipt and delivery of presents conformably to invariable eastern custom, the United States should be on a footing of equality, thus destroying the presumed claim hitherto held forth by China and Japan, that all presents to the respective emperors have been tendered as tributes to superior powers.

And lastly. I have endeavored to inculcate the idea that as the government of the United States is superior in power and influence to Japan, so its motives have been dictated alone by a desire to be on terms of amity with all nations, to give protection to our seamen and other citizens, and especially to cultivate a friendly intercourse with an empire whose geographical position has been brought by the power of steam commercially near to our Pacific ports.

Copy of letter of Commodore Perry to the Emperor of Japan, which accompanied the letter of the President and his letter of credence.

To His Imperial Majesty,
The Emperor of Japan.

The undersigned commander-in-chief of all the naval forces of the United States of North America, stationed in the East India, China, and Japan Seas, has been sent by his government to this country on a friendly mission with ample powers to negotiate with the government of Japan, touching certain matters which have been fully set forth in the letter of the President of the United States, copies of which, together with copies of the letter of credence of the undersigned in the English, Dutch, and Chinese languages are herewith transmitted.

The original of the President's letter and of the letter of credence prepared in a manner suited to the exalted station of your imperial majesty, will be presented by the undersigned in person when it may please your majesty to appoint a day for his reception.

The undersigned has been commanded to state that the President entertains the most friendly feelings toward Japan, but has been surprised and grieved to learn that when any of the people of the United States go of their own accord, or are thrown by the perils of the sea within the dominions of your imperial majesty they are treated as if they were your worst enemies.

The undersigned refers to the cases of the American ships *Morrison, Lawrence,*
and *Lagoda.*[22]

With the Americans, as indeed with all Christian people, it is considered a sacred duty to receive with kindness and to succor and protect all, of whatever nation, who may be cast upon their shores, and such has been the course of the Americans with respect to all Japanese subjects who have fallen under their protection.

The government of the United States desires to obtain from that of Japan some positive assurance that persons who may hereafter be shipwrecked on the coast of Japan, or driven by stress of weather into her ports, shall be treated with humanity.

The undersigned is commanded to explain to the Japanese that the United States are connected with no government in Europe, and that their laws do not interfere with the religion of their own citizens much less with that of other nations.

That they inhabit a great country which lies directly between Japan and Europe, and which was discovered by the nations of Europe about the same time that Japan herself was first visited by Europeans; that the portion of the American continent lying nearest to Europe was first settled by emigrants from that part of the world; that its population has rapidly spread through the country until it has reached the shores of the Pacific Ocean; that we have now large cities from which with the aid of steam vessels we can reach Japan in eighteen or twenty days; that our commerce with all this region of the Globe is rapidly increasing, and the Japan seas will soon be covered with our vessels.

Therefore as the United States and Japan are becoming every day nearer and nearer to each other, the President desires to live in peace and friendship with your imperial majesty, but no friendship can long exist unless Japan ceases to act toward Americans as if they were enemies.

However wise this policy may originally have been, it is unwise and impracticable now that the intercourse between the two countries is so much the more easy and rapid than it formerly was.

The undersigned holds out all these arguments in the hope that the Japanese government will see the necessity of averting unfriendly collision between the two nations by responding favorably to the propositions of amity which are now made in all sincerity.

Many of the large ships of war destined to visit Japan have not yet arrived in these seas, though they are hourly expected, and the undersigned, as an evidence of his friendly intentions, has brought but four of the smaller ones, designing, should it become necessary, to return to Edo in the ensuing spring with a much larger force.

But it is expected that the government of your imperial majesty will render such return unnecessary by acceding at once to the very reasonable and pacific overtures contained in the President's letter, and which will be further explained by the undersigned with the first fitting occasion.

With the most profound respect for your imperial majesty, and entertaining a

---

22. *Morrison,* David Ingersoll commanding, came to Edo Bay 30 July 1837, ostensibly to return seven Japanese castaways; and Dr. Samuel Wells Williams was on board. The Japanese, when they learned she was unarmed, drove her out of the bay by gunfire.

American whaler *Lawrence* of Poughkeepsie foundered off the Kuriles 27 May 1846. One boat with seven survivors reached Hokkaido on 3 June and the men were taken prisoner. The six men who survived two and a half years of privation and humiliation finally got out of Japan at Nagasaki in a Dutch ship.

When *Lagoda,* a famous New Bedford whaler, was near Matsumae, Hokkaido, in June 1848 fifteen crewmen went ashore in small boats and were taken prisoner. Twelve surviving captives were released at Nagasaki 26 April 1849 and rescued by Commander James Glynn, USN, in 18-gun corvette *Preble.*

106 sincere hope that you may long live to enjoy health and happiness, the undersigned subscribes himself.

> (signed) M. C. Perry
> Commander-in-chief United States
> Naval Forces in the East India,
> China, and Japan Seas.

> United States Steam Frigate *Susquehanna*
> Off the coast of Japan
> 7 July 1853.

In continuation of my journal I may insert here the names, titles, and employments of the several Japanese persons of distinction with whom we came more immediately in communication.

Toda, Izu-no-kami; or, Prince of Izu.

His coadjutor, Ido, Prince of Iwami.

The chief deputy of the Commissioners at Uraga, named Eizaemon Kayama.

The second in command at Uraga, Saburosuke Nakajima.

The chief interpreter, Hori Tatsnoske [Tatsunosuke Hori].

The second interpreter, Tateishi Tokoshuiro [Tokojuro Tateishi].

The secretary of the princes, present at the conference, seated on a line with them, was named Tsuzhimo Uyemon [Mouemon Tsuji.]

Au Revoir Edo

17 JULY 1853

We left our anchorage in Susquehanna Bay on 17 July. With *Susquehanna* towing *Saratoga* and *Mississippi* towing *Plymouth,* we passed rapidly by Uraga, neither vessel having a yard of canvas set.

On the second day out the wind, having been until this time from east to east southeast, began to increase in such force as to make it necessary to cast off the two sloops of war. Their commanders were ordered by signal to proceed on the duty previously assigned them, and they parted company. Commander Walker, in *Saratoga,* had previously received written instructions to make the best of his way to Shanghai, for the protection of American life and property and to look after the general interests of the United States in that vicinity. Commander Kelly, in *Plymouth,* was instructed to proceed to Lew Chew, and on his way to examine the western shores of O Shima.

The wind gradually increased to a strong gale. The two steamers were hove to on the port tack. The wind being at east by south, heaving up an ugly sea, *Susquehanna* was rolling very deeply but otherwise making tolerable weather. *Mississippi* apparently was doing better, but she lost two of her boats during the gale.

The gale began to abate on the third day and we reached Naha on the 25th where we ascertained from the officers of *Supply* that it had blown with great violence with them and had raged several days. It had been my intention to have surveyed the shores of O Shima, the island claimed by

ment of this object.

The current in our passages to and from Japan, from Lew Chew was setting invariably to the north and east, more or less strong, according to the direction and strength of the winds.

The weather during our stay in Edo Bay was fine, with a pleasant breeze up the bay during the day. The tides were regular, and set up and down the channel opposite Uraga, about 2½ knots.

In approaching Lew Chew from Japan, and the third time of my visiting Naha, the weather was so hazy that the land could not be discerned at any distance, and, night coming on, the two ships stood off but were carried very much to the south and west by the current, which according to the generally received accounts, should have been sitting in a contrary direction, and consequently an allowance for a northeast set was wrongly made.

The atmosphere continued hazy through the night, and as the day dawned no land was to be seen, and it was some hours before we could determine our position by getting sight at last of the Amakirima [Kerama] Islands.[23] During the morning we came upon a patch of breakers not laid down and at some distance from either of the islands, which we marked in our chart. The discovery of this patch, and other dangers amongst the Kerama Group, shows the necessity of a thorough survey of the islands lying west of Great Lew Chew, and I know of no better employment for the expedition under Commander Ringgold.[24]

We anchored on 25 July, having been absent since 2 July.

Again at this beautiful island, I renewed my negotiations with the authorities for obtaining from them further relaxations in their laws respecting strangers. Having been measurably successful with the Japanese, I felt confident of gaining additional concessions from the Lew Chewans, and without resort to any act of unkindness, or the adoption of *their* policy of lying and deceit.

The officers of the *Supply*—which vessel had been left at Naha during our visit to Japan—stated that the people had evinced no unfriendly feeling toward them, but were still very much reserved, and that the system of espionage was yet kept up. Supplies were, however, furnished through the agency of Dr. Bettelheim, and payment made through the same channel.

As my stay at the island on this occasion was to be very short, I lost no

*Return to
Lew Chew*

25 JULY–1 AUGUST 1853

23. Lying due west of southern Okinawa.

24. This expedition was commanded by Commodore Cadwallader Ringgold who set out from New York City on 2 June 1853 in *Vincennes* with four other ships for a survey and reconnaissance of the Bering Straits, North Pacific, and Chinese Seas. For reasons of health Ringgold was relieved of his command by Commodore Perry at Hong Kong in August 1854; he was succeeded by Acting Commodore John Rodgers who completed the expedition and returned to San Francisco in October 1865. Objects collected by this expedition were deposited in the Smithsonian Institution.

time in demanding an interview with the regent, which was immediately granted, and a day appointed to receive me. Previous to the meeting, I had caused the regent to be made acquainted with the nature of the propositions I had to make, as will be seen by the following instructions given to Commander Adams, and the Chinese interpreter Doctor Williams.

Instructions given to Commander Adams
and Mr. Williams, Naha, 25 July 1853.

Establish rate and pay for rent of house for one year. Say that I wish a suitable and convenient building for the storage of coal, say to hold 600 tons. If they have no such building, I desire to employ native workmen to erect one after the fashion of the island, or if the Lew Chew government prefers, it can be done under the inspection of the mayor at government expense; and I will agree to pay an annual rent for it; either one or other arrangement *must* be made.

Speak about the spies, and say that if they continue to follow the officers about, it may lead to serious consequences, and perhaps to bloodshed, which I should deplore, as I wish to continue on the most friendly terms with the authorities. That should any disturbance ensue it will be the fault of the Lew Chewans, who have no right to set spies upon American citizens who may be pursuing their own lawful business.

We must have a free trade in market, and the right to purchase articles from the shops.

It will be wise therefore for the Lew Chewans to abrogate those laws and customs which are not suited to the present age, and which they have no power to enforce, and by a persistence in which they will surely involve themselves in trouble.

Let the mayor clearly understand that the port is to be one of rendezvous, probably for years; and the authorities had better come to an understanding at once.

Thank the mayor for the kind act of the authorities of putting a tombstone over the remains of the boy buried from the *Susquehanna,* and ask the privilege of paying the cost of the same.

Require prompt and early replies to all these propositions and demands.

I also transmitted a formal communication to the regent, of which the following is a copy.

To His Excellency the *tsung-li-kwan,*
of the kingdom of Lew Chew.
    Sir,
    The commander-in-chief of the United States naval forces, in the East India, China, and Japan Seas, having returned to this port from Japan, is about sailing for China, and before leaving is desirous of communicating to his excellency, the *tsung-li-kwan,* a few observations having reference to the intercourse of persons under his command, with the authorities and people of Lew Chew.
    The commander-in-chief, while he thanks the officers of the Lew Chewan government for the services which they have already rendered in furnishing a few supplies to the ships of the squadron, cannot see the necessity of enforcing against strangers, a system of restriction which is altogether at variance with the customs and practices of all civilized nations, and which cannot at the present day be recognized as just or proper.
    The commander-in-chief is especially desirous of remaining on the most friendly terms with the government of Lew Chew, and of contributing all in his power to

the prosperity and happiness of the people; and he claims that the officers and 109
men under his command shall be received upon the same footing as are those
who arrive from China and Japan. That they shall have the privilege of purchasing in the market and shops whatever they may need, and for which they will pay
the prices demanded by the sellers. That the inhabitants, particularly the women
and children, shall not fly from us as if we were their greatest enemies, and finally
that our officers and men shall not be watched and followed by low officials acting
as spies. He declares that if this system of espionage is persisted in, he will on his
return to Lew Chew take the necessary steps to stop it.

It is repugnant to the American character to submit to such a course of unhospitable discourtesy, and though the citizens of the United States when abroad are
always regardful of and obedient to the laws of the countries in which they may
happen to be, provided they are founded upon international courtesy, yet they
never can admit of the propriety or justice of those of Lew Chew, which bear so
injuriously upon the rights and comforts of strangers resorting to the island with
the most friendly and peaceful intentions.

With the highest consideration.
(signed) M. C. Perry
Commander-in-chief United States Naval Forces
East India, China, and Japan Seas.

At the hour appointed, I landed with a suitable escort, and proceeded at
once to the *kung-kwa* [caravansary], where I found the regent and the
counselors in waiting, and though I was desirous of avoiding the detention
consequent upon one of their elaborate collations, I soon perceived that
escape was impossible and therefore prepared to submit with all possible
patience. But I could not hold out to the end of the feast.

On this as on some former occasions, Mr. Bayard Taylor was requested to
make notes of what passed, and the following is a copy of his account.

Interview between Commodore M. C. Perry and Shang
Hung-hsün, regent of Lew Chew, at Naha, 25 July 1853.

By previous arrangement, two o'clock P.M. had been fixed upon as the hour for
the interview, and the regent had sent word that he would leave Shuri at noon.
About half past one, however, a boat came off to the *Susquehanna* with the *pe-
ching,* Chang-yüen, on board to inform the Commodore that everything was in
readiness for his reception, and the regent already in waiting. The place selected
for the purpose was the *kung-kwua* of Naha, which is used on all official occasions.
The Commodore went ashore at two o'clock, accompanied by Captain Adams,
captain of the fleet; Lieutenant Contee, flag Lieutenant; Captain Lee, of the *Mississippi;* Captain Kelly, of the *Plymouth,* and twelve other officers, making a staff
of sixteen persons.

On landing he was received by a deputation of officers, headed by the *pe-ching*
and conducted to the place of reception, which is situated on the main street or
road leading from Naha to Shuri, and about a quarter of a mile from the beach.
It is a small but neat building, surrounded by a high wall which screens it from
all observation from without. The mayor of Naha with some of his attendant
officers stood at the entrance, and the regent advanced to the door of the enclosure
to receive the Commodore. Within the building, tables were already prepared for
a collation similar to that given at Shuri by the former regent, though not on so
extensive a scale. The feast was arranged in precisely the same manner; the Commodore and Captain Adams occupying the first table on the right hand, while the

regent and mayor took that on the left hand, opposite to him. After tea had been brought, the regent made a complimentary remark to the Commodore, hoping that he had returned in good health.

Ichirazichi [Itarajiki] acted as interpreter, and the conversation was carried on by Mr. Williams, through the medium of the Chinese language. The Commodore stated that he would leave in a few days for China, but should return again to Lew Chew in a few months. Before he left, however, he wished to have a settlement of all those matters concerning which he had addressed them. His demands were reasonable and proper, and he expected that they would be complied with. The Americans were persons of few words, but they always meant what they said. The regent answered that his reply would soon be read, and invited the Commodore in the meanwhile to partake of some refreshments. He was answered that we preferred business first, and the refreshments afterward. The requests made were fair and simple, and the Commodore was dissatisfied with any delay in granting them. We had been to Japan where we had been received in a very friendly manner. We had exchanged presents with Japanese governors, and were on friendly terms with the Japanese. We hoped now, to be on friendly terms also with the Lew Chewans. Mr. Williams then, at the Commodore's request, gave a brief narration of his reception by the princes of Izu and Iwami, and of our exploration and survey of the Bay of Edo. The regent observed in return, that his reply would very soon be delivered.

The dinner then commenced, and after seven or eight of the twelve courses of soups had been served, the letter was brought in and given to the regent, who took it, and, accompanied by the mayor and interpreter, advanced to the Commodore's table, where he presented it with every appearance of submission and humility. His demeanor during the dinner was even more constrained and impassive than on the occasion of his dining on board *Susquehanna*, previous to our departure for Japan. The letter was enclosed in an envelope, and stamped with the great seal of Lew Chew. Mr. Williams, at the Commodore's order, opened and read it on the spot.

It commenced by affirming the small size and poverty of the island, stating that Dr. Bettelheim's residence among them had given them much trouble, and that if we should erect a building for coal their difficulties would be greatly increased. Besides, they said, the temple which they had appropriated to our use was thereby rendered useless to them, and their priests were prevented from performing their worship in it. The productions of the island were few, as they derived all of their teas, silks, cloths, and many other articles from Japan and China. With regard to the shops and markets, that was a matter which depended on the people themselves, and if they chose to keep their shops shut, the regent could not interfere. He declared, moreover, that the persons who had followed us whenever we had gone ashore were not spies, but officers appointed to act as guides and to prevent us from being annoyed by the people. Since we had not found them to be of service, and objected to them, they would be directed not to follow us in future.

After the letter had been read, the Commodore ordered it to be delivered back to the regent, stating that it was not at all satisfactory, and could not be received. We had asked, he said, for no more than is accorded to us in other countries—for no more than we already had in China, and expected to have in Japan. With regard to the temple, they had themselves assigned it to our use, as they invariably had done for those foreigners who had visited them previous to our arrival. We would pay them rent for it, and expected to pay for everything that we obtained. We had traveled over their island, and knew that the soil was rich, the people thrifty and supplies of all sorts abundant. As we paid for all we received, our presence was an advantage to the people, who found in our vessels a good market for their productions. If they did not wish to erect a building for coal, we would send a vessel with materials, and put it up ourselves. The regent ventured to say, that there were some difficult points in the Commodore's communication, and they had had much deliberation concerning them, before the reply was written. The Commodore reiterated what he had previously said, that all his demands were plain and simple and ought to be granted without hesitation. The Lew Chewans should be satisfied by this time that we had no intention to injure them. They had not been molested in any way by any of our men, and if they persisted in following us with spies hereafter, he would not be answerable for the consequences.

The regent attempted to come forward and again present the reply, but the Commodore rose and prepared to leave, declaring that if he did not receive satisfactory answer to all his demands by noon the next day, he would land two hundred men, march to Shuri and occupy the palace there, and would remain until the matter was settled. With this declaration, he left; the regent attending him to the gateway where he remained until all the officers had taken their departure. The Commodore returned to the beach, attended by his staff, and immediately went on board the *Susquehanna*.

The next day I sent Commanders Buchanan and Adams, accompanied by Dr. Williams, to the mayor of Naha, instructing them to obtain categorical replies to all the demands made upon the regent yesterday. These were:

That a building should be erected for the safekeeping of coal, for which the United States government would pay rent or the cost of construction in full. That rent should be received by the authorities for the building assigned for the accommodation of the officers and men sent on shore on duty, and for the sick.

That the market people should be free to sell us what they had for sale.

That if the shopkeepers refused to open their shops (which I very well knew was not true) that the mayor should establish a sort of public bazaar at which articles, the production of the island, might be exposed for sale to the Americans, and at prices fixed by those who had them to dispose of.

That the fishermen should no longer be forbidden from taking their fish alongside the ships, where the officers and crews would pay them their own prices. And that the spies, who thronged about persons landing from the squadron, should be withdrawn by order of the authorities.

The reply of the mayor was that he would communicate with the regent and be on board the flagship the next day with the decision of his government. Accordingly he was on board by ten o'clock in the morning, with information that all my propositions had been acceded to, as far as the people could be controlled; that preparations for putting up a coal shed had already been commenced, and that the rent for the use of the temple was established at $10 per month. That a bazaar would be opened in two days (or Sunday, the day he came on board being Friday) where a variety of articles would be exhibited for sale. In reply to this he was told that Sunday was our sabbath, and we could not barter on that day, and as the squadron was to sail on Monday at 9 A.M. they might open the bazaar at five o'clock of that day,[25] and the officers would go on shore at that hour to purchase such articles as they saw worthy of obtaining.

In accordance with this arrangement everyone who felt inclined landed

25. Hawks *Narrative* (pp. 279 and 281) gives six o'clock as the hour for bazaar opening.

from the several vessels and selected whatever suited their taste, and were on board again in time to admit of our sailing at the hour appointed. There was no great display at the sale; indeed, it was not to be expected that the finer articles could be collected at such short notice. Everyone purchased something, however, paying the prices demanded by the Lew Chewans in gold or silver. These prices were sufficiently high to secure to the sellers good profits. But what gave greater interest and importance to the transaction was the fact that this dealing with foreigners was in direct opposition to one of the fundamental laws of the island; the abrogation of which cannot but be advantageous to the people.

At the time of our sailing, the building for the storage of the coal (commenced only two days before) had been framed and reared, and, as I have since learned from Captain Kelly, was entirely finished in two days more. It was of sufficient capacity to hold 500 tons of coal. The first cargo placed in it was that of the *Caprice,* which vessel arrived shortly after our departure from the island; subsequently *Southampton* landed a cargo taken from Macao.

The building is in dimensions about 50 by 60 feet, with a watertight thatched roof, with projecting eaves, and boarded up on the four sides more than half the distance from the ground to the eaves, leaving ample space for the admission of air for ventilation. It is in form and fashion somewhat similar to the recently erected coal sheds of the Peninsula and Oriental Steam Navigation Company at Singapore, though far from being so substantial. After the landing of cargo of the *Southampton* it was thought advisable to enlarge the building and accordingly the authorities added a wing on each side.

Conceiving it to be of the highest importance that a ship of the squadron should be stationed almost constantly at this place to keep alive the friendly interest and good feeling then subsisting between us and the islanders, and which was becoming daily more cordial, I determined to leave the *Plymouth*. Commander Kelly's instructions were also to run over to the Bonin Islands after the termination of the hurricane season for the purpose as well to visit the settlement at Port Lloyd, as to survey the southern cluster of the Bonins. These were originally called the Coffin Islands, after the master of the American whaling vessel *Transit,* who saw and named them in 1823. But Captain Beechey with the proverbial assurance and selfishness of most surveying officers, though admitting that they had been seen and named three years before by Mr. Coffin, took upon himself to substitute the name of Bailey for that of Coffin.

The following were the instructions given to Captain Kelly:

It is questionable whether these communications should be inserted in full or a synopsis of the whole introduced.

United States Steam Frigate *Susquehanna*
Naha, Lew Chew, 30 July 1853.

Sir,

You will be left with the *Plymouth,* until further orders, in command at this place, and will give every despatch to the *Supply* in getting her properly ballasted for a passage to Hong Kong.

I am in hourly expectation of the arrival of the storeship *Caprice* from Shang-

hai, and have to direct that steps be immediately taken for landing her cargo of
coal, even if the coal shed which is to be erected shall not have been completed; the coal can be put on shore (as much in bags as possible) and placed upon the spot which is to be enclosed by the four sides of the building.

It is requisite that the *Caprice,* being a hired vessel, and the terms of her charter expiring in September, should have preference to the *Supply* in being despatched. You will therefore please lend all your efforts to get her away as early as practicable.

Enclosed herewith are sailing instructions addressed respectively to Lieutenants Commandant Sinclair and Maury.

As you are familiar with all the circumstances connected with our relations with the authorities and people of this island, and of my object in bringing about a greater degree of confidence, and a more extended social and commercial intercourse with them, I have to request that you will avail yourself of every means of conciliating their friendship and good will. Exercise toward them a kind but firm bearing, insist on the fulfillment of all the stipulations agreed upon yesterday, and be careful to receive no aid or benefit from them which in other countries are paid for, without constraining them to receive compensation for the same.

And it will be indispensably necessary to the attainment of the objects in view that the officers and crews of the several vessels of the squadron should conduct themselves with great circumspection in their intercourse with the people, to the end that they may gradually relax in their unsocial habits, and become more familiar with our more friendly customs.

It will be necessary that two strong boats (scow-shape) should be built, purchased, or hired for the landing and shipping of the coal; this you will please attend to.

It will be optional with yourself to remain at Naha with the *Plymouth*—or other ships that may arrive whose commanders may be junior to you, and whose vessels are not otherwise disposed of—or remove to Port Melville. Should you adopt the latter course, it will be necessary that you leave a competent officer with a boat and crew to occupy the house hired on shore, to be in readiness to board vessels arriving, to pilot them in, and to watch and keep in their proper position the buoys which will be this day placed to mark the south channel.

When the weather promises to be fine and you have leisure, you will employ two of the ship's boats in surveying the eastern side of the island. Enjoin upon the officers in charge to run no risk, and to be careful to secure at night a good harbor for their boats and camping places on shore.

The reefs and islands which make off from the eastern side of Lew Chew are dangerous, and it is desirable that they should be carefully explored. Perhaps there may be some ports of refuge in bad weather that may be discovered by this examination.

It will be desirable during the absence of the surveying parties that you keep up a constant daily or semi-weekly communication with them overland, employing natives or Chinamen.

I would suggest that you cause to be constructed, based upon the data already in your possession, a skeleton chart on a large scale of the main island and islands immediately adjacent, to be filled up and corrected by the surveying party as far as they explore.

> I am very respectfully,
> (signed) M. C. Perry
> Commander-in-chief United States Naval Forces
> East India, China, and Japan Seas.

To Commander John Kelly.
Commander United States Ship *Plymouth.*

United States Steam Frigate *Susquehanna*
Naha, Lew Chew, 30 July 1853.

Sir,

When you may have considered the hurricane season to have passed, say about the 1st of October, you will (unless there should be strong public reasons requiring your continuance at this island) proceed with the *Plymouth* under your command to Port Lloyd, Peel Island, one of the Bonin Group.

You will on arrival inquire into the condition of the settlers at that place, and especially with respect to Nathaniel Savory and John Smith, two persons rated on the books of this ship, rendering to all the settlers such aid as you can proffer consistently with the nature of the service in which you are engaged.

Obtaining the services of one or more of the settlers as pilots and guides, you will proceed, either with your ship or boats as you may deem most advisable, to the cluster of islands lying to the south of Peel Island, and improperly called on Beechey's chart Bailey's Group instead of the legitimate name of Coffin's Group; they having been discovered and so named two years before Beechey saw them by a Captain Coffin, most probably an American, judging from the peculiar name. Therefore this name is to be retained and will be so noted in the chart you are to make.

To the principal island of the group or that which has the best and most commodious harbor, you will give the name of Hillsborough, and to the port the name of Newport.

You will cause the shores of the islands to be thoroughly surveyed in view of discovering ports and convenient anchoring places, especially with respect to a port suitable for a coal depot, the construction of sheds and wharves.

The interior of the islands will be fully explored, in which duty you will call into action the talents of the civil as well as the other officers of the ships.

It is desirable that you should obtain information respecting the geological formation of the islands, the character of the soil, its suitableness for cultivation, the indigenous timber and plants, the quality of the timber for mechanical purposes, the animals, birds, reptiles, etcetera, the kinds and description of fishes in the neighboring waters, including the families of cetacea, testacea, and mollusca. The convenience of obtaining wood and water, the *quality* of the water, in fine to obtain all and every information which may contribute to a full knowledge of the entire group.

Charts are to be made of the coasts and harbors with such explanations and meteorological observations as may the better enable you to report fully upon the subject. When these duties are accomplished, you will return to Naha, and await further orders. During your absence you will leave at Naha an officer with a boat and crew, suitably armed and equipped, whose duty it will be to look out for the hired house on shore, the coal sheds, and to board outside and pilot into port such vessels as may appear off the harbor, also to watch and keep the buoys in their proper places.

I will thank you to make enquiries as to the cattle and sheep. I placed the cattle on Peel, and the sheep on Stapleton Island.

Respectfully
Your Ob'dt Servt.
(signed) M. C. Perry
Commander-in-chief, United States Naval Forces
East India, China, and Japan Seas.

To Commander John Kelly.
Commander United States Ship *Plymouth*
Naha Keang, Lew Chew.

Naha, 30 July 1853.

Sir,

I omitted to mention in my letter of this date respecting the exploration of the Coffin Group of islands, that I desire you to take formal possession of them on the part of the United States, the act to be subject of course to the confirmation or otherwise of the government.

The group is to be called the Coffin Group, the principal island, Hillsborough Island, and the principal port, Newport.

You will receive two engraved plates, one of which you will nail to a conspicuous tree beyond the reach of any person standing on the ground; the other bury in such place at a certain distance and direction from said tree, known only to yourself and one or more officers; and a copy of the inscription to be placed in a bottle also at a well-marked place; records to be carefully made of all the circumstances, noticing exactly where these mementoes can be found.

Respectfully, etcetera,
(signed) M. C. Perry
Commander-in-chief United States Naval Forces
East India, China, and Japan Seas.

To Commander John Kelly
Commander United States Ship *Plymouth*

It was quite evident to everyone that a very marked change had taken place in the deportment of the islanders toward us. There was less of mystery about them, and some of the spies were becoming less reserved. They probably conjectured, and with good cause, that the trouble they had taken in their attempts to deceive us with respect to the condition of the government, the poverty of the island, and the harmless innocence of the people was futile, and so much labor lost, and though still adhering as by instinct to their system of deception, they were not so ready with their misrepresentations.

But after all, many allowances should be made for these misgoverned people, who have doubtless been taught from infancy, as were the Spartans of old, to practice duplicity and lying as necessary parts of an accomplished education and altogether essential to advancement in office. It is certain that they do not, any more than the Japanese, place the least confidence in each other, and the government in employing their agents, invariably send them forth in couples, one to watch the other.

This abominable system imposes great hardship on all classes, as those in power can never know how soon any of their acts, however harmless in their own estimation, may be construed into some offence against the state, and finding their lives consequently in jeopardy are compelled to purchase safety by humility, or a good share of their substance. These failing, they commit suicide to save their families from ruin, and their fortunes from confiscation. And it oppresses still more the lower classes, as they by their labor are required to furnish food for the armies of spies who infest every nook and corner in the island.

On the first day of August the *Susquehanna* and *Mississippi* sailed from Naha for Hong Kong, leaving the *Plymouth* as before mentioned. Lieutenant Commander Sinclair in the *Supply* was instructed to proceed to Hong Kong, touching on his passage at Amoy.

The day after our departure from Naha, we fell in with *Vandalia*, Commander John Pope, on her way to join the squadron, having recently arrived on station from Philadelphia. Captain Pope—who was ordered by signal on board the flagship to receive instructions to return to Hong Kong—informed me that *Powhatan* had also arrived out from the United States, and that Captain McCluney, her commander, was about leaving Hong Kong for Lew Chew to join me.

This information made me exceedingly anxious to reach port before the departure of *Powhatan,* as her trip to the north would be utterly useless, and the consequent consumption of coal a serious loss to our limited stock. But she had unfortunately sailed only the day before our arrival, taking the Formosa passage, or we should have intercepted her, and she did not return to Hong Kong until the 25th, having been detained ten days at Naha in the repair of her machinery. Similar delays, and for like *alleged* cause were found necessary in the opinion of the chief engineer at almost every port at which the ship touched on her outward passage. *Vandalia* got back to Hong Kong on 15 August.

As the typhoon season was approaching and the ships all required a general overhaul with some indulgence to their crews—sixty working days being alone asked for by the engineers to put the machinery of the *Powhatan* in order—I determined in consideration of these circumstances to give them all a thorough refitment, to which I was the more induced as the merchants of Canton were in constant apprehension of an outbreak in the city and consequent danger to their lives and property, and had applied for further protection. Their wishes could thus be gratified, and the overhauling of the ships proceed at the same time.

See following copy of correspondence.

Canton, 18 August 1853.

A notice of this correspondence will only be necessary, or rather a synopsis inserted.

To His Excellency Commodore Perry
Commander-in-chief of all United States Naval Forces
in the East India, China, and Japan Seas
    Sir,
    We the undersigned American merchants beg leave to offer your excellency our congratulations upon your safe return to China, and upon the satisfactory result of your initiative visit to Japan.
    We hear with great satisfaction that you will remain here and retain most of the ships under your command upon these coasts until the period of your proposed return to that country, in prosecution of the further objects of your mission in the ensuing spring; and we esteem it a most fortunate circumstance for the material interests of our country, that so powerful and efficient a force, commanded by an officer so justly entitled to the confidence of his government, will be held available for the protection of interests of such magnitude during the next six months: a period which has in it all the uncertainties incident to the state of complete disorganization into which this empire has fallen.

We can, indeed, scarcely magnify the importance of the present crisis in the affairs of this country or the influence of such a state of things upon the prosperity of our commerce and the safety of our intercourse.

It is, we believe, now apparent to all observers that we are witnessing the overthrow of the government of the Tartars; whilst, as yet, we look in vain for a power to replace it upon a settled and firm basis. Although the majority of the Chinese people are distinguished by a disposition to cultivate the peaceful pursuits of industry and commerce, and although we have every reason to believe that the revolutionists are favorably disposed to foreign intercourse, and these are elements of great promise for the future prosperity of our trade, yet it cannot be disguised that should the present convulsed state of things be prolonged, this mutually beneficial trade will continue to dwindle away; if it does not in respect to the importation of American goods, which is of great importance to our country, suffer a complete extinction; but whilst we allude to these more remote consequences of this struggle for empire, our more immediate purpose and wish is to call your attention to the present condition of affairs here, with a view of obtaining more available protection for a large amount of property that is here constantly exposed to the violence of a mob or the strife of contending forces.

We are sensible of your vigilance in behalf of these interests, and acknowledge with extreme satisfaction the prompt sending of the steamer *Mississippi* to the lower reach of Whampoa on your arrival at Hong Kong. We are the more ready to address you upon these points because we see every indication of a desire to render all possible protection to the interests in our charge,—our purpose, indeed, is rather to convey information as to the most available and efficient modes of affording such protection, than to suggest a course of proceeding.

We wish in this sense to state that so completely paralyzed is the power of the government that it may be said that the whole country about Canton is swarming with thieves and desperate fellows, who are lying in wait for an opportunity to attack and plunder the foreign residences, if not to wreak their vengeance upon the persons of their occupants. We have long been protected in common with British subjects, by a steamer or sloop of war of Her Britannic Majesty stationed near the factories in the Macao passage, or directly in their front; and we beg to say that we believe the *Vandalia* might be anchored in the Macao passage with perfect safety as respects the draft of water, or that even the *Mississippi* might proceed up the Blenheim Reach to a point within about two miles of the factories, where H.B.M.S. *Blenheim* of 70 guns was anchored for a number of weeks in 1841. In either of these positions the force would be made available with perfect ease in case of a fire or of any other cause of a sudden outbreak; whereas from the present position of the *Mississippi* no aid could be furnished in time to protect life and property efficiently: and we beg to add for your information that the freshes are much less strong in the Macao Passage than in the Junk River, and that the southwest monsoon or summer wind is much more regular, so that in all respects the stations we indicate are preferable to the lower reach.

With these remarks, and the offer to give you any further information or assistance in our power

We are, Sir,
With great respect
Your Obedient Servants

(signed) Nye, Parkin & Co.
    "   Augustine Heard & Co.
    "   James Purdon
    "   Henry H. Hubbell
    "   Wm. D. Lewis & Co.
(signed) Thos. Walch

(signed) Russell & Co.
    "   Wetmore & Co.
    "   King & Co.
    "   W. C. Hunter
    "   Lionel Moses

Macao, 26 August 1853.

Gentlemen,

I have had the honor of receiving your communication of the 18th inst. in which you describe the present threatening aspect of political affairs in China, and speak of the necessity of prompt assistance should sudden commotions arise in Canton.

I hardly need assure you in reply to the flattering expressions contained in your communication that as it ever has been my desire during a long course of service to dispose of the forces placed at my command in such manner as in my judgment would best subserve the honor and interests of our common country, so I shall be prepared for the present, and until a special duty calls me elsewhere, to adopt every means of securing the lives and property of American citizens in China; and I trust that a lapse of a few weeks will furnish information enabling us to judge more advisedly of the probable issue of events.

It will be perceived by reference to the enclosed copy of an order, that I have directed an examination of the river above Whampoa in view of moving the *Mississippi* higher up. Meanwhile if the merchants of the city deem it expedient, a guard of Marines and one or more pieces of artillery can be sent from that ship to remain at the factory, and Commander Lee will be prepared upon requisition of the acting vice consul Mr. R. S. Sturgis, to land at a moment's notice an advance guard, to be followed, if need be, by a much larger force composed of detachments from the other ships in the river.

On enquiry of Captain Endicott and others, I learn that the *Mississippi*, drawing as she does when light nearly 19 feet, cannot ascend to the point indicated in your letter, but I expect in a few days the storeship *Supply*, which vessel has an efficient armament and room for the accommodation of 150 men. She can reach the city, and if it be found necessary will on arrival be immediately despatched.

Thus, having a large ship at Whampoa in readiness to land her officers and crew and one of lighter draft abreast the city, sufficient protection will be afforded, not only to the property of our own countrymen, but to that of all the foreign residents, as it is equally my wish to render assistance if required, to the people of all nations whose safety may be endangered by unlawful violence.

> With great respect,
> I have the honor to be
> Your most Obedient Servant
> (signed) M. C. Perry
> Commander-in-chief United States Naval Forces
> East India, China, and Japan Seas.

To Messrs. Nye, Parkin & Co.
    "   Augustine Heard & Co.
    "   Wetmore & Co.
    "   King & Co.
    "   Russell & Co.
    "   Wm. D. Lewis & Co.
    "   James Purdon
    "   Henry H. Hubbell
    "   W. C. Hunter
    "   Lionel Moses
    "   Thos. Walch

P.S. If there should be any delay in the arrival of the *Supply*, I shall send the storeship *Southampton* to the city as soon as she can be partly discharged.

The *Mississippi*, Commander Lee, was despatched, by an order bearing date the 9th of August, to Blenheim Reach, as well for the purpose of protecting

the shipping at Whampoa against the numerous pirates infesting the river,
as to be as near to Canton as she could reach in readiness to send a force to
the city.

Macao, 25 August 1853.

Sir,

I enclose herewith an extract of a letter from the American merchants resident
at Canton addressed to me, and have to direct that you examine in person the anchorage described therein, and report to me whether it may be considered a safe
and commodious position, having regard to depth of water, room for swinging
and veering, looking to the great length of the steamers, and especially with respect to its healthfulness.

You will take the surgeon and master with you, the one to examine and report
as to the healthful position of the anchorage at this season, and the other to prepare a sketch of the place, to be forwarded with your report.

You will direct Captain Slack to be ready at any moment to proceed to Canton
with 30 rank and file of Marines, also a lieutenant with two pieces of artillery
with their crews, should requisition be made on you by the acting consul for aid,
being also prepared to follow yourself with all the force that can be spared from
the ship, consistently with her safety at the same time despatching an express boat
to me at this place with information of any disturbance.

Respectfully,
Your obedient servant
(signed) M. C. Perry
Commander-in-chief United States Naval Forces
East India, China, and Japan Seas.

To Commander S. S. Lee
Commander United States Steam Frigate *Mississippi*
Whampoa

And on the 29th the following order was issued to Lieutenant Commander
Sinclair of the *Supply,* just arrived from Amoy, to take his vessel to the
anchorage opposite the city.

Macao, 31 August 1853.

Sir,

As soon as the *Supply* is prepared as directed in a former letter you will proceed
with her to Blenheim Reach and there communicate with Commander Lee of the
Mississippi, who will put on board of her a sergeant, a corporal and twenty-three
privates of the Marine guard attached to that ship.

On receiving these on board you will proceed up the river and anchor your ship
opposite the factory of the merchants, or at such point as may be pointed out as
most suitable.

The object of your being sent to this point is to give protection to the lives and
property of the American and other merchants resident at Canton, and you will
confer fully with the United States Vice Consul, Mr. Spooner, as to the most effec-
tive means of carrying out these intentions.

The Marines will be in charge of Captain Slack.

Report to me your arrival at Canton, and make semiweekly reports of all transactions, informing me of every circumstance on shore and on board, and should
serious disturbance occur despatch an express boat to me with the intelligence
immediately.

It is highly desirable that you should reach Canton with all possible despatch.

To prevent sickness and insubordination, allow of no liberty to your men
whilst at Canton.

See that your guns are all mounted and in readiness, as also your small arms for immediate service.

I have directed Commander Lee to send a piece of artillery with the detachment. Select a crew for it and place it in charge of a passed midshipman, who if he lands, will, to secure harmony of action, report to Captain Slack for orders.

You had better remain on board to receive persons and property sent for protection.

Respectfully,
Your Obedient Servant
(signed) M. C. Perry
Commander-in-chief United States Naval Forces
East India, China, and Japan Seas.

To Lieutenant Commander A. Sinclair
Commander United States Storeship *Supply*.

Meanwhile the remainder of the squadron were ordered to rendezvous at Cum Sing Moon,[26] a port lying between Hong Kong and Macao. It is safe and commodious, and more healthy than either of the ports or anchoring places in the vicinity, and from its being the rendezvous of the opium vessels belonging to the merchants of Canton, it possesses the advantage of constant communication with the neighboring towns.

Having myself much laborious work before me, in arranging the materials which had been collected during our trip to Japan and the islands, and as it was necessary that *Susquehanna*, as well as *Powhatan* should take their turns at Whampoa, where a stay of a month invariably causes large numbers of the officers and men to fall sick of intermittent fever, I took a house at Macao as an office, and for the accommodation of the surveying officer and the artists to bring up their work. A hospital was also established in the town under the superintendence of the fleet surgeon, Dr. T. S. Smith.

I found myself more conveniently stationed here than I could have been on board either of the ships or at Canton or Hong Kong. Macao being an intermediate or rather central port between those two places and Cum Sing Moon, with mails arriving and departing daily, and steamers and despatch boats almost hourly, I could hold constant and daily communication with them all.

The hospital soon had a good number of inmates sent from the different ships, and at the house hired for the purpose, the several apparatus of the magnetic telegraph, the daguerreotype, and the talbotype[27] were established and put in full operation. Lieutenant Bent was employed in preparing fair copies of the charts which had been constructed during our recent cruise. Messrs. Heine, Brown, and Patterson were constantly engaged in bringing up and completing their sketches and drawings, of which more than two hundred have already been made. Messrs. Draper and Williams were also busy in exhibiting the telegraphic apparatus to the many who expressed a desire to witness its operation.

In the supervision of all these occupations—with an immense amount of

26. Also known as Chin-hsing Men, this anchorage, just north of Macao, is at latitude 22°20′ N, longitude 117°35′ E.
27. A photographic process patented in 1844 by W. H. F. Talbot.

writing growing out of the duties of my command, and a large correspondence rendered more extensive by the disturbed state of China and the apprehensions of danger entertained by the merchants—I found that my strength ere long broke down under this accumulation of labor. A severe attack of illness completely prostrated me for a time, though I managed not to allow my work to fall astern.

But I was not the only sufferer by illness. Scarcely an officer or man escaped an attack of more or less severity and some few deaths occurred. Among those who died was Lieutenant Joseph H. Adams of *Powhatan,* as also the master of the *Mississippi's* band.

Macao had hitherto been considered a remarkably healthy place, and the usual summer resort of families from Canton and Hong Kong, but the epidemic which prevailed in 1853 proved that it was not always to be exempt from those destructive visitations to which the cities and towns of the east are so much exposed.

Canton

AUGUST 1853

It is, however, remarkable that Canton should be looked upon, and justly so, as a comparatively healthy residence, and especially as the people are constantly breathing the miasmatic atmosphere, arising from the luxuriant fields of rice and other grains, which surround the city in all directions. What is still more extraordinary, many parts of this far-famed provincial metropolis are periodically overflown by the rising of the river.

At the time so much sickness prevailed at Macao, the public garden of the factory [at Canton] was covered with water, which approached the very doors of the merchants, and at a season too, when in all intertropical latitudes, local fevers are to be expected. And though the officers and crews of the other ships of the squadron suffered more or less from epidemical diseases, those of *Supply,* at anchor off the city and within the influence of all these suppositious causes, remained perfectly healthy.

Various speculations have been advanced to account for this singular exemption of the people of Canton from the effects of malaria. Some have ascribed it to the vast amount of smoke produced by the burning of wood for domestic purposes; others to the abstemiousness of the inhabitants; but these reasons are absurd, because in the city of New Orleans, though of a much smaller population, there is a greater consumption of fuel producing smoke, and with respect to abstemiousness, the masses are abstemious from necessity. If narrow, filthy streets, inconvenient and crowded houses, and nastiness of person can produce disease, then the people of Canton should be sorely afflicted. But all these predisposing causes seem to have no effect, either upon the myriads who live and die in crowded boats upon the river, or those who are domiciliated on shore; and years pass away without any serious epidemic.

As for the abstemiousness of the Chinese, this virtue as I have just mentioned is altogether a matter of necessity. They are fond enough of flesh of every description, and of all sorts of food, however gross. Never have I seen such inordinate feeders as they are.

The poorer classes are accustomed only to boiled rice, mixed with small proportions of dried fish, and occasionally with other simple condiments, of which preparation they consume enormous quantities, if they have the means of procuring it.

Dogs and cats which are carried about the streets for sale must be considered delicacies above the reach of the poorer classes, judging from the prices demanded for them. Rats, mice, and other vermin are also eagerly sought for and made into savory dishes. To the families belonging to the fast boats attached to the ships, a rat is a highly esteemed present, which they prepare and mix as a condiment to their rice.

Those who have been employed in the ships of the squadron, have found the navy ration insufficient to satisfy their gluttony; and our navy ration is far superior to that of any other country. A mess of ten American seamen usually refuse two rations, for which they receive the commutation in money.[28] Though there are none more sordid than the Chinese, they not only devoured the entire ration, but went about the decks collecting what they could pick up from the leavings of the messes, and invariably beset the ship's cook for the scrapings of the coppers.

The Chinese servants employed in my cabin eat in miscellaneous food—including rice, bread, beef, pork, and the leavings of my table—three times as much as do the others. In truth the enormous quantities of rice they consume with whatever else they can seize upon is almost incredible; and as for sugar and other sweets, there would be no end to their pilfering if they were not carefully watched by the steward. And this gross feeding exhibits its effects upon them precisely as it does on dumb animals: they soon become fat and lazy, and consequently idle.

Most of the Chinese servants employed in European and American families, engage to find their own food. The wages of men are from four to six and seven dollars per month. Cooks receive from seven to ten dollars. In the establishments of the merchants—who are called upon as forming part of the expenses of their business to keep up abundant tables—great waste must necessarily take place; but as the expenditure goes to the profit-and-loss account of the concern it is of little consequence. With the missionaries and others who live quietly within themselves, much discreet management is required.

All articles for household consumption are procured through the agency of a person called a comprador, who hires the servants, pays them their wages, is security for their honesty, keeps a regular account of the domestic expenditure, and settles with his employer at established periodical seasons. In the large mercantile houses where the expenditure is profuse, the profits of these compradors are very considerable. However ample a dinner table

28. A ship's company was organized in mess groups—usually of ten men each—for meals. Shipboard servings were so generous that eight servings usually satisfied a ten-man mess; they shared a cash payment for the unused servings. Chinese employed by the squadron were entitled to the same messing arrangement and ate their entire allotment.

may have been furnished, it would be difficult to secure (at some of the establishments where little attention is paid to the economy of the household by the proprietors) anything for a late guest arriving half an hour after the meats had been removed. Scarcely are the dishes taken from the dining room, than they are on their way to the neighboring eating houses, there to be concocted into stews to be sold to the middle classes.

In the establishments of merchants in which there are no ladies, female servants are unknown, [and what would seem to be repugnant to our notions of delicacy there are some English and American families without female domestics, though ladies form part of the household. The reason assigned for this singular practice, is the difficulty of obtaining trusty maid servants.][29]

But I have observed that in all the families having children, either foreign maid servants or women of Macao—called amahs or ayahs—are employed. The wages of the latter at Macao, are four dollars per month, but if they are taken to Canton or Hong Kong, they demand additional compensation. Many of these women speak a little of the lingua called Chinese English, which is very amusing to those first hearing it, but one soon finds himself drawn necessarily into this manner of making himself understood. The women possessing this elegant accomplishment demand higher wages.

There is certainly some excuse for employing male attendants about the bed chambers and dressing rooms when it is known that these lords of creation are the only tailors, dressmakers, washers and ironers, and doers up of fine linen and fine dresses. In Canton, women are hired by the tailors to do the plain sewing, and their pay is from five to seven cents per day. A male tailor will go to anyone's house and work all day for twenty-five cents, finding his own food or, as they call it, *chow-chow*.

It is not unusual to see a dirty, small-footed female sitting in some nook in the street, ready to sew up a rent, or put a patch upon the filthy garments of anyone who needs her services, for which she is provided with sewing materials and a few rags. Toward night she is seen with her stock in trade, hobbling home upon her disgusting stumps, of which she is very proud, and professes the greatest contempt for the vulgarity of a big-footed woman.

I have been told that girls of seven, eight, and nine years, importune their parents to compress their feet, as promising them a higher position in society, though we see everywhere many of the lower orders with small feet; these may possibly be persons reduced from higher stations. It is difficult for strangers to get a sight of these singular deformities, as the China women show the greatest reluctance to expose them. Dr. Parker prevailed upon a girl of thirteen, a patient in his hospital, in the presence of her mother, to unbandage her feet for my inspection, and my curiosity was soon satisfied.

A fashionable dressmaker is in as much demand in China amongst the foreign ladies, as these consequential persons are in Philadelphia and New York, and it is necessary to bespeak his services in time. These men usually

29. Curiously, these words were struck through in the manuscript, but they appear almost verbatim in Hawks *Narrative*, p. 291.

require what they call a muster or pattern, which they can imitate precisely, whether of London or Paris fashion, and fit them very neatly to forms of all descriptions. It is singular to observe on passing one of the dark, and by no means cleanly, tailor shops at Macao, a greasy half naked Chinaman, late at night, busily employed upon some splendid dress, wanted probably for a forthcoming ball or dinner party. In such estimation are these male dress-makers held by European and American ladies, that instances are not unfrequent of their having been taken from the country to be employed exclusively as women's tailors.

The ordinary compensation of all operatives in Canton, who find their own food, varies from twelve to twenty cents per day. Farm hands who are fed, receive about six cents. Day laborers and porters, if not hired by the job, and chair bearers are paid from twenty to twenty-five cents per day.

Porters and other crafts, in Canton, form themselves into guilds and appoint leaders or headmen, who contract for labor of various sorts. Boat-men are paid from one and a half to two and a quarter dollars per month, and fed, living always in the boat, and generally having their wives and children with them.

Nearly all those who belong to the lower orders, recognize some system of organization amongst themselves. Like the gypsies, the beggars have their king, who assigns to them their particular beats; and what is singular, the laws of China secure to these vagabonds certain rights and privileges. These laws give them the right to approach and knock at the door of any domicil, or to enter shops, and there to strike together two sticks, similar to those used by the night watchmen, frequently employed by families to guard their premises against thieves, and which produce a loud and disagreeable sound, and though the beggars may continue this annoyance for an indefinite time, they cannot be legally ejected, until they are paid the usual gratuity, the smallest coin in use, a *cash,* which is about a twelfth of a cent. They then pass to the next house or shop and repeat the same trick.

It is said that one hundred of these mendicants are assigned by their king to Old China Street, which is occupied altogether by wealthy shop keepers, some of whom pay a certain sum for exemption from these provoking annoyances. Others refuse to do this, and hold out as long as their patience will allow in view of wasting the time of the suppliant, who having a right to visit all the shops, makes the most money when he can accomplish the greatest number of calls and pay into the general treasury at night the greatest amount of cash. This well organized fraternity takes care of their sick and supports the old and infirm. The number of these professional gentlemen is unknown to strangers, but it must be large if one may judge by the crowds that infest those parts of the city accessible to foreigners.

Each city has its own laws with respect to mendicants, and each its own charitable institutions. In Canton there are four, one for widows, one for foundlings, one for furnishing coffins to indigent families, and the fourth for lepers. All these are so badly managed that they answer very indifferently the purposes for which they are intended. It is very much the same in China as in Christianized countries, those who have the management of these institutions generally contrive to embezzle the revenues, and thus, "make themselves rich by *taking care of the poor.*" Whether these beggars are also thieves, I am unable to say, but as a Yankee, I might make a very pretty correct guess that they are, and quite as accomplished in small pilfering, and the picking of pockets, as the most expert in any other part of the world.

Each ship of war, and most merchant vessels employ what is called a fast boat, always in charge of an experienced pilot. This man's family, if he has one—and they are almost universally married—live in the boat with him, and assist in rowing, steering, and managing the sails. Their children are born and grow up in the boat, rarely leaving her, and in proportion to their number and strength, contribute to the profit of the father, both sexes laboring alike. Without these children six or eight rowers are necessarily employed, but with their assistance only four or five are hired, and at the rate of wages above mentioned. The hire of one of these boats is at the rate of forty dollars per month.

There are several other descriptions of boatmen and women in the Canton River, such as those who manage the flower boats, the *hong* boats, the pullaway boats, the various fishing boats, and the tankia [*tanka*][30] boats; but of all these I shall further speak only of the last named. These are owned and managed entirely by females, many of them quite young. Each boat has two who are probably joint proprietors, and they frequently have an apprentice of twelve or thirteen years, obtained from her parents either by purchase or for instruction in boatcraft and food.

The *tanka* boats are quite short with a sort of canopy made of matting in the center, under which the passengers sit or recline. One of the girls sculls and steers the boat at the same time, and the other sits in the bow and rows. The younger one employs herself in attending to the seats of the passengers, and receives the fare.

These girls rarely leave their boats except to land to purchase their simple food of rice, dried fish, and leeks, which they cook on board. In very boisterous weather, when it becomes necessary to haul their craft on shore, they mutually assist each other, and form little clusters along the shore or upon the quays, availing of these occasions of leisure to gossip and visit each other in what might seemingly be termed their amphibious domicils.

Drawings of these boats with portraits of their proprietors will be found amongst the illustrations appended to this journal. It may be well to remark now, that with reference to these illustrations, I have thought that it would require more writing and occupy greater space than would be desirable without any particular advantage, were I to call attention to each particular sketch. I therefore merely observe that drawings illustrative of almost every subject spoken of will be found in their proper places in this journal. It is my intention that each volume shall be illustrated with one hundred original drawings, all taken from life, from nature, or from the actual inanimate objects depicted.

30. Cantonese for "egg home," from the shape of the boat's protective cover.

Volumes might be written to describe the peculiarities of the Chinese, and volumes *have* been written, but no one can form any correct idea of their habits, manners, and institutions who has not mixed intimately with them. The missionaries have without doubt the better opportunities of acquiring correct information. Merchants come in contact only with those engaged in trade. Such is the character of their laws and customs—which exclude from the domestic circle all who are foreigners, and indeed the males of their own nation—that little is known of those laws which govern the social order of society. Indeed, it may be inferred that they have little or no social domestic intercourse. The men resort to the tea and opium houses for recreation, and the women like so many slaves confine themselves either by necessity or choice to their domicils.

Polygamy is allowed by law in China, and so is concubinage. Since wives as well as their less fortunate adjuncts are rather expensive appendages, however, none but the wealthy indulge in the ostentation of more than one. Though with them, as it is in many other parts of the world, the extent of the household of a man gives prima facie evidence of his greatness. So upon the western coast of Africa the wealth of a king or chief is always estimated by the number of wives he is enabled to purchase and support, though in China the ladies are more costly.

With respect to the lower classes, I have been agreeably disappointed. It is true that honesty is a conventional virtue with them. If they stipulate to be honest and furnish security for their good conduct, they may in most cases be depended on. But if there is no formal understanding of good faith, they conceive that they have the right to lie, cheat, and steal.

When they engage themselves as servants, it is required that they should produce securities for their good conduct and honesty, who hold themselves accountable for their well doing and are bound for their defalcations. Without this sort of endorsement I doubt whether the lower orders of Chinese could well be employed by foreigners for domestic purposes. Of the integrity of the higher classes, I have had no opportunity of forming an opinion.

Macao Sojourn

SEPTEMBER 1853–JANUARY 1854

Macao, once so famed for its extensive and profitable commerce and for its wealth, is now entirely divested of these advantages. It seems to be supported only by a small coasting trade, the expenditures of a limited garrison, and the families of the English and American merchants. Also many single gentlemen attached to mercantile pursuits make it a summer resort. They have an abundance of money and are free in its disbursement.

The Portuguese jurisdiction is confined within very narrow limits. The Chinese settlements crowd close upon them, indeed the larger portion of the population of the town is composed of Chinese men and women, who perform most of the menial duties in the families, both of the Portuguese and foreigners. They are also the shopkeepers, tradesmen, and market people. It would be difficult to ascertain what are the avocations of the native

Macao, *Tanka* (egg-house) boat. By Patterson

PASSENGER BOAT MACAO.

Macao, passenger boat. By E. Brown, Jr.

Portuguese, most of whom are very much impoverished and yet too proud to work. Numbers of the men are employed as clerks in the foreign mercantile houses, but a large portion of them spend their time in idleness, living upon the remnants of the once princely fortunes of their ancestors, and still occupying the stately mansions erected in bygone times.

The hills about the city are crowned with military works, constructed after the fashion of the 17th century, and these are quite sufficient to keep the Chinese in awe. But with a particle of energy the governor of the province could at any time dislodge the Portuguese, for whom they have no love, and drive them altogether from the country.[31] The garrison consists of about 200 regular soldiers, and as many local militia, all of whom are under excellent discipline; in truth I have never seen better dressed or more orderly men.

It will be recollected that the English East India Company before the abolition of its charter made Macao a sort of entrepôt for its China trade, and some of the finest buildings were erected either by that munificent corporation or by the wealthy Portuguese. One of those magnificent dwellings, with a garden of more than an acre, tastefully laid out, and still kept in order at considerable cost, can be hired at this time for five hundred dollars per annum. It is in this garden that the tomb of Camoens has been reared.

The power of the church of Rome, and the baleful influence of the inquisition, were in former times in full force at Macao, as at Goa; but the present-day Church and its impoverished priesthood are in a most distressed condition. It was from Macao that many of the commercial expeditions of the Portuguese were despatched to Japan.

Since the construction of vessels of greater draft than those of former times few that now resort to the place can enter the inner harbor. It is sufficiently commodious for the lorchas engaged in the coasting trade. These vessels under the Portuguese flag are of curious construction and rig, a sort of nondescript craft. Chinese junks also enter the inner port, and occasionally a brig or schooner. The storeship *Southampton,* drawing thirteen and a half feet, anchored inside. Thirteen and, at high tides, fourteen feet can be carried into this inner port, and about as much into a small harbor opposite the city, called the Typa [Taipa].

It was in this Taipa that the Portuguese corvette *Don John the Second,*[32] was lying when blown up,* on which occasion the United States sloop of war *Marion,* at anchor nearby, rendered much service in saving the lives of many.

Ships of war and large merchant vessels resorting to Macao anchor in the

* It was generally thought that this ship was purposely blown up by the gunner, who had been punished in the morning by the captain for neglecting some necessary preparation to do honor to the day, a national anniversary. [The birthday of the King of Portugal.]

31. This situation still prevails.

32. Not "*Don Juan II,*" but *Donna Maria II,* a tanker, blew up at Taipa Island on 29 October 1850 when her magazine, loaded with 300 barrels of powder, exploded. The cause is unknown. Noble rescue work was performed by several nearby ships—including *Don Juan I, Iris,* and U.S.S. *Marion*—but of the 267 men on board only one officer and seven seamen were rescued.

Camoens' Tomb, Macao (front) . H. Patterson   Camoens' Tomb, Macao (rear) . H. Patterson from W. Heine

road, a distance of three to five miles from the city, and in depths from 16 to 27 feet, muddy bottom. This makes the communication with the shore at all times inconvenient, and in blowing weather altogether impracticable. It was for this and other reasons that I recommended the removal of the naval depot to Hong Kong. See following communication.

United States Steam Frigate *Mississippi*
bound to Shanghai
At sea, 1 May 1853.

Sir,

In considering the inconvenience and consequent delay and increased expense of landing and shipping at Macao, articles sent from the United States for the use of the squadron, and more especially the coal, I at once saw the necessity of having a depot of the latter at Hong Kong, and I can see no reason why every article of public property should not be deposited at that place, as infinitely more convenient and less expensive.

It is known to the department that the depot for United States Naval stores was originally at Hong Kong, and was removed, as I have been informed by Commodore Parker, for reason of the troubles at that time expected to grow out of the Oregon question. No difficulties are at present anticipated, and public property at that place would be actually more safe than at Macao, a small, badly defended town, surrounded by a numerous population of Chinese.

In no one particular has Macao any advantage over Hong Kong, excepting perhaps its superior healthfulness, but this should not be considered of any weight, as the vessels need remain no longer in port than to complete their re-equipments, and Hong Kong is by no means unhealthy for those living on shipboard, and indeed not particularly so to its inhabitants.

At Hong Kong the largest ships of the squadron can anchor in perfectly smooth water within 1000 yards of the depot; in Macao, not nearer than $3\frac{1}{4}$ miles, and in an open road. All articles required at the latter place from the public store are sent off in lighters to the ships, and this can be done only in calm weather, as with a good topgallant breeze boats cannot lie alongside.

Store vessels arriving with government stores can approach very little nearer than the ships of war, and are subject to the same inconvenience, hence the delay in discharging their cargoes is taken into account in estimating at home the amount of freight money. But it is still more inconvenient and expensive with respect to the landing and re-shipping of coal, an article of so much bulk, besides the risk of getting it wet during the time of its transit to and from the shore.

Again, Hong Kong is the market for all articles of provisions and stores, which it is found to be more desirable to purchase in China, rather than to send them from the United States. It is also the place to effect repairs, such as caulking, repairing engines, etcetera, hence the ships must necessarily resort to it.

In the necessity of despatch, steamers can at Hong Kong replenish their coal in 24 hours; at Macao, no calculation can be made as to time. This is a most important consideration with respect to active cruising.

If the coal and stores are at Macao, vessels must go there for them and, apart from the cost and delay of taking them on board at that place, the cost of the coal consumed by the steamers in running to and from Hong Kong would in the course of the year pay fourfold the cost of the storage at either place.

Under these circumstances I have thought it my duty as a measure of unquestionable economy and expediency to cause the coal, the propeller and shaft, and other heavy articles shipped in the *Supply,* and merchant vessel *Talbot,* to be landed at Hong Kong with directions to Mr. De Silver to take charge of them, and

Macao, fruit seller. By W. T. Peters from a daguerreotype by E. Brown, Jr.

PUNTA ST. FRANCISCO, MACAO.

Macao, fisherman at Punta St. Francisco, 1853. By W. Heine

to arrange that the coal now on its way to Macao shall on arrival be landed at Hong Kong, provided the master or consigners shall make no objection.

I have bargained for the hire of a storehouse and large enclosure; the storehouse large enough to hold from 1000 to 1200 tons of coal, and the enclosure more than sufficiently extensive to accommodate all articles which may not be injured by exposure to the weather.

For this I have agreed to pay through the storekeeper, at the rate of $40 per month, $480 per annum, exclusive of the cost (about $90) of the construction of a landing place for stores. Judging therefore from the low rate of this rent, the probability is that the aggregate rent for all purposes will not be much greater at Hong Kong than at Macao.

I have thus explained in detail the reasons which have governed me. I await instructions from the department approving or disapproving the entire removal of the depot from Macao to Hong Kong, not by actually freighting the stores from one place to the other, but by landing at Hong Kong all that may hereafter arrive, and by consuming those left at Macao until they are all exhausted, and then to abandon it as a place of deposit, though visiting it occasionally with the ships as a suitable place for refreshment and for indulging the men on shore liberty.

In a word, I respectfully recommend this change of depot, and ask for the decision of the department upon the subject.

I enclose herewith sketches of the ports of Hong Kong and Macao, showing the respective anchorage places of vessels landing or receiving coal or stores.

With great respect,
Your obedient servant,
(signed) M. C. Perry
Commander-in-chief United States Naval Forces
East India, China, and Japan Seas.

To The Honorable
Secretary of the Navy
Washington, D.C.

The city and batteries of Macao present from the outer anchorage an agreeable and imposing appearance, and the town itself has many attractions. During my stay there I made the acquaintance of many of the residents, among whom were the families of several of the Canton merchants having summer establishments in the town, to which they retreat during the hot months, and where they exercise most kind and liberal hospitality.

Monsieur de Bourboulon, the French Minister to Canton, had also his residence at Macao, and with his wife, formerly a Miss MacLeod, whom he married at Washington,[33] contributed much to the interest of an agreeable society.

The French Commodore, Monsieur de Montravel, came with his squadron to the outer road, and I had the pleasure of forming his acquaintance, and of interchanging as well with him as with Monsieur de Bourboulon, and indeed with all the residents of the place, those acts of hospitality and kindness which are invariably allied to a just appreciation of mutual cour-

33. Washington, D.C. marriage records reveal no certificate issued for this marriage. Information from the French Embassy shows that on 17 March 1851 (three weeks after being named Minister to China) he requested permission of his Foreign Minister to marry Miss Kate MacLeod, "ecossaise de race et française de coeur, niece de Mme. Calderon de la Barca, femme du ministre d'Espagne aux Etats-Unis." Needless to say, the permission was granted.

Chinese beggar. By H. Patterson

Chinese woman with children

Tanka (egg-house) woman

Face of *Tanka* woman

tesy. Indeed I received nothing but kindness from all, and shall recollect with much satisfaction the pleasant days passed at this place.

With Governor Guimarães, an officer of the Portuguese Navy, whom I had before met on the coast of Africa, I was so fortunate as to be equally intimate. It is with cordial sincerity I now bear witness to his gentlemanlike and courteous deportment in all the official transactions which passed between us.

A large experience in public life has long ago satisfied me that nothing is to be lost by meeting the advances of foreign functionaries with prompt and friendly cordiality. Practicing this doctrine in my present cruise, I have found all my interviews with the English, the Portuguese, and the Chinese authorities in every way satisfactory. I shall defer alluding to my intercourse with the Japanese and Lew Chewans until I see more of them. With Sir George Bonham and Sir John Bowring, the British superintendents of affairs in China and governors of Hong Kong, and with the military and naval commanders-in-chief, and with the high mandarins of China with whom I have been in contact, the utmost good feeling has prevailed.

Two most remarkable incidents occurred at Macao in 1849 and during the administration of Governor Amaral, an officer of distinction and highly esteemed by all who knew him. Both these events were fully described by the Hong Kong newspapers at the time of their respective occurrence. I shall merely refer to them here to illustrate the fallen fortunes and depressed national character of the Portuguese.

The first grew out of one of those contemptible acts of stupid folly, which are sometimes exhibited by foolhardy religionists in foreign countries, in view of acquiring for themselves a certain sort of notoriety; when brought into bodily danger by their own insolence they invariably prove themselves cowards as well as fools.

A young Englishman attached to a missionary school at Hong Kong, made a visit to Macao,[34] and shortly after landing espied one of those religious processions so common in Roman Catholic countries, in which the symbol of the Host is conducted with great pomp through the principal streets, attended by numerous priests and others in full costume with lighted torches. On witnessing, perhaps for the first time, this singular exhibition of what, to his imagination, seemed to be an insult to common sense, and altogether at variance with his own preconceived notions of religious propriety, he conceived the idea of showing his contempt for such pageantry by placing himself conspicuously in the way of the procession and refusing to take off his hat when the Host passed, which every well bred gentleman would always do; or if his conscience forbade him to show such mark of respect for the opinions of others (and I always suspect the honesty of such alleged scruples) to stand aloof or pass into another street. But this aspirant

34. On the evening of 7 June 1849, Mr. Summers, a Protestant missionary, refused to remove his hat for the Corpus Christi processions, even when warned by a police officer under order of Governor Ferreira do Amaral of Macao.

for distinction—though as it afterwards appeared by no means ambitious of martyrdom, even of his stomach—when mildly requested by a priest, well known to the foreign residents as a gentleman, to take off his hat or move away, refused to do so, but with fine dramatic effect pressed his hat closer upon his head and held his ground. When again warned by a police soldier to stand uncovered or retire, repeated his impertinence until he was at last arrested and taken to the guardhouse.

Here was a catastrophe, one of her Majesty's subjects shut up in a Portuguese guardhouse. Such an outrage aroused the indignation of a Captain Keppel, commanding H. M. S. *Dido,* then at anchor in the road, and a demand was made on Governor Amaral for his unconditional release. This officer pleaded a short delay, for reason of the necessity of consulting the ecclesiastical council. Also a regatta of boats belonging to the United States ship *Plymouth,* and the vessel commanded by Captain Keppel—who had been appointed one of the judges—was to take place on the same day, on which occasion the governor and many officers of the garrison would be absent on board the *Plymouth.* Captain Keppel taking advantage of these circumstances quietly withdrew himself from the race, and with a party of marines and some volunteer officers, left the outer harbor, pulled on shore and landed opposite the house of a Mr. Patrick Stewart. Avoiding the principal street leading to the guardhouse, bypassing through an unoccupied house and garden, they came suddenly upon the guard, and rushing upon the sentinel[35] rescued by force the trembling dastard, who had by his insolence brought about this abominable military outrage.[36]

The second incident, and one which caused the death of the governor, was of equally surprising character. It appears that Amaral was a man of great energy, and ambitious of improving the city by opening carriage roads through and around its limited space, and in doing this was charged by the Chinese with desecrating their ancient burial places. He had received several obscure hints that his life was in danger, but paid little or no attention to such warning, and according to his usual practice, was riding in the afternoon [of 22 August 1849] in the outskirts of the town, the daily resort of equestrians. That day he was accompanied by his aide, Lieutenant Seite, also on horseback, and several other horsemen were in the vicinity.[37] As he came to a part of the road skirted by a few bushes, one or more Chinamen (the number has never been ascertained) rushed from behind these bushes, seized the bridle from the one hand of the governor—who had but one arm,

35. The British killed one guard, and wounded the sergeant of the guard and two other soldiers.

36. An extra edition of the Macao *Bulletin* for 8 June 1849 reported the event and the taking of Summers "to the steamer *Canton* which was surrounded with American boats [that were assembled there for the regatta]" noting that the bracketed words were inserted in the next regular edition with an explanatory note:

> It seems proper to add here this circumstance, which did not occur to us while writing the Extra, in order that people at a distance may not think that the Americans took the least part in this affair.

37. Messrs. Nye, Spooner, Lewis, King, Parker, Williams, and several English families.

having lost the other in battle—hurried him from his horse, cut off his head and his remaining hand, and disappeared.

Though persons were on the spot immediately, no traces could be had of the murderers, and to this day they have not been made known to the city council, though the Chinese authorities must have been acquainted with their identity, as upon the repeated demands of the council, the mutilated head and hand of the unfortunate governor were sent in to the city. This sad event happened but two months after the feat of Captain Keppel, which had greatly chagrined the gallant Amaral.

By the latter end of October, the machinery of the *Powhatan* had, according to the report of the chief engineer, been put in good working condition, and she was ordered to take the place of the *Susquehanna,* which vessel had previously relieved the *Mississippi* at Whampoa. Each steamer in turn despatched an officer of Marines with a competent guard, and one of the boat howitzers to remain at Canton during the stay at Whampoa of the vessel to which the Marines respectively belonged. The guard lived on board the *Supply,* whilst the officer remained at the house of Messrs. Rupert & Co. to be in readiness in case of disturbance at night. But during all this time there was not the slightest incident that could in any way justify an opinion that a revolt was seriously contemplated by the people, and up to the day of my departure everything remained as quiet in Canton as at the moment of my first sending vessels and a guard to the city. Nor has there been any outbreak at either of the consular cities, which has in the least affected Americans or foreigners of whatever nation.

However the Chinese may have quarrelled amongst themselves and cut each others' throats, not a foreigner properly conducting himself has been in the smallest degree molested.

Japan Return Hastened

JANUARY 1854

About the close of November [1853], the French commodore, in the frigate *Constantine,* then lying at Macao, suddenly put to sea, under sealed orders. It was at the time well known that in a day or two he was to have departed for Shanghai with the French minister, Monsieur de Bourboulon, and wife as passengers, but on the arrival of the mail from Europe he hurried away, no one knowing in what direction.

The Russian Admiral Pontratine [Putiatin], in the frigate *Pallas* [*Pallada*], with three other vessels was at this time at Shanghai, and just arrived from Nagasaki. Suspecting his design of returning again to Japan, and apprehensive that he might ultimately go to Edo, and there interfere very seriously with my operations, and believing also with many others that the French commodore had been ordered by his government in the same direction, I became exceedingly anxious for the arrival of *Lexington,* and of some articles of presents for which I had sent to Paris. I determined—rather than allow either the French or Russians to gain an advantage over me—to encounter all the inconveniences and exposures of a cruise to Japan with so

El Campo. The country beyond San Antonio Gate, Macao. H. Patterson from W. Heine

Fishing boats, Macao. H. Patterson from W. Heine

large a force in mid winter, regardless of the terrible accounts given by writers, of the storms and fogs and other dangers to be met with on this inhospitable coast in the inclement season.

It had been my intention to have waited until the spring had set in before going to the north, but the intelligence mentioned above induced me to alter my plans. *Lexington* fortunately arrived, after an unusually long passage, and she was ordered to Hong Kong, there to land such part of her cargo as would not be required for the Japan service, and to take on board in its place four hundred tons of coal. This being accomplished, I sailed in *Susquehanna* on 14 January for Lew Chew, in company with *Powhatan*, *Mississippi,* and storeships *Lexington* and *Southampton,* the two latter in tow respectively of *Powhatan* and *Mississippi.*

Macedonian and *Supply* had been a few days before despatched for the same place, there to meet *Vandalia*. *Plymouth* was at Shanghai, and *Saratoga* had orders to join the squadron at Lew Chew.

On the day and hour of our sailing from Hong Kong, the mail steamer arrived with the overland mail, bringing me instructions to detach one of the steamers from the Japan expedition and place her at the disposal of Mr. R. M. McLane, recently appointed commissioner to China, and soon expected out from the United States. As these orders caused me great embarrassment, and would in their execution very seriously derange my plans, and act injuriously to the success of my mission, I determined not to act upon them immediately, and thus weaken my force, but to wait until I had made a preliminary demonstration in Edo Bay.

The following are copies of the letter of the department, with my hasty reply; hasty because it was written and despatched by the pilot, after the squadron was fairly under way and standing out of port.

Navy Department
28 October 1853.

Sir,

For some months past, the department indulged the hope of being able to despatch a steamer to China to be at the service of the commissioner representing our government, and to afford him facilities for accomplishing the great purposes of his mission, rendered much more interesting and important by the startling revolutionary movements in that country.

The United States steamer *Princeton* was especially set apart for that purpose. But the steamers *Princeton, San Jacinto,* and *Alleghany* have all proved miserable failures. This accounts, therefore, for the delay of a previous order similar to this.

The President trusts that it may not seriously incommode your operations in regard to Japan to cooperate with our commissioner in the interesting undertaking to bring about free intercourse with the government of China—to form commercial treaties of vast benefit to the American people, and introduce a new era in the history of trade and commerce.

The mission in which you are engaged has attracted much admiration and excited much expectation. But the present seems to be a crisis in the history of China and is considered by many as throwing around China, at least, as much interest and attraction as Japan presents. To have your name associated with the opening of commercial intercourse with Japan, may well excite your pride, but to be identified also with the great events that we trust may yet transpire in connection with China may be well esteemed a privilege and an honor.

Hoping that it may not interfere seriously with your plan of operations, you will on receipt of this communication immediately despatch one of the war steamers of your squadron to Macao, to meet the Honorable R. M. McLane, our commissioner to China, to be subject to his control until other orders reach you. Mr. McLane will bear with him further instructions to you. In the meantime, however, you will act as heretofore in the matter of your mission—only despatching the vessel as above mentioned. Mr. McLane will probably leave on the 19th proximo.

Your very interesting despatches of 25 June last have been received, and the department is much gratified with your successful operations thus far, and indulges the hope that in regard to Japan and China there is in store for you much additional honor and fame.

I am very respectfully,
your obedient servant
(signed) J. C. Dobbin.

To Commodore M. C. Perry
Commander United States Squadron in the
East India and China Seas.

United States Steam Frigate *Susquehanna*,
Hong Kong, 14 January 1854.

Sir,

On the eve of getting under way for Japan, with all my arrangements made to leave in an hour, and a large portion of my force actually gone, I am placed in possession by the arrival last night of the overland mail of the letter of the department of the 28th of October, directing me under certain views of the government respecting China, to detach one of the steamers of my command to be placed at the disposal of Mr. R. M. McLane, recently appointed commissioner to that empire.

Such an arrangement at this moment would be seriously inconvenient and highly injurious to my plans, the action of which has already commenced; indeed it could not be done without deranging the operations of the whole squadron, and I feel assured that if the department were to be made acquainted with the true state of things in China, and the importance of my carrying the three steamers with me to Japan, and knowing as it now does of the events of my former visit, it would at once revoke the order.

But it is my duty to obey, though it cannot be done at this moment without serious consequences to the success of my mission.

I will detach one of the steamers from the Bay of Edo, and send her to Macao, where she can be of use only in contributing to the personal convenience of the commissioner, as her draft of water will render it impossible for her to ascend any of the rivers for any useful purposes.

My various letters to the department will, I think, have demonstrated the correctness of this assertion. However, I have no alternative, though I cannot but express the deep disappointment and mortification to which I am subjected.

Although Mr. McLane will[38] not find the steamer at Macao when he arrives, I will order her to the coast of China the moment I can do so consistently with the public service.

I am sure the department will not object to the exercise of this discretion; no possible inconvenience can arise from the delay. Mr. McLane may probably be de-

38. In Hawks *Narrative* "may" is substituted for "will."

tained some time in Europe, and the steamer can be back probably in time to meet him on arrival, or before he will be prepared to act.

I must confess that this order has dampened my hopes very much, but, I must do the best I can.

> With great respect,
> Your obedient servant,
> (signed) M. C. Perry
> Commander-in-chief United States Naval Forces
> East India, China, and Japan Seas.

To The Honorable
James C. Dobbin
Secretary of the Navy
Washington, D.C.

As an apparent auspicious offset to these unexpected and annoying instructions, the same mail steamer brought the packages expected from Paris, but too late to be taken with me. I therefore requested Messrs. Williams, Anthon & Co.—after obtaining first the kind permission of Admiral Pellew—to send them to Shanghai, in her Majesty's steamer *Rattler,* to sail for that place in two days, there to be put on board *Saratoga,* by which means they reached me in time to be distributed on the occasion of my Japan treaty.

Before sailing I had established a most cordial understanding with the Canton merchants, and in consideration of the necessity of withdrawing the *Supply* from that city, and the *Powhatan* from Whampoa, I determined to assume the responsibility of hiring and arming a small steamer to remain for their protection during my absence. Conformably to this determination, a new and very suitable vessel was chartered for six months at $500 per month, with the privilege of extending the term of engagement at the same rate of hire.

To this vessel was assigned a sufficient armament and crew, and she was placed in command of Lieutenant Alfred Taylor, of the *Mississippi.* He had as his officers Passed Midshipman Barrand, acting as master, and, to superintend and manage the engines, First Assistant Engineer Whipple who was aided by the requisite number of firemen and coal heavers.

I regretted not to have been able to leave more officers, but the deficiencies in all the ships made it impracticable to do so. Lieutenant Commander Taylor had authority to engage others as master's mates, and to ship more men if he found such resort necessary.

See following correspondence.

Canton, 5 November 1853.

His Excellency
Commodore Perry.
Commander-in-chief United States Naval Forces
East India, China, and Japan Seas
Sir,
Upon the occasion of your return from Japan in August we had the honor of offering you our congratulations, and the expression of the satisfaction we derived from knowing that you would remain here and retain your forces upon these coasts for a considerable period of time.

We then briefly sketched the state of affairs in this country, as in our view characterized by much insecurity, and as showing the opportuneness of your arrival with a powerful force—one so commanding, that the moral effect of its presence would tend to avert apprehended dangers.

The course of events at Shanghai and in this neighborhood, while it has confirmed our apprehensions as to the precarious condition of affairs, leaves to yourself the satisfaction of having afforded the protection which the important interests of our country required.

You now inform us that the special service with which you are charged requires your early departure from this river with the vessels of your squadron, which, collectively, you consider no more than sufficient for your purposes.

As there appears no reason to apprehend an early outbreak of hostilities, and we understand that a new and efficient steamer can be chartered at Hong Kong, we beg leave to suggest to you the substitution of her in place of the storeship *Supply,* now used as the guard ship near the factories here.

We consider that from the greater adaptedness of a steamer to service in this river, she may be made more efficient than a larger sailing vessel, by the placing of proper officers, crew and armament on board of her; and we trust that you may consider yourself authorized by the importance of the interests at risk here to charter and commission her accordingly.

We take great interest in the special mission with which you are charged, and should very much regret any occurrence in this country compelling the weakening of the force necessary to ensure your success. We hope, indeed, that your able initiatory steps have so impressed the peculiar people with whom you have to deal, that you may now readily attain the principal objects of the undertaking, and thus achieve a success equal to your own deserts, and commensurate with the liberal scale upon which the government entered upon the expedition—a result at once satisfactory to our country, and worthy the applause of all other nations.

With the expression of this hope, which is inspired by the high respect and sincere personal regard derived from the intercourse we have held with yourself, as well as by our patriotism,

We remain, Sir, Your countrymen,
and obedient servants

(signed)	Henry H. Hubbell	(signed)	Nye, Parkin & Co.
"	Wm. D. Lewis & Co.	"	Wetmore & Co.
"	Lionel Moses	"	King & Co.
"	Russell & Co.	"	Augustine Heard & Co.

Canton, 9 November 1853.

Gentlemen,

I have had the honor of receiving your communication of the 5th inst. and have now the pleasure of informing you that in accordance with the suggestions contained therein, I have chartered the new steamer *Queen,* and shall take immediate steps to put her in commission and station her off this city, as a substitute for the *Supply.*

Again, Gentlemen, let me thank you for the kind and complimentary manner in which you have alluded to my public services, and to the brief intercourse which it has been my good fortune to enjoy with you: an association made doubly gratifying to me in bringing me more intimately acquainted with so many of the most distinguished merchants of our country; and of knowing from your flattering letter that I have gained your friendship and esteem.

In the delicate and responsible duties so frequently devolving upon a naval officer serving abroad, the good opinion of those with whom he may be called to act, superadded to the approval of the government, is a reward not always at-tained, but with you, Gentlemen, my way has been smooth and pleasant, and I trust that the kindly feeling at present subsisting between us may long continue.

Whatever may be the result of the special mission with which I have been charged, the conviction that I shall carry with me your good wishes will be a source of high satisfaction.

> With great respect and esteem,
> I am, dear Sirs,
> Your friend, and fellow countryman,
> (signed) M. C. Perry
> Commander-in-chief United States Naval Forces
> East India, China, and Japan Seas.

To Messrs. Wetmore & Co. To Messrs. Augustine Heard & Co.
"   King & Co.   "   Henry H. Hubbell
"   Russell & Co.   "   Wm. D. Lewis & Co.
"   Nye, Parkin & Co. "   Lionel Moses

Canton, 23 November 1853.

Sir,

The object of placing the chartered steamer *Queen* (to the command of which you have been appointed) at her present anchorage is with reference to her particular adaptedness to the service, and her capability of being at any moment in readiness to give shelter and protection to the lives and property of our fellow countrymen resident at Canton, and you are accordingly instructed to exercise every vigilance in holding the steamer in constant preparation for immediate action and movement.

You will keep yourself in communication with the U.S. Commissioner to China, with the secretary of legation when resident at Canton, and with the U.S. Consul; and will consult with those functionaries; and so far as it can be done consistently with your instructions, and the rules and usages of the Navy, will follow their advice with respect to your proceedings; always bearing in mind that your station is off the city of Canton, which you are not to leave, excepting to carry persons or property beyond the reach of danger.

Though the *Queen* has been stationed by me in the river for the protection of American life and property, and though this object will receive your first attention, it may be hoped that in case of danger you may have the means of extending your services to all who may be in jeopardy, and who may need your assistance.

That your vessel may be in constant readiness, I have to direct that no officer belonging to her, shall remain out of her after 11 o'clock at night, and no one of the crew after sunset; and that in no case shall yourself and the master be out of the vessel at the same time, even for a moment.

Funds will be left in your hands by Purser Speiden to defray the ordinary expenses of the *Queen,* for the expenditure of which you will be held accountable to the government.

> Respectfully
> Your obedient servant,
> (signed) M. C. Perry
> Commander-in-chief United States Naval Forces
> East India, China, and Japan Seas.

To Lieutenant Commander Alfred Taylor
Commander United States Steamer *Queen*
Canton River.

I was somewhat surprised to learn from Sir George Bonham, a few days prior to my leaving Hong Kong, that my visit to the Bonin Islands had

attracted the attention of the British government. He had called on board
to confer with me upon the subject, remarking that he had been instructed
by Lord Clarendon to ask of me some explanation of my designs. I told
him I would very cheerfully communicate to him the information he desired, and gave him verbally to understand my objects in visiting the islands, at the same time suggesting to his excellency that I should prefer to
have the purport of our conversation put in writing. To this proposition, he
at once assented, and accordingly addressed me on the following day a letter
recapitulating what he had verbally stated, to which I replied.

See following copies.

Superintendency of Trade
Hong Kong. 22 December 1853.

Sir,

With reference to my interview with your excellency, respecting your visit to
the Bonin Islands, and to your proposal that I should address you officially on this
subject, I have now the honor to enclose for your information, copy of a letter
and its enclosure from a Mr. Simpson, wherein it is stated that you have purchased ground from a resident there, for a coal depot, for the use of the government of the United States of America.

After our conversation yesterday, your excellency will I am sure, clearly understand, that it is not my desire nor intention to dispute your right, or that of any
other person to purchase land on the Bonin Islands; but as it is generally understood that this group was some time ago taken possession of in the name of the
government of Great Britain, I think it desirable to acquaint your excellency
therewith, in an official form, that you may, should you see fit, favor me with an
explanation of the circumstances referred to by Mr. Simpson.

I have the honor to be, sir,
your excellency's
most obedient
humble servant,
(signed) J. G. Bonham.

His Excellency
Commodore Perry, United States Navy
United States Steamship *Susquehanna*

Beauly, Invernesshire
1 October 1853.

My Lord,

I observe it stated in the public prints that the officer commanding the United
States Japan expedition had touched at the Bonin group—that he had made purchase from a resident there of land for a government coal depot.

Permit me to call Your Lordship's attention to the fact that this group of islands, so advantageously situated for opening up intercourse with Japan, really
appertains to Great Britain.

Having had some connexion with it while acting temporarily for Her Majesty's
government in the South Seas, its importance was impressed upon my mind, and I
respectfully bring under your lordship's notice the particulars, which will be
found narrated in the enclosure herewith.

I have etc.
(signed) Alex Simpson

To Lord Clarendon
etc.—etc.—etc.

THE BONIN ISLANDS.

This small but interesting and, from its situation, valuable group of Islands, lies in latitude 27° north, longitude 145° east, within five hundred miles distance from the city of Edo in Japan.

It appertains to Great Britain, having been discovered by an English whaling vessel in 1825 and formally taken possession of by Captain Beechey, of H.M.S. *Blossom,* in 1827. There were no aboriginal inhabitants found on the islands, nor any traces that such had ever existed. Their aggregate extent does not exceed 250 square miles; but their geographical position—so near to Japan, that mysterious empire of which the trade will one day be of immense value—gives them a peculiar importance and interest. The climate is excellent, the soil rich and productive, and there is an admirable harbor well fitted for the port of a commercial city.

The first colonists of this eastern group were two men of the names of Millechamp and Mazarro,[39] who having expressed to Mr. Charlton, the British consul at the Sandwich Islands, their wish to settle on some uninhabited island, in the Pacific Ocean, were by him recommended to go to this group, of the discovery and taking of which he had been recently informed. They sailed accordingly in 1830, took with them some Sandwich Island natives as laborers, some livestock and seeds, and landing at Port Lloyd, hoisted an English flag which had been given to them by Mr. Charlton.

The little settlement has been visited by several whaling vessels since that period, and also by a vessel from the British China squadron. Mr. Millechamp returned to England, and Mr. Mazarro, anxious to get additional settlers or laborers to join the infant colony—the whole population of which only numbers about twenty—came to the Sandwich Islands in the autumn of 1842 in an English whaling vessel. He described the little settlement as flourishing, stated that he had hogs and goats in abundance, and a few cattle; that he grew Indian corn and many vegetables, and had all kinds of tropical fruits; that, in fact, he could supply fresh provisions and vegetables to forty vessels annually.

Mr. Mazarro, who in virtue of his first arrival receives the appellation of governor, finds the task of governing even this little colony no easy matter. He applied to me for assistance in this task, and thankfully received the following document which I drew up for his assistance and moral support.

"I hereby certify that Mr. Matthew Mazarro was one of the original leaders of the expedition fitted up from this port under the protection of Richard Charlton, Esq., her Majesty's consul, to colonize the Bonin Islands; and I would intimate to the masters of all whaling vessels touching at that group, that the said Mazarro is a sober and discreet man, and recommend them to support him by all means in their power against the troublers of the peace of that distant settlement, recommending also to the settlers to receive Mr. Mazarro as their head, until some officer directly appointed by her Britannic Majesty is placed over them.

Woahoo [Oahu], Sandwich Islands
27 December 1842.
(L.S.) Alex Simpson.
H.B.M. Acting Consul for the Sandwich Islands.
God Save the Queen!!"

A small body of enterprising emigrants would find this group a most admirable place for settlement. Its colonization, indeed, I consider to be a national object.

39. Note, as does Perry below, that this British document makes no mention of Nathaniel Savory, the leading American colonist.

Sir,

Referring to the conversation which I yesterday had the honor of holding with your excellency, as also to your written communication with accompanying papers this moment received, I beg to remark that the account given by Mr. Simpson is far from being correct.

That gentleman has omitted to name *all* the white persons who embarked in the enterprise to form a settlement upon Peel Island. The names and places of birth of these men may be enumerated, as follows;—

Matthew Mazarro, the leader, a native of Genoa; Nathaniel Savory, born in Massachusetts, United States; Alden B. Chapin, also a native of Massachusetts; John Millechamp, a British subject; and Charles Johnson, a Dane.

These five men, accompanied by about 25 or 30 natives of the Sandwich Islands, male and female, landed at Port Lloyd, in the summer of 1830. Of the whites, Nathaniel Savory is the only one remaining on the island. Mazarro, Chapin, and Johnson are dead as I am informed, and Millechamp is now residing at Guam, one of the Ladrone group.

It would therefore appear that so far as the nationality of the settlers could apply to the question of sovereignty, the Americans were as two to one compared with the three others, who were subjects of different sovereigns.

Since the first occupation of the island, the early settlers have been occasionally joined by white persons landing from whaling ships, some few of whom have remained; and at the time of my visit, there were, I think, about eight whites in the settlement.

After my departure these people met together and established a form of municipal government, electing Nathaniel Savory their chief magistrate, and James Mottley and Thomas H. Webb councilmen.

With respect to any claim of sovereignty that may be founded upon the right of previous discovery, there is abundant evidence to prove that these islands were known to navigators as early as the middle of the 16th century, and were visited in 1675 by the Japanese who gave them the name of Bune Shima.

In 1823, four years before the visit of Captain Beechey, in H. M. Ship *Blossom,* the group was visited by a Captain Coffin in the American whaling ship *Transit.* *

Thus it is plainly shown that the government of her Britannic Majesty cannot claim the sovereignty upon the ground of discovery, and it only remains to determine how far this right may be derived from the ceremony performed by Captain Beechey.

But these are matters only to be discussed by our respective governments, and I refer to them now merely in explanation of our conversation yesterday.

With respect to my purchase of a piece of ground from Nathaniel Savory, though conceiving myself in no way bound to explain such arrangement, I do not hesitate, in all due courtesy, to say that the transaction was one of strictly private character.

In acquiring the fee of the land I had not the slightest idea of personal profit, but made the purchase for a legitimate object, and to withhold the only suitable position in the harbor for a coal depot from the venality of unprincipled speculators, who might otherwise have gained possession of it for purposes of extortion.

And now let me assure your excellency that the course pursued by me has been influenced solely by a settled conviction of the necessity of securing ports of refuge and supplies in the North Pacific for our whaling ships, and a line of mail steam-

* I have ascertained the name of this vessel from a Captain Morris, commanding an American whaling vessel now in this port.

ers, which sooner or later must be established between California and China. I have no special instructions from my government upon the subject, and am yet to learn whether my acts will be approved.

The recognized sovereignty of these islands would only entail an expense upon the power undertaking their occupancy and protection, and whether they may ultimately fall under the American, the English, or a local flag would be a question of little importance, so long as these ports were open to the hospitable reception of the ships of all nations seeking shelter and refreshment.

And I may venture further to remark that it would seem to be the policy as well of England as the United States to aid in every possible way in the accomplishment of an arrangement that would fill up the remaining link of the great mail route of the world, and thus furnish the means of establishing a semimonthly communication around the entire globe.

> With great respect, I have the honor to be,
> your most obedient servant,
> (signed) M. C. Perry
> Commander-in-chief United States Naval Forces
> East India, China, and Japan Seas.

Accompanying notes to be added to this letter taken from the diplomatic correspondence.

To His Excellency
Sir J. George Bonham, Bart.,
Chief Superintendent of
British Trade in China, Hong Kong.
On leaving Hong Kong by the Lymoon Passage, I thought it desirable to get well to northward before striking over for the south end of Formosa. Fortunately the monsoon was not very strong and we made a favorable passage with the two storeships in tow as far as the northeast point of the island just mentioned. There they were cast off with orders to follow us to Naha, at which port the steamers arrived on the 20th of January, and the two storeships on the 24th. Here we found *Macedonian, Vandalia,* and *Supply.* The *Saratoga* had not yet made her appearance.

The northeasterly current which is constantly setting with great rapidity round the south end of Formosa, and with decreased velocity along its eastern coast was especially noticed on our passage, and careful observations were made upon its force and direction.

As it is my intention to cause every possible information to be collected respecting this stream, which in all its characteristics assimilates very closely with the peculiarities of the Gulf Stream upon our own coast, and proposing to speak more at large in another part of this journal upon the currents of the Japanese seas, I shall at this time allude no further to the subject.

Lew Chew

20 JANUARY–7 FEBRUARY 1854

A very marked change had taken place at Lew Chew during my absence of six months. The authorities still continued to furnish whatever was required, at just prices; and the people were evidently, though slowly, relaxing in their disposition to avoid a more friendly intercourse. The women no longer fled from the market places, but remained in charge of what they had for sale.

Exploring parties were again despatched into various parts of the island, and one in particular to seek for coal. All of them made written reports which have been carefully preserved.

Mr. Chaplain George Jones, who was sent to examine a locality giving every indication of the existence of coal beneath the surface, came to the conclusion that by proper mining, this valuable product could doubtless be found, and I am inclined to think that Great Lew Chew, as well as O Shima, contains coal and other valuable minerals and earths.

Numerous botanical specimens were collected, but unfortunately we have no one in the squadron well acquainted with botany. A few of those which seemed to be the most rare have been sketched, and others preserved according to our means and acquaintance with the method of preparing them.

Being detained at Naha by business with the regent and in discharging and preparing the *Supply* for a trip to Shanghai, I thought it advisable to despatch the other sail ships for Edo Bay in advance, making my calculations to reach the appointed rendezvous with the steamers about the time of the arrival of the former in the bay. Accordingly, Captain Abbot in the *Macedonian* sailed on 1 February in company with *Vandalia, Lexington,* and *Southampton,* and on the 7th I followed with the *Susquehanna, Powhatan,* and *Mississippi.*

The *Supply,* being ready, was to have sailed the following day with the wife and children of Doctor Bettelheim on board, for Shanghai, there to take on board a cargo of coal and some livestock, and proceed to rejoin the squadron at Edo Bay.

I had been for some days in expectation of the arrival of the *Saratoga* from Shanghai, and thinking it probable she would be met outside, I caused the steamers to pass to westward of Lew Chew in view of intercepting her track. As good fortune would have it, we had scarcely cleared the harbor when a sail was discovered standing toward the island, which on her approaching nearer was ascertained by signal to be the long-looked-for ship.

Captain Walker came on board and received orders to proceed direct to the American Anchorage, Edo Bay, and after sending from his ship some livestock which he brought from Shanghai for the squadron, and three packages containing presents for the Japanese authorities, he bore away with the intention of taking the passage east of Lew Chew.

Judging it politic to accustom the people of the capital to the visits of Americans to the palace to weaken the very strong opposition they at first evinced to our entrance within the gates of the royal residence, I gave notice that it was my intention before leaving Naha, on this my fourth visit to the island, again to pay my respects to the regent at Shuri. In answer to this, a proposition was made that I could be more conveniently received at Naha. But the regent was informed that I considered it more respectful to go to the palace, and requested that horses, *kagos* [palanquins], and *kago* bearers should be in attendance on the morning of the day of my contemplated visit. To all these demands objections were offered, whether because the authorities did not wish to comply or whether it was to interpose their crooked policy of deceit, which experience ought to have satisfied them would have been fruitless, I knew not. I simply replied to all their excuses, that the requisitions upon them were reasonable and just, and I would receive no excuses or equivocations. Accordingly all things were arranged as I desired, the visit made, and every mark of respect manifested by the regent, at whose palace we called after leaving that of the queen. At the first, as on a former occasion, slight refreshments were served, but at the regent's a profuse feast was in readiness and, having become somewhat accustomed to the Lew Chew cookery, we managed to do better justice to the viands than on former similar occasions.

At this visit I informed the regent that I was desirous of obtaining for the United States Mint, in exchange for pieces of American coinage of equal value, all the coins in use in the island, well knowing that the imperial coins of Japan were in circulation, though they had hitherto concealed them from us.

Both the regent and treasurer declared that there were no coins in the island, excepting a few in the possession of the Japanese residents, who would not part with them. This declaration, like most of those coming from them, I knew to be false, and insisted on their complying with my request. Leaving with them American coins to the amount of $49.24, I remarked that before sailing I should expect to receive an equal value in Japanese and Lew Chew coins. But at the last moment, the interpreter sent me word that the coins could not be had, and desired to return those I had left. These I refused to receive, and so the matter now stands. As a measure of policy I must persist and shall doubtless succeed. As a first failure to carry a point with these people would lead to many others, and to show my dissatisfaction, I refused to receive on board some poultry and other refreshments, which the authorities sent as presents.

The passage of the steamers until we made the islands lying in front, or rather at the entrance of the great Bay of Edo, was pleasant and by no means protracted. We passed in full view of the northern group of the Lew Chew chain, composed of the islands O Shima (Ta-tao), Tok-Sima [Toku Shima], Ratona Shima, and Kikai Shima, and had opportunities of establishing with some accuracy the positions of several of the headlands on the western side of O Shima, and the islets named by Captain Guerin of the French corvette *Sabine,* Cleopatra Isles.

In passing these islands I was reminded of an order I had received from the Secretary of the Navy to investigate and report upon a question touching the original discovery of O Shima by Commander Glynn, at the time in command of the United States sloop of war *Preble,* in February 1846; and, as the subject is one which may be appropriately introduced into this journal, I subjoin a copy of my communication to the department, setting forth the views and opinions entertained by me with respect to the entire chain of islands, extending from Formosa to Kiu-Siu [Kyushu].

Sir,

In the hope of obtaining more satisfactory information from personal examination, I have hitherto deferred a reply to the order of the department, directing me to report upon the contents of a letter addressed by Commander James Glynn to Commodore Thomas ap Catesby Jones,[40] and bearing date 21 February 1850, in which he communicates the fact of having as he supposed discovered an island in the Japan seas not before known to modern navigators, and upon such conjecture claims the right under certain reservations of giving it the name of the ship he then commanded.

The island represented to be seen in June 1849 and described in the letter just referred to as bearing in a southeasterly direction from the *Preble* is called in the Japanese charts O Shima (Great Island), and by the Chinese Ta-tao. The islets in sight at the same time bearing NNW were examined in 1846 by Captain Guerin, of the French corvette *Sabine,* and named by him Cleopatra Isles.

These islands as well as O Shima and others lying contiguous were distinctly seen from the decks of the ships of the squadron on passing them yesterday, and of which sketches were taken, herewith enclosed.

The Cleopatra Islands are two in number, are small, cone shaped, uninhabited, and lie near to each other. They are evidently of volcanic formation, the craters being clearly visible. In height, the largest has been estimated by Monsieur Guerin at 1,650 English feet.

O Shima is the principal of what I shall call the northern group of the Lew Chew chain, which in connection with the Miyako Shimas and another chain commencing with the Cleopatra Isles extend from near the north end of Formosa to Kyushu, the southwestern extremity of Japan proper.

The positions of the Cleopatra Isles and O Shima, as established by cross bearings taken from the *Susquehanna,* at noon on the 8th day of February 1854, after good observations, were as follows:

South end of Cleopatra Isles, latitude 38°48′ N, longitude 128°59′30″ E.

North end of O Shima, latitude 28°29′ N, longitude 129°30′ E.

The Miyako Shima islands have been more than once visited by foreign vessels, and more recently by *Saratoga* of this squadron, whose officers describe the inhabitants as being in language, manners, customs, and appearance almost identical with those of Great Lew Chew. If we are to judge by what we have seen of this island we may suppose the entire chain—those I mean capable of sustaining a population—to have been peopled many hundreds of years.

We know that the Miyako Shima group are governed by officers appointed by the king and council of Great Lew Chew, and that they are frequently changed in conformity with the insidious and jealous policy practiced throughout Japan and its dependencies. We also know that these islands are subject to Lew Chew, to the government of which they pay an annual tax, and we are moreover told that Lew Chew is a royal fief of Japan, though it is asserted by some writers that it owes fealty only to the prince of Satsuma.

With regard to the people and government of O Shima, and the neighboring and probably dependent islands of Toku Shima, Ratona Shima and Kikai Shima we as yet know but little, but it is fair to assume that they are also subject to

40. Commander of the United States Pacific Squadron 1849–1850, and thus Glynn's superior officer. The *ap* is a short form of the Gaelic *map* meaning "son of."

Great Lew Chew, and the government of the latter exercises an intermediate sovereignty between them and the empire, or possibly the prince of Satsuma.

From what Von Siebold asserts, it seems pretty clear that this prince receives, at least, the income derived from the Lew Chew Islands, which he says amounts to the annual sum of 2,240,000 guilders, nearly 900,000 dollars.

He also sustains the opinion to which I have been irresistably led, that the three groups of Miyako Shima, Great Lew Chew (or Okinawa Shima) and O Shima should be denominated the southern, middle, and north Lew Chew Islands; the central government being established at the city of Shuri, in the island of Great Lew Chew.

The geographical positions of these islands form, as before mentioned, a continuous chain from Formosa to Japan proper, seem to be so arranged and as to suit the convenience of the commerce of the unskillful Japanese, who sail in their frail, open-sterned vessels, from island to island, always being careful to have a port under their lee, into which to escape on the approach of foul weather.

O Shima, to which this communication should more particularly refer, is in circumference nearly 150 English miles. It is mountainous, resembling indeed the appearance of Lew Chew.

It is represented by Von Siebold and other writers to be thickly populated, having all the advantages of cities, towns, villages, and commodious ports, and the wonder is that it has never, as far as we can learn, yet been visited by a Christian voyager. I may hope to have that satisfaction and to be able to communicate to the department further information with respect to these interesting islands.

The recorded history of Great Lew Chew goes back to the 12th century, when its line of kings became allied by marriage with the Japanese dynasty. Ruins of extensive and massive castles are still found in the island. The one occupied by the present royal family is in good repair, and in architectural proportions, extent, strength, and massiveness of structure is quite equal to many of those reared in Europe in the early and middle ages.

The roads and bridges throughout the island are of admirable structure, all giving indication of great antiquity. Many of the roads are paved with square blocks like those in the ancient cities of Italy, and are shaded by avenues of pines and other forest trees.

The remains of fortified works, apparently intended for defense of the port of Naha, go to show that in the art of engineering, the people were not deficient, and though these works are no longer armed, they could still be made available.

To each of the principal towns belongs a commodious buliding, called in the Lew Chew language, *kung-kwa,* and similar in object to the caravansaries of the East. These are constructed and kept in repair at the public expense; and here travelers can always find shelter and refreshment. It was to these public inns that the officers of the squadron, prosecuting their explorations in the interior of the island, were conducted by their guides, and where they invariably found hospitable entertainment.

In addition to a mass of hydrographical information which has already been obtained to be forwarded in due time to the department, and to which we are constantly adding, I shall cause to be prepared as illustrative of the opinions expressed in this communication a sketch of the chain of islands particularly referred to.

It should be considered nothing more than just to Commander Glynn to assume that if he was mistaken in the conclusions to which he was very naturally drawn—considering the very imperfect charts with which the ships on this station are provided—he deserves commendation for a laudable desire to contribute all in his power to the improvement of hydrographical knowledge.

It is in truth by such observations that the attention of the navigator is called to investigate questions thus agitated; no one should relax in the prosecution of similar enquiries, because they may not always be founded on data altogether correct.

With great Respect
I am, sir,
Your Obedient Servant,
 (signed) M. C. Perry
Commander-in-chief United States Naval Forces
East India, China, and Japan Seas.

To the Honorable
James C. Dobbin
Secretary of the Navy
Washington, D.C.

Volume 3 February – June 1854

The space embraced between Cape Nagatsuro on the west, Cape Serafama [Shirahama] (or Cape King) on the east, and Odawara, Kamakura, and Cape Sagami on the north—and which has hitherto been considered and so mentioned in the charts and in this journal, as forming part of the great Bay of Edo—I shall hereafter denominate the Gulf of Edo, and consider the bay to commence at Point Rubicon. The channel between Cape Sagami and Uraga I shall call Uraga Straits. By thus subdividing and naming the three most distinctive parts of this magnificent sheet of water, its navigation and the hydrography of its shores, will be the better understood by strangers.

On entering the gulf this time the steamers encountered a severe blow from northward and eastward, but, keeping during the night under the lee of O Shima, avoided its greatest violence. The previous afternoon we had passed near to a cluster of three dangerous rocks, showing above the surface from ten to twenty feet. These we supposed to be what are called in the charts Broughton Rocks. If this conjecture be correct, their positions are very erroneously laid down; and if they are not the same, then they are *not* marked on any of the charts known to us. This is not at all remarkable, as few European or American navigators have ever visited the southern and eastern coasts of Japan. It ought not to be expected that the very imperfect charts which have been compiled from the meager information furnished by Broughton, Gove, and Krusenstern, and by the three or four American and English vessels visiting Uraga within a few years back, can be in any manner correct. [See bibliography for Broughton and Krusenstern; Gove has not been identified.]

It is true that the Japanese have charts, constructed after a plan of their own, without meridian or scale, nor do they mark the soundings. They never venture, if they can possibly avoid it, beyond sight of land, and always seize upon favorable seasons and appearances for making their longest runs from island to island. Their junks skirt the coasts and rarely make a run of longer than 24 hours.

The largest Japanese junks that have come under my notice could not have drawn more than eight feet of water, and as before remarked they run from port to port, invariably seeking shelter on occasions of adverse winds or appearances of bad weather. Their pilots need no charts, familiar as they are with every nook upon the coast into which a junk can enter. There can be no better evidence of the antiquity of the coasting trade of this empire than is furnished by the conveniencies offered in these little harbors for securing the crafts as they run in from the sea. Everywhere holes are artfully made through the angles of the rocks for passing their cables. Where this cannot be done, upright pillars or posts are hewn or morticed in the rock, or small projections or detached parts are rounded and made smooth to prevent the chafing of the moorings.

It may be hoped that the information obtained from actual observation, surveys, and other authentic sources by myself and the other officers of the squadron may contribute very considerably to a more intimate acquaintance with those parts of the coast visited by the vessels of the squadron.

156   On the morning of the 12th, the weather became more settled and the steamers stood up the bay, and at noon discovered two vessels close in with the land and apparently at anchor. On approaching them they proved to be *Macedonian* and *Vandalia*. The latter displayed a signal that *Macedonian* was aground. On enquiry I soon ascertained that Captain Abbot, on the day previous, mistaking the indentation in which he was aground for the entrance of the passage leading to Uraga and Edo had, in venturing too near the shore, grounded on a ledge of rocks. These were not, of course, laid down on the imperfect chart which he had. It was nothing more than a copy of one of Von Siebold's maps, compiled from Japanese authorities, with a few notes upon it, made on our former visit. He ought not to have depended on it.

Japanese boat in Edo Bay. Pencil sketch by William Speiden, Jr., from his journal. (Courtesy Naval Historical Foundation)

Finding his ship in this dilemma, he adopted the usual means of getting her again afloat by starting the water, getting her guns ready for throwing overboard, and actually heaving over the side many miscellaneous articles of which I apprehend there was no account taken. Commander Pope in *Vandalia,* at the time in company, immediately anchored and sent his boats to the assistance of *Macedonian*. The providential arrival of the three steamers at once gave assurance of effectual aid. Commander Lee in *Mississippi* was ordered to approach as near as he could safely venture to the ship on shore, and run lines to her in view of hauling her off by the power of steam. This duty he executed with his usual promptitude and judgment, and before night she was towed into safe anchorage. Meanwhile the other ships were brought to anchor for the night, having been joined on the same afternoon by *Lexington*, which vessel it will be recollected sailed from Naha in company with *Macedonian*.

During the same night a boat came alongside, despatched by Lieutenant Commander Boyle of the *Southampton*, which vessel—another of Captain Abbot's division—had arrived the day before at the American Anchorage. The Japanese authorities had sent information to Lieutenant Boyle that two ships had arrived off Kamakura, and that one of them was ashore. He very promptly and very properly despatched the launch of *Southampton*

View of Uraga, Edo Bay, July 1853: Sinclair lithograph from Heine. (Courtesy Mr. and Mrs. W. John Kenney)

"Passing the Rubicon," 11 July 1853. Lieutenant Silas Bent's survey cutter confronts Japanese guard boats. Driftwood in lower left bears wrong date. Heine watercolor. (Courtesy Mr. and Mrs. J. William Middendorf II)

Commodore Perry comes ashore in Japan for the first time, 14 July 1853, at Kurihama. Note boys with red boxes containing credentials. Heine watercolor. (Courtesy Mr. and Mrs. J. William Middendorf II)

Delivery of President Fillmore's letter, 14 July 1853. Sinclair lithograph from Heine (Courtesy Mr. and Mrs. W. John Kenney)

Two storm-tossed ships of Perry's squadron in Bay of Odawara, Japan, 12 February 1854. Sarony lithograph from Heine and Walker
(Courtesy Mr. and Mrs. W. John Kenney)

Delivery of American presents at Yokohama, 13 March 1854. Sarony lithograph from Peters. Pump, ¼-scale locomotive, Francis lifeboat, farm implements, whiskey keg assembled ashore near Treaty House. Note telegraph wires. (Courtesy Mr. and Mrs. W. John Kenney)

Dinner given to Japanese commissioners on board *Powhatan*, 27 March 1854. Duval lithograph from Heine. (Courtesy Mr. and Mrs. W. John Kenney)

Landing of Commodore Perry at Yokohama, 8 March 1854, to meet the Imperial Commissioners. Treaty House is at left. Camphor tree at right was almost totally destroyed in 1923 earthquake and fire, but from a surviving root the tree flourishes in the British Consulate compound at Yokohama. (Courtesy Mr. & Mrs. J. William Middendorf II)

Commodore Perry paying farewell visit to Shimoda. 8 June 1854. From Heine watercolor. (Courtesy Mr. and Mrs. J. William Middendorf II)

Shimoda from American graveyard, April–May 1854. Sarony lithograph from Heine painting. (Courtesy Mr. and Mrs. W. John Kenney).

Hakodate from Snow Peak, May 1854. Sarony lithograph from Heine painting. (Courtesy Mr. and Mrs. H. John Kenney)

Hakodate Scolopax

Shimoda pheasants.

Dogs presented to Perry at Shimoda, June 1854. (Courtesy Mrs. George Tilton)

Shimoda

Dog Miako From Japan

Miyako

Exercise of troops in Ryosenji temple grounds, Shimoda, 8 June 1854. From Heine lithograph. (Courtesy Naval Academy Museum) (Courtesy Naval Academy Museum)

with two officers to render all practicable assistance. When the officer in command reached the vicinity he discovered the presence of the squadron and consequently made his report to me.

It is worthy of remark that the Japanese on observing that *Macedonian* was on shore, offered their assistance, and subsequently picked up a hogshead of bituminous coal, which had been thrown overboard in lightening the ship, and was washed upon the beach. This they took the trouble to send to the squadron, a distance of twenty miles.

On the following morning the ships moved up to the American Anchorage, about twelve miles above Uraga, the three steamers each taking a sail ship in tow. On passing the city, we saw a few officials come out and motion to us that they wished to come on board, but this I did not permit. Early in the afternoon the whole squadron was safely anchored at the position selected by me as the appointed rendezvous, and which has before been repeatedly referred to.

As a correct account of our transactions from this time until the signing of the treaty is contained in a series of notes prepared and transmitted to the government at Washington, I prefer to embody these notes in this journal, the rather to save unnecessary writing.

> *Notes of transactions which occurred on the occasion of*
> *the second visit to Japan by the United States Squadron*
> *in command of Commodore M. C. Perry.*

The squadron sailing in a line ahead—*Lexington, Vandalia,* and *Macedonian* being in tow respectively of *Susquehanna, Powhatan,* and *Mississippi* —arrived off Uraga about two P.M. on 13 February 1854.

As orders had been given similar to those issued by me in July last, no communication was allowed with anyone from shore. Although the ships, in passing the city, were intercepted by government boats, the officials on board of them were beckoned not to venture alongside. They followed us, however, to the position designated in my instructions as the rendezvous of the squadron, and called in our chart the American Anchorage, and there the six above-named ships anchored, *Southampton* having arrived in advance.

Beginning
Negotiations

It was not long before the government or mandarin boats were alongside the flagship with a request from the Japanese officers that they might be admitted on board.[1] But as I had caused the extra or Captain's cabin to be removed from the *Susquehanna* to *Powhatan*—in view of changing my flag to that ship, preparatory to the return of the former to China—and as I could not consistently with the system of exclusiveness which I still pursued, of not seeing any of the subordinates, admit them into my cabin, I directed Captain Adams to receive them on board *Powhatan*.

1. This delegation, headed by Kahei Kurokawa, consisted of two interpreters and three *metsuke*, or spies as Perry called them.

158   Accordingly he proceeded to that ship, accompanied by Messrs. Williams and Portman, interpreters, and Mr. Perry, my secretary. Captain Adams had been charged by me with precise and special instructions to hear all the Japanese had to say, but to give them no unnecessary information, nor to promise them anything.

These people, who seemed to be mandarins of middle rank, with their Dutch interpreters, stated that the Emperor in expectation of our arrival had given orders to receive us in the most friendly manner, and had appointed commissioners of high distinction to meet and confer with me upon the propositions of the President presented in July last. A town called Kamakura, about twenty miles from Uraga—and the place where *Macedonian* had got on shore—had been designated for the meeting.

I had anchored off this town for the purpose of giving my personal attention to the extrication of *Macedonian* from the perilous situation in which I found her, and saw enough to satisfy me that it would be absurd to take the ships there. Suspecting some artful design on the part of the Japanese, I directed Captain Adams to say that it was altogether unsuitable.

For this answer they were evidently prepared as, after a little more quibbling, they declared that although the Emperor preferred Kamakura still he would have no objection to the negotiations being conducted at Uraga. There, in fact, a pavilion had been expressly erected for the purpose, and persons of high rank appointed to receive me, but to this end it would be necessary for all the ships to return and anchor off that town.

This proposition I also declined upon the ground of the inconvenience and actual unsafety of the anchorage at this boisterous season. I directed other and the following reasons to be assigned: that I felt myself bound to go to Edo, or to approach with the ships as near to it as possible; that the anchorage was better higher up the bay, and I was desirous of securing a smooth place to anchor the ships in view of stopping a leak in *Mississippi,* and to examine the bottom of *Macedonian* with the sub-marine apparatus to see whether she had sustained much injury whilst on shore.

They replied that Uraga was the only place at which the conferences could be held. The Emperor had issued a decree to that effect, and it could not be changed.

Captain Adams at this stage of the conference sent Mr. Perry to communicate to me this apparent ultimatum of the Japanese. I immediately ordered him back with a message that, for reasons already assigned, I would not go to Uraga, but would consent to meet the commissioners anywhere between the American Anchorage and Edo, and that I would not recede from the point then occupied by the squadron, but would be more disposed to move higher up the bay. During this interview many compliments and acts of courtesy were interchanged between the American and Japanese officers, refreshments were served, and offers of supplies made by the latter, but in adherence to my instructions not a single point was conceded.

On 15 February the same officials accompanied by others again visited *Powhatan,* where they were received by Captain Adams, assisted as before.

The same arguments were urged to induce the removal of the ships to Uraga, but with no better success. An offer was again made of supplying wood and water and such other refreshments as the ships needed. They were told that we had abundance of provisions though in the course of time we should require wood and water, which we would be disposed to receive as an article of necessity, even if they declined taking pay for it. But nothing else would be admitted on board the ships so long as they refused payment for the same, and for reasons that the government of the United States could well pay for whatever might be furnished to its Navy, and would not consent to receive supplies gratuitously.

Parties of officials visited *Powhatan* on the 16th and 18th, ostensibly to enquire after my health and to bring me delicacies of fresh oysters, eggs, and confectionary, but in reality to renew their arguments and persuasions for the ships to remove to Uraga, proposing as a sort of compromise that I should go there with one or two of my squadron, but I still resisted. I was convinced that if I receded in the least from the position first assumed by me, it would be considered by the Japanese an advantage gained. Finding that I could be induced to change a predetermined intention in one instance, they might rely on prevailing on me by dint of perseverance to waver in most other cases pending the negotiations. Therefore it seemed to be the true policy to hold out at all hazards, and rather to establish for myself a character of unreasonable obstinacy than that of a yielding disposition. I knew that upon the impression thus formed by them would in a measure hinge the tenor of our future negotiations, and the sequel will show that I was right in my conclusions. Indeed, in conducting all my business with these very sagacious and deceitful[2] people, I have found it profitable to bring to my aid the experience gained in former and by no means limited intercourse with the inhabitants of strange lands—civilized and barbarian —and this experience has admonished me that with people of forms it is necessary either to set all ceremony aside, or to out-Herod Herod in assumed personal consequence and ostentation.

I have adopted the two extremes by an exhibition of great pomp when it could properly be displayed, and by avoiding it when such pomp would be inconsistent with the spirit of our institutions. I have never recognized on any occasion the slightest personal superiority, always meeting the Japanese officials, however exalted their rank, with perfect equality, whilst those of comparative distinction of their own nation were cringing and kneeling to them. For motives of policy, and to give greater importance to my own position, I have hitherto studiously kept myself aloof from intercourse with any of the subordinates of the court, making it known that I would communicate with none but the princes of the empire. Up to this time, I have succeeded far beyond my expectations in maintaining this extreme point of diplomacy, and as I believe to very great advantage.

That there should be no misapprehension of my intentions, I prepared and directed the following note to be read to the Japanese.

2. Words "and deceitful" are circled in manuscript, as though considered for deletion.

United States Steam Frigate *Powhatan*
                                   American Anchorage, Edo Bay.
                                       18 February 1854.
     The Commodore expects to be received at Edo agreeably to the customs of all
countries.
     In consideration of the size of our ships, and their great value, he cannot return
to the anchorage at Uraga, nor even remain at this place much longer, but will
have to go higher up the bay toward Edo, where the vessels can be more secure.
     If the great man (chief commissioner) will appoint an officer of proper rank to
meet Captain Adams on shore near where the ships are now lying, to determine
when and where the interview with the Commodore shall take place, he must let
us know by noon of Tuesday next.
     The Commodore will be happy to place a ship at the disposal of the great man,
to bring him up to the place of interview and take him back again to Uraga if he
wishes it.
     When the officer comes to meet Captain Adams, he had better bring a letter to
show that he has proper authority, and a person must be sent to conduct Captain
Adams to the place of meeting.

                                                          (signed) M. C. Perry.

     Visits were made to *Powhatan* by the officials on 19 February (Sunday)
bringing with them presents of refreshments.[3] They were told that the day
was set apart by the Americans as their sabbath, but as they had come a
great distance in cold and boisterous weather on an errand of kindness, they
would on that account be politely received, but in future no official intercourse would be allowed on that day. At this interview one of the principal
interpreters, after the others had retired, took Captain Adams aside and
informed him in strict confidence that the Emperor had given orders to his
commissioners to receive and entertain most favorably the propositions of
the President presented by me, but nothing would be done to further the
desired object, unless I consented to have the meeting at Uraga.
     Receiving no satisfactory reply to their suggestions of yesterday, the
officials visited *Powhatan* again today, the 20th, and were told that out of
respect to the commissioners, who were detained at Uraga, in expectation of
seeing me, I would send Captain Adams to that place in one of the ships to
call upon them, and to assure them personally and by letter that I would not
go there myself. Accordingly, on the 21st the same officers came from Uraga
to accompany Captain Adams to that place, and to introduce him to the
Japanese commissioners. They were invited to take passage in *Vandalia,*
and did so.
     Captain Adams was the bearer of a note from me, of which the following
is a copy:

                                             United States Flagship *Powhatan*
                                             American Anchorage, Edo Bay
                                               20 February 1854.
The undersigned is highly gratified to learn through the officers of his Majesty,
who have vistited the flagship, that the imperial court has come to the conclusion
to respond in the most cordial manner to the propositions of the President of the
United States, which the undersigned had the honor to present in July last.

     3. The visitors were Kahei Kurokawa and his subordinates.

Inasmuch as the anchorage at Uraga is unsafe and inconvenient, and consider- 161
ing the great size and value of the steamers composing a part of the command of
the undersigned, he does not consider himself justified in removing to that place.
On the contrary he deems it necessary to seek a more commodious harbor higher
up the bay, and as his instructions direct him to present himself at Edo, it is desirable that he should approach as near as possible to that city, as well for the better convenience of communication, as with reference also to the arrangement and
exhibition of the various presents sent by the President to His Imperial Majesty.

As the mission of the undersigned is of a most friendly character, he is not prepared to anticipate any objection to his reception at the seat of government, conformably to the usages of all the nations of Europe and America, and he hopes
that when the steamers shall have reached the vicinity of the city and secured
more suitable moorings, he may have the honor of receiving on board his ship,
such distinguished members of the imperial court, as may be desirous of viewing
the steamers and witnessing the working of their machinery.

This communication will be presented by Commander H. A. Adams, captain of
the fleet, who is empowered to receive any written proposition addressed to the
undersigned, and place at the disposal of the commissioners of His Imperial Majesty one of the vessels of the squadron.

With the highest respect
(signed) M. C. Perry
Commander-in-chief United States Naval Forces
East India, China, and Japan Seas.

It was quite calm in the morning [21 February] and *Vandalia* did not get
under way until near noon, but before she had reached Uraga a strong gale
from the southwest and directly ahead prevented her from reaching the
port, making it necessary for her to anchor under Point Rubicon, and
Captain Adams with his party did not land at the town until the following
day, the 22nd.

He was courteously received by one of the commissioners, Izawa, prince of
Mima-Saki [Mimasaka], at the pavilion, erected purposely for my reception,
and presenting my note, was told that a reply would be handed to him on
the following day. After partaking of some slight refreshments, he returned
to the *Vandalia*, which he had scarcely reached before it again began to
blow, causing much anxiety to Commander Pope, the anchorage proving
very much exposed and consequently unsafe.

Captain Adams particularly noticed the position of the building erected
for the meeting of the commissioners, as being placed in a deep gorge near
to the shore, and fenced in by palisades or stakes. On this being told to me, I
at once declared that such obstructions would not have been tolerated, and
Captain Adams, as he informed me, assured the Japanese that if I had
landed at Uraga, my first act would have been to have ordered the demoli-
tion of this barricade.

The 22nd being the anniversary of the birth of Washington, all of the
ships of the squadron fired the usual salute. Many of the Japanese gentlemen came by permission on board the flagship to witness the firing, with
which they were much interested. The most intelligent among them had
heard of the name of Washington, though they had very vague notions of his
history and character.

As I had little hope of any favorable result from this visit of Captain Adams, I determined to carry out my threat, from which I anticipated much advantage, and actually removed the squadron during his absence to within sight of Edo. So near indeed that from the masthead we could distinctly hear the striking of the city bells during the night.

I may as well remark here, that from the moment of the anchoring of the squadron in the bay, the surveying boats were actively employed in exploring the upper part of this magnificent sheet of water—magnificent beyond anything of the kind I have ever before seen.

As a measure of precaution, these boats always sounded in advance of the ships. When *Vandalia,* with Captain Adams on board—charged with the reply of the Japanese commissioners to my letter—had rejoined the flagship, the boats were absent engaged in further explorations toward the city. Though this letter intimated the impossibility of holding the conference at any other place than Uraga, it had not been in my hands an hour, before Eizaemon Kayama, governor of Uraga, made his appearance on board *Powhatan* with the alleged object of receiving a reply from me, but actually, as it will appear, for another purpose.

Here follows a translation of the letter of the commissioners.

To Admiral M. C. Perry,

The undersigned, ambassadors of the Emperor of Japan, have perused and understood the letter of the Lord Admiral, and in reply may remark:

The Lord Admiral is right in going up to Edo to be received there according to the custom in Europe and America. According to the Japanese custom ambassadors are commissioned, and a building erected for the reception of ambassadors from foreign countries in a friendly manner and with high consideration.

The Emperor has sent us to Uraga to receive the Admiral with the highest honor, and to extend the Japanese hospitality toward him, and have the interview at that place in compliance with the order of the Emperor, regardless of the customs of foreign countries.

We wish this to be well understood; we desire the Admiral to come to Uraga, there to have the interview with us in the building aforesaid, and would gratefully acknowledge the friendly meeting of the Lord Admiral in complying with this order of the Emperor, and our own wishes.

Our best wishes for the health of the Admiral.

(signed) Hayashi, *Daigaku no kami.*[4]

The 27th Siogoots [Shogatsu],[5] 1854.

Kayama first commenced by inquiring whether I was still determined not to return to Uraga, and being answered in the affirmative, he again offered supplies, and was again told that we would receive wood and water, to which he said that these articles would be cheerfully furnished, but they could be obtained only at Uraga. He was informed by my order that it was a matter of indifference to us from whence they came, as I should not go to Uraga, and if the Japanese did not bring water to us, I would send on shore and procure it by some means.

4. Rector of the university.
5. Lunar calendar equivalent of 24 February.

Seeing that I was immovable in purpose and evidently inclined to approach nearer to Edo, he suddenly abandoned the previous assumed ultimatum of the commissioners as to the place of meeting, and suggested as a substitute a very convenient spot, directly opposite the ships. To this proposition I at once acceded, the situation suiting my views in all respects, being near to Edo, with safe and commodious anchorage at a mile distant from the shore, and affording abundant space for the landing, preparing, and arranging of the presents.

Now let us look into the deceitful conduct of these people. For the last ten days they have interposed all possible objections to the movement of the ships higher up the bay and endeavored by every means to persuade me to return to Uraga. When they found that I could not be deceived by their cajolery, and had actually approached within eight miles of the capital, they suddenly abandoned the position from which they so often assured me they could not be moved, and proposed unconditionally to concede what I had with equal but more successful pertinacity contended for.

Before deciding positively upon accepting this last proposal, I sent Commander Adams with other officers to examine the place last appointed for the conference, and they soon returned with a most favorable report.

The surveying boats shortly after came in with information that they had found six fathoms of water within four miles of Edo. This intelligence at once gave me the clue to the sudden change of policy of the Japanese, but as I had never entertained the idea of abandoning the intention of getting as near with the ships to this famed capital as the depth of water would allow, and as the place of meeting last proposed suited exactly, I was satisfied with the arrangement. Accordingly, I prepared the following letter to be presented to the commissioners on the first day of meeting, as a reply to the one addressed to me from Uraga, and sent by Captain Adams.

> United States Flagship *Powhatan*
> At anchor off the town of Yokohama
> Edo Bay, 1 March 1854.

To His Highness,
Hayashi, Daigaku no kami
etc   etc   etc

Your Excellency,
The letter of your excellency from Uraga was duly delivered by Captain Adams and shortly after when it was ascertained that I could not agree to return to Uraga, Eizaemon Kayama suggested that the negotiations might be conducted at a village opposite to the present anchorage of the squadron.

Being exceedingly desirous of meeting the wishes of your excellency in every way consistent with the honor and interest of my country, and learning that the place pointed out was in all respects convenient for the purpose, I at once consented to defer my visit to Edo, until after the completion of the negotiations.

I the more readily entered into this arrangement as on examination of the port by the surveying boats, it has been found that the ships can approach near to the city, where I propose at some future time to anchor them, as well to do honor to his Imperial Majesty by salutes, etc., as to be in full view of the palace and convenient to be visited by such of the court as may desire to examine the steamers and their machinery. I hardly need say that they will be kindly and politely received.

> With the most profound respect,
> (signed) M. C. Perry
> Commander-in-chief United States Naval Forces
> East India, China, and Japan Seas,
> and Special Ambassador to Japan.

It struck me that it was better to have no treaty than one that would in the least compromise the dignity of the American character. To agree to any arrangement that would recognize in the remotest degree the restrictions submitted to by the Dutch could not for a moment be thought of.

As soon as the weather would permit, the surveying boats were sent to examine the anchorage opposite the place agreed upon for the conference and the erection of another council house. After receiving a favorable report, I directed the squadron to be moored in a line abreast, within a mile of Yokohama, and covering with their heavy guns an extent of shore of five miles. On anchoring we observed great numbers of workmen busily employed in the erection of a large irregular edifice intended as a substitute for the one abandoned at Uraga.

It is probable that arrogance may be charged against me for persisting as I did; and, against the judgment of all about me, in changing the place of conference, and thus compelling four princes of the empire to follow the squadron, and subjecting the government to the trouble and expense of erecting another building, but I was simply adhering to a course of policy determined on after mature reflection, and which had hitherto worked so well.

The ships had not been long at anchor before a number of the Japanese officials came on board the flagship and stated that the imperial commissioners would be ready to receive me as soon as the building should be finished. They made daily visits to the ship and brought me the names of the dignitaries who have been empowered by the Emperor to meet me.

Here follow their names and titles:

Hayashi *Daigaku no kami,* member of the council.

Ido, prince of Tsus sima [Tsushima].

Izawa, prince of Mimasaka.

Udono, *Mimbu shoho* [member of the board of revenue].

Subsequently a fifth, Michitaro Matsuzaki, was added to the number, so that being myself alone, the odds were as one to five.

Second Landing in Japan

8 MARCH 1854

It was not long before the building was completed and furnished, and I was duly notified that the five commissioners would be ready to receive me on Wednesday, 8 March, at noon. Accordingly, every preparation was made in the squadron to distinguish the occasion of our second landing in Japan by all necessary parade, knowing as I well did the importance and moral influence of such show.

At 11:30 A.M. on the day appointed, the escort—consisting of about 500 officers, seamen, and Marines fully armed—embarked in twenty-seven barges in command of Commander Buchanan, and, forming a line abreast, pulled in good order toward the shore. The escort having landed and drawn up, I followed in my barge under an appropriate salute. Upon landing I was received by the escort and a party of Japanese officials and conducted to the hall prepared for the conference, where I found in waiting the five commissioners, and was invited to be seated opposite the chief personage.

At this moment salutes were fired from the howitzers mounted in the launches, of twenty guns in honor of the Emperor, and seventeen for the Japanese commissioners. This display in landing was made altogether for purposes of policy in accordance with the reasons already assigned.

After suitable interchanges of courtesy, I was requested to retire with my suite to an inner apartment where the necessary business could be conducted undisturbed. Accordingly—accompanied by the captain of the fleet, the two interpreters, and my secretary—I withdrew with the commissioners to an adjoining room separated from the principal hall by a flag suspended across the entrance. Refreshments having been served, a reply to the letter of the President, presented in July last, was handed to me and translated from the Dutch by Mr. Portman and I replied to it orally. I then handed to the chief commissioner a draft of a treaty which I had previously prepared as the basis of one which I was desirous of negotiating with the imperial government. This was accompanied by three other papers, one being a reply to the communication of the chief commissioner addressed to me from Uraga, a copy being appended and marked B. Another was a statement of my views with respect to the policy of bringing about a mutually advantageous compact between the United States and Japan, a copy also appended and marked C. The third was a memorandum—likewise appended, and marked D—in further explanation of the motives which would govern me in conducting the negotiations, and asking for certain relaxations of the Japanese laws with respect to the squadron.

As it would happen, a Marine[6] belonging to *Mississippi* had died two days before this conference, and the very first matter to be discussed was the suitable interment of the body. I had apprehended much difficulty upon this point, and had in my own mind determined—if the Japanese persisted in forbidding the interment within either of their numerous burial places—to have effected the object, let what might occur, upon the small island called in our charts Webster Island and lying convenient to the American Anchorage. I was pretty well satisfied that once the body was in the ground it would not be disturbed, and as others of the squadron might die during our stay, it

First American Burial
9 MARCH 1854

6. Private Robert Williams.

would be a very appropriate place of interment for all. I was moreover anxious for special reasons to acquire an interest in this island to subserve some ulterior objects.

The proposition seemed to perplex the Japanese commissioners, and after some consultation they retired to discuss the question alone. On leaving they requested that in their absence we might partake of a few Japanese dishes.

I observed that we should be most happy to do so, but it would be more consonant to our notions of hospitality if the commissioners were to join us, as the breaking of bread together was amongst many nations considered an evidence of friendship. They replied that they were unacquainted with foreign customs but would cheerfully join us. Upon this they all retired, but shortly after, the second and third in rank of the number returned, and the collation was served, and all went off in apparent kindness and good nature.

It was not long before the entire board was again in session and a written reply to my request respecting the interment was presented by the chief commissioner. Its purport was that as a temple had been set apart at Nagasaki for the interment of strangers it would be necessary that I should send the body to Uraga, whence at a convenient season it might be conveyed in a Japanese junk to the former named place.

To this I objected, remarking that undisturbed resting places for the dead were granted by all nations, and then proposed to send boats and inter the body at Webster Island. To this they evinced strong objections, and after considerable discussion amongst themselves finally consented to allow the interment to take place at Yokohama, at a spot adjoining one of their temples, and in view of the ships. They observed that as the novelty of the scene might attract an inconvenient crowd, the authorities would send on board *Mississippi* in the morning an officer to accompany the funeral party.

Accordingly on the following day, one of the interpreters made his appearance and the corpse was taken on shore in the usual manner and placed in a grave near to a Japanese temple with all religious ceremony,* conformably to the forms of the Episcopal Church, since which a neat enclosure of bamboo has been put up by the Japanese authorities.

Treaty Articles Considered

17 MARCH 1854

The day after the conference a formal reply to the letter of the President was sent to me together with a Dutch translation. An English translation is appended, marked E, as also a copy of my reply, marked F. [See Appendix A]

It will be seen that the imperial government is prepared to concede much more than was anticipated by many, but, entertaining the opinion that something still more advantageous might be gained, I thought it good policy to hold out for a specific treaty.

* Black-and-white sketch of funeral procession by Japanese artist. Date was 9 February 1854.

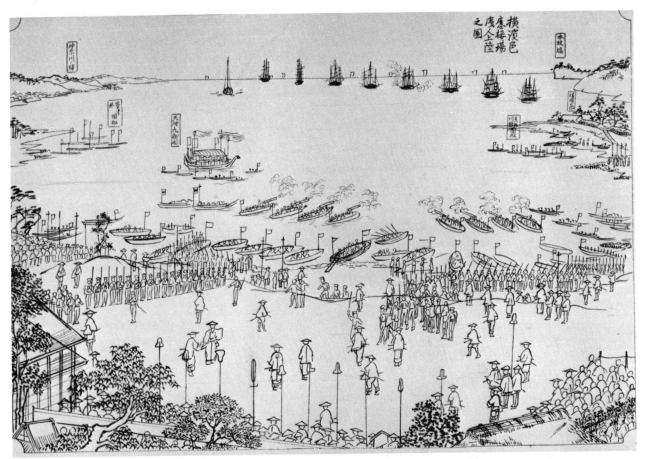

Japanese sketch of the 8 March 1854 landing at Yokohama. (Courtesy Shiryo Hensanjo.)

Yokohama Funeral Procession of Private Robert Williams, USMC. Japanese sketch. (Courtesy Shiryo Hensanjo)

In delivering the reply to the letter of the President, they stated that the commissioners would be ready for receiving the presents on Monday the 13th. Accordingly they were landed with much ceremony by a detachment of twenty-four boats, in command of Captain Abbot, and safely placed in a building adjoining the conference house. Engineers and operatives were sent from the ships to put together and arrange the various articles preparatory to the work of instructing the Japanese in their several uses.

On the 13th, the day the presents were landed, I sent a message to the commissioners requesting them to meet me at the conference house on the 15th to discuss the several articles of the treaty which they had submitted for my approval and signature. They replied that they should be much employed until Thursday, and suggested that day as more convenient provided it was fair. The messenger remarked that the Japanese did not like to expose themselves to bad weather.

It stormed on Thursday and consequently the meeting did not take place until the following day, 17 February. The commissioners arrived about noon from Kanagawa in a magnificent barge or rather galley covered with banners.

On landing I was conducted immediately to the private room set apart for the discussion, and we at once proceeded to business. A paper written in Dutch was now presented, similar in purport to one which had been previously sent me in the Chinese language. From the latter version Mr. Williams had made an English translation, which being compared with the Dutch copy may be read, with the replies respectively submitted by me, as follows:

*Propositions of Japanese Commissioners
with replies of Commodore Perry.*

1st Japanese proposition.

From the first of next month, wood, water, provisions, coal and other things, the productions of this country that American ships may need, can be had at Nagasaki; and after five years from this, a port in another principality shall be opened for ships to go to.

Commodore Perry's reply.

Agreed to; but one or more ports must be substituted for Nagasaki, as that is out of the route of American commerce; and the time for the opening of the ports to be agreed upon must be immediate or within a space of sixty days. The manner of paying for articles received shall be arranged by treaty.

2nd Japanese proposition.

Upon whatever part of the coast people may be shipwrecked, those people and their property shall be sent to Nagasaki by sea.

Note. When after five years shall have expired, and another harbor shall be opened, those shipwrecked men will be sent either there or to Nagasaki, as may be most convenient.

Commodore Perry's reply.

Agreed to excepting as to the port to which the shipwrecked men are to be carried.

3rd Japanese proposition.

It being impossible for us to ascertain who are pirates and who are not, such men shall not be allowed to walk about wherever they please.

Commodore Perry's reply.

Shipwrecked men and others who may resort to the ports of Japan, are not to be confined, and shall enjoy all the freedom granted to Japanese, and be subject to no further restraints. They shall, however, be held amenable to just laws, or such as may be agreed upon by treaty.

It is altogether inconsistent with justice that persons thrown by the providence of God upon the shores of a friendly nation should be looked upon and treated as pirates before any proof shall be given of their being so, and the continuance of the treatment which has hitherto been visited upon strangers will no longer be tolerated by the government of the United States so far as Americans are concerned.

4th Japanese proposition.

At Nagasaki they shall have no intercourse with the Dutch and Chinese.

Commodore Perry's reply.

The Americans will never submit to the restrictions which have been imposed upon the Dutch and Chinese, and any further allusion to such restraints will be considered offensive.

5th Japanese proposition.

After the other port is opened, if there be any sort of articles wanted, or business which requires to be arranged, there shall be careful deliberation between the parties in order to settle them.

Commodore Perry's reply.

Agreed to, so far as it applies to ports other than Nagasaki.

6th Japanese proposition.

Lew Chew is a very distant country, and the opening of its harbor cannot be discussed by us.

Commodore Perry's reply.

As there can be no good reason why the Americans should not communicate freely with Lew Chew, this point is insisted on.

7th Japanese proposition.

Matsmai [Matsumae] is also a very distant country, and belongs to its prince; this cannot be settled now, but a definite answer on this subject shall be given when the ships are expected next spring.

Commodore Perry's reply.

The same with respect to the port of Matsumae, for our whaling ships, steamers, and other vessels.

Choosing Open Ports

These propositions and replies were consecutively discussed, the commissioners interposing all possible difficulties, contending that the laws of the empire were of such character as positively forbade the concessions I demanded. They remarked that Nagasaki was set apart for the admission of strangers, that the inhabitants and authorities of that city had been trained to enforce the laws with respect to foreigners, and if the Americans were to have another port assigned to them, five years would be required to make similar preparations.

I replied that that was one of my reasons for objecting to this port; that its inhabitants and authorities having been so long accustomed to the servility of foreigners would doubtless exact more from the Americans than they would be inclined to submit to, and serious consequences would follow. Moreover, it should be well understood that my countrymen visiting Japan must be free from all those oppressive laws which have hitherto been enforced upon strangers. In a word, I would not think of accepting Nagasaki as one of the ports.

I told them that I should expect in the course of time, five ports to be opened to the American flag, but at present would be content with three, as follows: one on the island of Nippon, and suggested either Uraga or Kago-shima; another in Yesso (or Matsumae) [Hokkaido]; and a third in Lew Chew (Naha); and would defer all discussion with respect to the other two until some future time.

To this, after many evasions, they answered that as I positively refused to accept Nagasaki, and having themselves objections to the selection of Uraga, they proposed the port of Shimoda, in the principality of Izu as one in every way suitable and convenient, remarking at the same time that Lew Chew was a distant dependency, over which the crown had limited control, and consequently they could not entertain the proposition. Matsumae also stood very much in the same relation to the imperial government.

Notwithstanding all these objections I still persisted in my demands, and seeing me determined to hold out, they proposed to retire to another room to consult upon the matter. After an absence of an hour the whole board again convened in the council room, and gave as the result of their delibera-tion that longer time would be required to decide upon the expediency of opening the port of Matsumae.

They further remarked that it was not in the power of the crown to grant the required privilege of this port, without consulting the prince under whose hereditary right it was governed; that to do this would require a year, at the expiration of which time they would be prepared to give a reply. I told them I could not leave Japan without a reply of some sort; that if the prince to whom they referred was an independent sovereign, I would go to Matsumae and negotiate with him.

Finally the interview ended by their saying that they would give me a definite answer on Thursday, 23 March. Before adjourning, however, it was agreed that one or more vessels of the squadron should be despatched to the port of Shimoda, to be met by a Japanese officer of rank for the purpose of examining the harbor, in view of determining its fitness for the required purposes. It was clearly understood that if it did not answer my expectations in all respects I should insist on another somewhere in the southern part of Nippon.

plying between California and China, and for whaling ships cruising in this part of the Japan seas could not be more desirable, lying as it does just within Cape Izu or Nagatsuro, with clear and open navigation toward the sea. It is easy of access and vessels would be taken but a short distance from their route in resorting to it. The commissioners represent it as safe, commodious, and convenient for obtaining such supplies as the country can furnish, which are limited, owing to the remarkable abstemiousness of the Japanese in the use of animal foods.[7]

Matsumae is equally convenient in position for vessels passing more to the north and through the Strait of Sangar, a vicinity much frequented by our whalers. It is a question whether in making the passage from San Francisco to Shanghai this may not be the nearest though certainly not the safest route.

The department has already been fully informed by me of the superior advantages of securing a port in Lew Chew.

Thus if I succeed in obtaining free access to the required ports in Japan, we shall have three very convenient places of resort and refreshment for our ships, nearly equidistant from each other and belonging to an empire from which our flag has hitherto been by law excluded. Peel Island, one of the Bonin Group, would make the fourth.

Before separating from the commissioners, I called their attention to the details of our conversation, remarking that my secretary had taken full notes, and suggested that to prevent mistakes they should send me a written statement of their understanding of the oral agreements already arranged between us. To this proposition they at once assented and accordingly the chief interpreter brought on board a paper of which the following is a translation, strongly indicative, it would seem, of the good faith in which they intend to act.

*Japanese statement of points agreed upon
in the interview of Commodore Perry with the
Japanese commissioners on 17 March 1854.*

1st. The citizens of the United States will not submit to degradations like those imposed upon the Dutch and Chinese in their confinement at Nagasaki. That place is not convenient for ships to resort to, and does not answer the purpose.

2nd. Lew Chew is a very distant country, and a definite answer cannot be given.

3rd. Matsumae is a very distant country and belongs to a prince. This point cannot be settled now; some time will be required for negotiation· until the first month of our next year. Because the concurrence of our

---

7. The Gyokusen Temple in Shimoda has a tablet marking the spot where cattle were first slaughtered for food in Japan. Prior to the opening of the country by Perry and the arrival of Townsend Harris in 1856 as first United States minister to Japan, the Japanese ate only fish and fowl.

central government and of the prince of that country are both necessary to effect a result, a negotiation of the Admiral with that prince, therefore, would be to no purpose.

It was stated that an answer had better be given at once. There was time enough to have that harbor opened by the above-mentioned time; but it was not probable that in the first years that harbor would be resorted to by many ships, because some time would be required to communicate this decision to the government, and to have it generally known. In consideration thereof it was agreed that a final answer should be given on 23 March (the 26th of the Japanese month.)

It being mentioned that besides Matsumae and Lew Chew, more harbors in Nippon would be required, it was suggested that the harbor of Shimoda could be opened for the ships of the United States, and agreed that two ships of the squadron would sail on 19 March to make a survey of that harbor, and further that some Japanese officers, to go by land, would arrive at that place on the 22nd instant, and that the captains of those ships would await the arrival of those officers, before proceeding to survey and get permission to land.

That shipwrecked men should meet with kind treatment, and be free as in other countries.

Agreement made upon due consideration.

Daily Notes   Wednesday, 22 March 1854. The chief interpreter visited *Powhatan* today to inform me that owing to an error in referring to the Japanese calendar, a mistake had been made as to the next day of meeting of the commissioners on which occasion I was to have had a definite answer with respect to Matsumae; but inasmuch as such answer was promised on the 23rd it would be sent on board, and on the day succeeding the commissioners would be prepared to receive me on shore, and to present in due form the return presents from the Emperor, to be sent to the United States.

The chief interpreter also informed me that the commissioners had appointed Saturday, 25 March, to dine with me on board the flagship, in accordance with my invitation and request that they would fix a day. To this I suggested that as Saturday might prove stormy, and our sabbath following—on which day I could not receive company—I would prefer to have the honor of their presence on Monday, and it was so arranged.

Thursday, 23 March. The chief interpreter, according to appointment, came on board *Powhatan* today accompanied by several other officials, and brought the reply of the commissioners to my demand for the opening of a port for the admission of American vessels in the Strait of Sangar, island of Matsumae or Hokkaido.

The document was written in the Japanese, Chinese, and Dutch languages, and the one in Japanese signed by the four principal commissioners. Here follows a translation from the Dutch:

Ships of the United States of North America, in want of provisions, wood, and water shall be supplied in the harbor of Hakodadi [Hakodate] as has been desired. Some time will be required to make preparations, inasmuch as this harbor is very distant; consequently a commencement can be made the 7th month of next year. (17 September 1855.)

> Kayei [Kaei] *sitsinen* [*shichinen*] *shogatsu.*
> Seal attached by order of the high gentlemen.
> (signed) Moryama Yenoske [Einosuke Moriyama][8]

I informed the interpreter that I would consent to the proposition of the commissioners assigning this port in the island of Matsumae or Hokkaido as a northern port of resort for American ships, provided on examination it proved to be equal to the favorable description he gave of it, and the time for throwing it open should be fixed at an earlier period, and further remarked that I would discuss these matters with the commissioners at our next business interview.

Hakodate is situated at the eastern entrance of the Strait of Sangar, at about 42 degrees of north latitude, and is in all respects a convenient geographical position as a stopping place for our whaling ships cruising in that region. Many of them pass annually through this channel into the Sea of Japan in pursuit of whales.

Von Siebold states that sixty-eight square-rigged vessels were counted by the Japanese as passing Hakodate and Matsumae in one year; nearly all, it is presumed, were American, and not one dared to approach the shore within gunshot. Golownin [Golovnin][9] also refers to it, as follows:

The city of Hakodate, the second in magnitude on the island, is situated on its southern coast on the declivity of a high circular hill, which rises above the peninsula there formed; it is washed on the south by the Bay of Sangar, on the north and west by the bay of Hakodate, which is very convenient for receiving a large fleet. The peninsula forms its junction on the east by a narrow strip of land, so that there is at once a view of both the open sea and the low grounds.

The necessity of despatching *Susquehanna* early in the morning to enable her to get clear of the bay before dark, makes it proper that I should bring this paper to a close. Details of all future transactions during the remainder of the squadron's stay in these seas will be continued in the same form.

I may remark in conclusion that in the short time we have been in this bay (about five weeks), we have conciliated in a great degree the confidence of the authorities and people. We have established a magnetic telegraph upon the land almost as perfect as any in the world, a mile in a direct line, by which words in English, Dutch, and Japanese have already been conveyed. We have laid down the entire railroad track sent from the United States, and put the steam engine, tender, and car in excellent practical operation, carrying round the circle many of the astonished natives. We

8. Moriyama spoke English well, but with a heavy accent, and was fluent in Dutch. He had interpreted for Commander Glynn (1846), the *Lagoda* visit (1848), and later for Townsend Harris.

9. Captain Vasily Mikhailovitch Galovnin surveyed Pacific shores in Russian sloop *Diana* and was taken prisoner in Hokkaido in July 1811. He was set free in 1813, and compiled a three-volume narrative of his Japanese experiences and observations, which was published in English as *Memoirs of a Captivity in Japan,* London, 1824.

have exhibited and explained the use of numerous useful inventions of our country, especially implements of husbandry, and all without the occurrence of the slightest unfriendly act from either side. [Written 23 March 1854.]

*   *   *

1 April 1854. *Susquehanna* sailed on the morning of the 24th for Macao, and was seen by *Vandalia* to pass Shimoda at 3 P.M.

On the same day a number of presents were sent on board for the President, for myself, and other officers of the squadron. All were carefully packed, marked, and put on board the storeship *Supply* to be sent to Washington, conformably to the laws of the United States.

On the 27th, the five commissioners with their respective retinues and followers, about seventy in number, dined on board *Powhatan* by special invitation from me. They were received with salutes and all the honors due to personages of their rank. Conforming on this occasion to the Japan custom which forbids the sitting at meals of subordinates with their superiors, a table was arranged in the cabin for the commissioners, and another on deck for their retinues, many of whom were of comparative distinction.

The captains, my secretary, and Dr. Williams, the Chinese interpreter, were the only persons invited by me to dine with the high functionaries. Every effort was made to entertain the entire party, and the day passed with much hilarity and good feeling.

The following day was appointed for another interview on shore to settle the final details of the treaty. The meeting took place and, after much discussion and many evasions on the part of the commissioners, an arrangement was agreed upon, and Friday the 31st fixed for the signing of the treaty. This was accordingly done about noon and, at the house erected especially for the conferences. The commissioners gave me three copies of the treaty in the Japanese language, duly signed by the four especially delegated by the Emperor. In return they received from me three copies in English, with my signature, translations in Dutch and Chinese certified by the Dutch and Chinese interpreters, Messrs. Portman and Williams, for the United States.

It will be observed that the practice usually pursued in affixing signatures to treaties was departed from on this occasion, and for reason assigned by the Japanese, that their laws forbade the subjects of the empire from putting their names to any document written in a foreign language. As I did not consider that this omission to sign the English version of the treaty could effect in the slightest degree the validity of the instrument, I made no very strenuous objections to the course they proposed and seemed determined on. Especially as they gave me triplicate copies of their version with certified translations, I was well satisfied that all the stipulations as agreed to by them and in their own way would be scrupulously carried out by their government.

Indeed throughout the negotiations I was met at every step by objections to forms, and application and use of words, which though of little or no importance, were tenaciously insisted on by them; such for instance as to

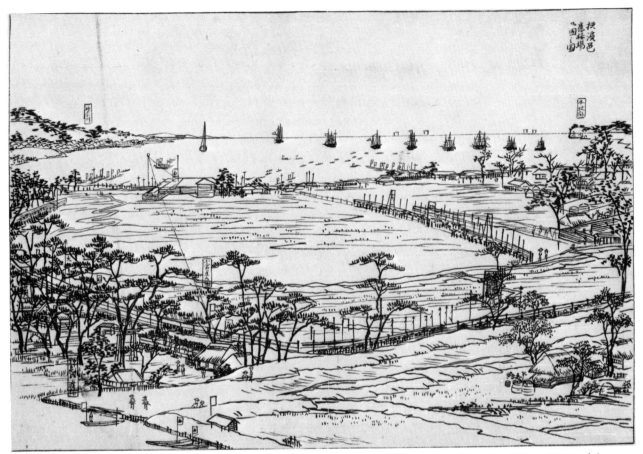

Yokohama telegraph station one mile inland from Treaty House. March 1854. (Courtesy Shiryo Hensanjo)

Telegraph line to Treaty House terminal. (Courtesy Shiryo Hensanjo)

substitute the word "goods" for "merchandise" and numerous other trivial alterations of like import. By these changes the phraseology of the treaty will not be found as perfect as it would otherwise have been. And so in the concluding article, I was constrained to frame the sentence in a manner to meet their watchful avoidance of agreeing to any feature in the treaty that could commit them with their government.

The great object, however, of effecting an advantageous compact with this most singular people has been fully accomplished. This compact secures protection and kind treatment to all Americans who may by chance or design find themselves in any part of the empire. It also stipulates to give shelter and supplies to vessels of the United States, and to grant to American citizens privileges never conceded to any foreign people in the two preceding centuries. The government of the United States may well claim the honor of being the first to open friendly and *independent* relations with a nation hitherto claiming the right of entire exclusion from all foreign intercourse, unless the immunities granted to the Dutch and Chinese at Nagasaki, may be considered in such light.

It may be remarked here that at all our interviews on shore, whatever may have been the number of officers from the ships, usually ranging from 20 to 50, refreshments prepared in the Japanese fashion were served to all, and on the day of signing the treaty greater preparations were made. On all occasions, visitors to the ship on business with me have been provided with refreshments.

Supplies of wood and water, poultry, eggs, and vegetables have been furnished by the Japanese in limited quantities to the several ships of the squadron, for which they have, in accordance with my positive demand, received payment. It is quite probable they will in a short time lose all their scruples in this way, as at Lew Chew, where they soon learned to charge and receive good prices for their supplies.

[These notes] respectfully submitted,
(signed) M. C. Perry
Commander-in-chief United States Naval Forces
East India, China, and Japan Seas.

United States Flagship *Powhatan*
At anchor off the town of Yokohama
Edo Bay, Japan. 3 April 1854.

American Gifts

During our stay in Edo Bay, all the officers and members of the crews had frequent opportunities of mingling freely with the people, both ashore and on board, as many of the natives visited the ships in the business of bringing water and provisions, and on official matters.

For the first few days after our arrival at Yokohama, Mr. Gay, the chief engineer of *Mississippi,* assisted by First Assistant Engineer Danby, with the requisite number of mechanics, was employed in unpacking and putting in working order the locomotive engine, whilst Messrs. Draper and Williams were equally busy in preparing to erect the telegraphic posts for the extension of the magnetic lines. Dr. Morrow was also engaged in unpacking and arranging the agricultural implements, all intended for presentation to the Emperor, after being first exhibited and explained.

The Japanese authorities offered every facility. Sheds were prepared for sheltering the various articles from the weather; a flat piece of ground was assigned to the engineers for laying down the track of the locomotive. Posts were brought and erected as directed by Messrs. Draper and Williams, and telegraphic wires of nearly a mile in a direct line were soon extended in as perfect a manner as could have been done in the United States. One end of the wire was at the treaty house, the other at a building allotted for the purpose, and communication was soon opened between the two operators in the English, Dutch, and Japanese languages, very much to the amazement of the spectators.

Meanwhile the implements of husbandry had been put together and exhibited, the track laid down, and the beautiful little engine with its tiny car set in motion. It could be seen from the ship, flying round its circular path exciting the utmost wonder in the minds of the Japanese. Although this perfect piece of machinery was with its car finished in the most tasteful manner, it was much smaller than I had expected it would have been, the car being incapable of admitting with any comfort even a child of six years. The Japanese therefore who rode upon it were seated upon the roof, whilst the engineer placed himself upon the tender.

These various exhibitions, with the singular groups of American officers, sailors and Marines, intermingled with the native mandarins, officials, and laborers presented an animated spectacle which is happily represented in the drawing which faces this page. [No such drawing in Journal.]

Japanese Curiosity

The Japanese are remarkable for their inordinate curiosity and, in the display of so many of the inventions of our ingenious countrymen, they had ample means of gratifying this propensity. They were not satisfied with the minutest examination of all these things, surpassingly strange as they must have been to them, but followed the officers and men about, seizing upon every occasion to examine every part of their garments, and showing the strongest desire to obtain one or more of their buttons. Those who were admitted on board the ships were equally inquisitive, peering into every nook and corner accessible to them, measuring this and that, and taking sketches after their manner of whatever they could lay their eyes upon, though it would be difficult to discover from their drawings what they were intended to represent.[10]

Notwithstanding that the Japanese are themselves so fond of indulging

10. Perry probably saw only Japanese sketches. Objects portrayed in finished Japanese works were unmistakable and in some cases artistic.

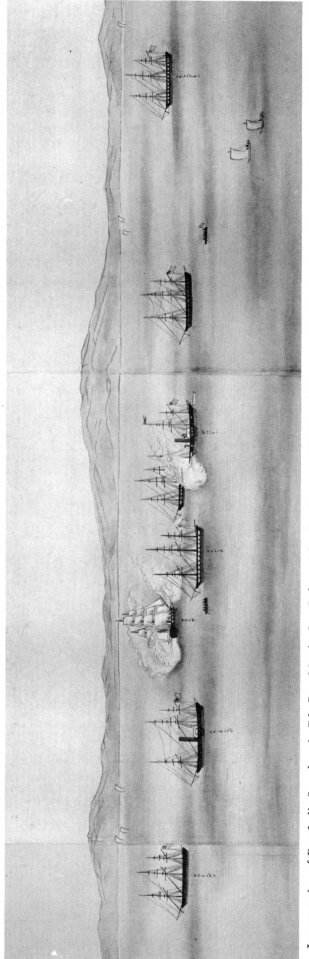

Japanese view of East India Squadron in Edo Bay, March 1854. Left to right: *Southampton, Mississippi, Saratoga, Macedonian, Susquehanna, Powhatan, Vandalia, Lexington.* Compare with Heine painting of Perry landing at Yokohama, 8 March 1854. (Courtesy Shiryo Hensanjo)

Japanese painting of sloop-of-war *Saratoga* and steamer *Powhatan* (Courtesy Mr. Paul Blum)

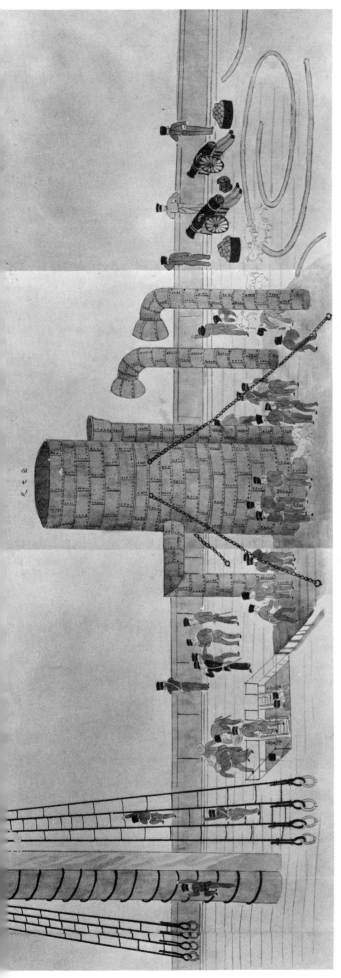

Steamer *Powhatan*, deck detail by a Japanese artist. Note livestock and pivot circles for gun-carriage wheels. (Courtesy Mr. Paul Blum)

Steamer *Powhatan*, below-deck detail by a Japanese artist. Note battle lanterns, gun carriages, barrels, ammunition, dice game beneath storage racks, chow time for some, others warming hands at cannonball stove. (Courtesy Mr. Paul Blum)

their curiosity, they are by no means communicative when information is required of them, alleging as a reason that their laws forbid them to communicate to foreigners anything relating to their country or its institutions. We have had much better opportunities of picking up here and there, and from time to time, many interesting particulars respecting the laws, customs, and habits of these people than others who have preceded us. Yet a long time will elapse before any full and authentic account of their internal laws and regulations will be obtained; certainly not until we can establish men of intelligence in the country in the character of consular agents, merchants, or missionaries who, to enable them to make any progress, should acquire a knowledge of the language.

We found the common people more disposed to fraternize than were the mandarins or officials. It was evident that nothing but a fear of punishment deterred them from entering into free intercourse with us; but they were closely watched, and it may be inferred that the higher classes would be equally inclined to greater intimacy if they in their turn were not also watched. In truth every native has a spy set upon him in this country, as in Lew Chew. No one is entrusted with public business of any importance without having one or more associated with him, who are ever on the alert to detect and take note of the slightest suspicion of delinquency.

Countryside Stroll

6 APRIL 1854

Though they were very shy.

In moving through the village of Yokahama, and traversing the paths leading in all directions, the officers and such of the crews as wandered from the boats were treated with great civility. The universal smoking apparatus and tea were always ready to offer to every succeeding visitor. The women did not, as at Lew Chew, run from us, their curiosity overcoming [all authority and] all feelings of fear.[11]

On an occasion of taking a long stroll in the neighborhood of the treaty house, accompanied by several of the officers and the chief interpreter Moriyama, with other Japanese officials, I noticed that on entering any of the villages or hamlets, a person was sent ahead to order the women and rabble (for in most eastern countries they are placed pretty much upon the same footing) to keep out of the way. When I mentioned this to the interpreter he adroitly ascribed it to their modesty or shamefacedness. But on telling him I did not believe a word of what he said—a charge not considered reproachful to a Japanese interpreter whose duty it is to lie—he promised that at the next village we came to, where he had ordered some refreshments to be prepared, the women should not be required to avoid us. Accordingly on entering the village, everyone crowded to see us—men, women, and children—and being conducted to the house of the mayor, our party was very politely received. The mayor officiated himself in helping us to whatever he had to offer such as tea, cakes, confectionary, and *saké,* which

11. Bracketed words inserted by Commodore Perry.

was served with a kind of hot waffle made of the flour of rice or some other grain.

These were served by the wife and sister of the mayor, who while in our presence remained on their knees moving themselves from one guest to the other with the *saké* kettle, bowing their heads to the floor and displaying their disgusting blackened teeth. The lady mayoress brought in her unwashed baby—a genus found everywhere—for me to caress, which I did with the best grace possible. When I handed him a piece of the confectionary, he was bidden to bow his little shaven head, which evidence of precocious politeness called forth the greatest apparent pride and admiration of the mother and all the ladies present.

On preparing to depart, I proposed the health of the whole household in a cup of *saké*, which brought into the room the mayor's mother, who squatted herself in one corner and bowed her thanks for the compliment paid to the family of which she was the oldest member.

These women were barefooted and barelegged, dressed very much alike in a sort of dark nightgown secured by a broad band passing round the waist. They had black hair and eyes, with fat dumpy figures, their lips being painted, making their black teeth and corroded gums the more conspicuous.*

"There is no accounting for taste," is a truism made plain to us every day, and I think it cannot be more strongly illustrated than by reference to this fashion of the Japanese women, who would be tolerably good looking if they were not to practice this singular custom. The young girls are well formed and rather pretty, their teeth not being blackened until they are married, but it would be folly to compare them with the females of corresponding rank and position in most parts of Europe, and in any part of our own country. In truth I can hardly be charged with national partiality in claiming that with respect to all the elements which constitute feminine—I say feminine not physical—beauty, the women of the United States undoubtedly deserve the palm. This may be accounted for by the admixture of the

---

* The color with which they paint themselves is called "bing," and is kept in little round porcelain bowls; with this they paint, not their cheeks as the Europeans do, but their lips, and lay the color on according to their own fancy. If the paint is very thin the lips appear red, but if it be laid on thick they become of a violet hue, which is here considered as the greater beauty. On a closer examination I found that this paint is made from the *carthamus tinctorious*.

That which distinguished the married women from the single were their black teeth which in their opinion were extremely beautiful, but in most other countries would be sufficient to make a man take French leave of his wife; to me at least, a wide mouth with black shining teeth had an ugly and disagreeable appearance.

The black which is used for this purpose is called *Ohaguro* or *Canni*, and is prepared from urine, filings of iron and *saké*: it is fetid and corrosive. It eats so deeply into the teeth that it takes several days and much trouble to scrape and wash it away. It is so corrosive that the gums and lips must be well covered while it is laid on, or it will turn them quite blue. Some begin to make use of this ornament as soon as they are courted or betrothed.

Thunberg, Vol. III, p. 78

European races, and the genial and generous climate in which they are reared, saying nothing of the respect and veneration by which they are held by the entire community.

Yokohama is a populous village, situated at the head of a bay (called, in our charts, Treaty Bay) which is formed by Point Hope on the southeast and the neck of land extending northeast from Kanagawa to the southern suburb of the city of Edo, Sinigawa [Shinagawa], and near to which the junks resorting to the capital usually anchor.

It may be said that the towns and villages lying upon the shores of the gulf and bay of Edo are continuous, excepting only where the projecting heads of high lands naturally forbid their erection. These places unavailable for domestic habitations are chiefly occupied by batteries of cannon, none of them, as I could judge, of caliber superior to five-inch bore.

Treaty House Kanagawa is quite a large town, and was the residence of the commissioners, pending the negotiations of the treaty. I should have selected this place for the erection of the treaty house, if it were not that the ships could not approach within gun shot of its front toward the bay, and therefore preferred to confirm Captain Adams' choice of Yokohama, since he had been sent to examine and report upon the most eligible anchorage for the squadron. At the position in front of Yokohama there was just sufficient room to anchor the whole squadron in a line of battle. The guns of the several ships commanded an extent of shore equal to their entire range.

At this time the squadron consisted of steam frigates *Powhatan* (flagship), *Susquehanna,* and *Mississippi,* and sail ships *Macedonian, Vandalia, Southampton,* and *Lexington.* This force was soon after joined by the *Saratoga* and *Supply,* making in all nine efficient vessels, a very respectable force, but much smaller than I had expected to have had.[12]

It has often been said and written by me, that this force was quite sufficient for all purposes of defense, and for the chastisement of insult, but not large enough to make any great moral impression, especially after the ostentatious display at home of the intentions of the government with respect to the Japan expedition. I claim the greater credit, however, in effecting more than the government anticipated, with the reduced means placed at my disposal, and under all the discouraging circumstances under which I labored.[13]

It is true, there has been no call for an exercise of force; and why? An interrogatory easily answered by replying that the Japanese government, without the slightest doubt in my mind, came to the conclusion after due deliberation not to bring about an issue of arms. Consequently from the moment of the passing of the flagship beyond Point Hope, all military show was studiously concealed. The great object of the commissioners was to

12. *Supply* arrived 19 March with coal and stores for the squadron.
13. Concluding four words of the paragraph added by Commodore Perry.

induce me to return to Uraga and not to ascend higher up the bay to
discover the defenseless condition of their capital. When they found that I
could not be deceived by their misrepresentations, they at once and with
apparent grace submitted to my ultimatum. From that time they discontinued a military work which had been commenced on Point Hope, and
destroyed by fire in the night as if by accident the sheds which had been
erected for the accommodation of the numerous workmen noticed to have
been employed before the passing of the ships toward Edo.

This policy was easily seen through. They found that resistance would be
useless, and very wisely determined to adopt peaceful measures and the
exercise of a system of diplomacy peculiarly Japanese to evade by every
possible means of falsehood and deceit the reasonable concessions demanded
by my government. The result proved that they had at last to concede even
more than was expected by the most sanguine of those through whose means
the expedition was set on foot.

In July last, on the occasion of our former visit, every means was adopted
to impress us with the extent of their military defenses. New works were
commenced, additional guns mounted and troops were constantly moving in
military array in view of the ships. I have little doubt that it has been
seriously discussed in the Japanese councils whether or not to resist by force
all intercourse with us.[14]

The building erected for the accommodation of the Japanese commissioners and myself—as well as the numerous persons in attendance—and which
I have called the Treaty House was placed upon a level plain near to the
shore. It was distant from Kanagawa three miles, and probably nine English
miles from the center of the city of Edo, and five from its southern suburbs.

The Treaty House was of one story and covered a large extent of ground,
having a reception hall about 40 by 60 feet, and several adjoining apartments and offices. In one of these rooms leading from the upper end of the
reception hall, our discussions took place, and it was here also that the treaty
was finally concluded and signed.

As another evidence of the suspicious nature of the Japanese character,
the entrance to the room in which we had our discussions had no door, and
was separated from the hall by a transparent flag, through which the attendants might see what was passing within.

It was said that the building would be taken down after our departure
from the bay, though I noticed on passing Kurihama, that those put up at
that place on the occasion of my reception in July last were still standing.

I shall endeavor briefly to describe the five commissioners, four of whom
signed the treaty, although the fifth was always present, apparently as counselor, or probably spy.

14. Commodore Perry was perfectly right. The Japanese had considered resisting by force
of arms and other wiles and stratagems as well. See Morison, "Old Bruin," p. 358.

The first, Hayashi, *Daigaku no kami* (i.e., prince counselor) aged about 55, well formed, of middle size, of grave and reserved deportment, was evidently looked upon as the chief, as all matters of importance were referred to him. He might be likened in appearance to Mr. Reverdy Johnson of Baltimore.[15]

The second, Ido prince of Tsushima, aged about 50, tall and rather corpulent, with a pleasant expression, resembling somewhat Mr. Buchanan,[16] our present minister to London.

The third and youngest, Izawa, prince of Mimasaka, aged 41, according to his own account, and the best looking of the number; he was quite gay, fond of fun and frolic, and had the reputation of being a Lothario. According to the representation of the interpreters, he entertained more liberal views with respect to foreign intercourse than either of his coadjutors, and seemed to be a favorite with the Japanese, as he certainly was with us. He manifested a great fondness for our music, and could not keep his hands and feet quiet when the bands were playing enlivening airs.

He resembled somewhat Mr. Tho. Corwin.[17]

The fourth, Nagatoshi Udono, a member of the Board of Revenue, about 55 years of age, tall, having prominent features, could be compared in appearance to Mr. Cave Johnson[18] of Tennessee, though probably not as tall.

The fifth, Michitaro Matsuzaki, of whose rank and title I am ignorant, is about 60 years of age, tall and lank, and very nearsighted; in outward appearance grave and unsociable, but from what we saw of him, rather fond of the [gaudy and] good things of the world, a prevailing propensity I should judge with all of high rank in this country. I refrain from comparing him with anyone at home, although I have his double in my mind's eye. The precise business of this man in the commission I could not learn. He sat with the other commissioners, but at the end of the divan, nearest the entrance to the room, and had before him, crouched upon his knees, a scribe who was constantly employed in taking note of what was passing, occasionally under the promptings of his superior.

As he was far from handsome.

The room in which the business of the treaty was transacted could not have been more than twelve feet square, having at one end the entrance as before described, and at the other a window with sashes similar to those in our country, but instead of glass, oiled paper was used. Across the end of this little apartment, and at both sides, divans or wide covered benches were placed. Hayashi, the chief commissioner, was seated nearest the window,

15. This prominent attorney, Senator from Maryland, 1845–1849, later served as minister to England and negotiated the Johnson-Clarendon Treaty.
16. James Buchanan, Minister to London, 1853–1856, was 15th President of the United States, 1857–1861.
17. Thomas Corwin, Secretary of the Treasury, 1850–1853.
18. Cave Johnson, Postmaster General, 1845–1849.

and at the right of his associates, and they in succession, according to their rank.

Directly opposite to Hayashi, and on a corresponding divan, I was seated. The four officers—Commander Adams, my secretary Mr. Perry, and the two interpreters Messrs. Williams and Portman—occupied corresponding positions opposite the four other commissioners.[19]

Between Hayashi and myself, the chief interpreter, Einosuke Moriyama, placed himself upon his knees, and all the communications were made through him. First I spoke in English to Mr. Portman, who communicated the same in Dutch to Moriyama, and he translated it to the first commissioner in the Japanese tongue. The replies were communicated to me in the same way. My written communications were addressed in the English, Dutch, and Chinese languages, and the replies came to me in Japanese, Dutch, and Chinese. The translations were always verified by the chief interpreter.

See drawing following this page.[20]

No people in the world exceed the Japanese in politeness and courtesy as well to strangers as to each other, and they are as systematic in that as in all other matters, suiting the forms of their salutations to the rank and position of the person saluted. Indeed such are the gradations of rank and place among them that all seem to understand as well the respect due to themselves as that which they are bound to pay to the classes above them. They have often reminded me of an amusement of children, of placing a number of bricks on end in a row. In knocking over the first against the one next to it, the whole are in succession prostrated, and so from the peasant of Japan to the Emperor, one makes obeisance to the other. The only difference is, the Emperor, being the cornerstone of all temporal power, is supreme and bows only to some pagan idol.

The prefect, Kahei Kura-kawa [Kurokawa], and the chief interpreter were always prostrate before the commissioners, with downcast eyes. These in their turn had their satellites, and never passed beyond the sight of the greater luminaries than they expected to be reverenced by inferiors.

It should be remarked that the crouching position in which the inferiors place themselves when addressing those of higher rank, seems to be to them one of ease, and acquired by practice from infancy, though to us it would be one of torture. The position taken by all who were in attendance at the treaty house was to crop their feet under them with the heels up, and to rest the body upon the knees, the upper part of the toes, and the instep; with the hams and calves of the legs brought together. Another mode and one of less ceremony is to rest upon the soles of the feet, and to bring the hams down in contact with the calves of the legs. This is followed more generally at Lew

19. The Japanese artist of the adjoining scene is unknown but he depicted the same setting as did interpreter Portman. The principal difference is the seating order of the Americans.

20. This pencil sketch by Dutch interpreter Portman comes from the journal of William Speiden, Jr., assistant to his father, the purser of *Mississippi*. It must be the "drawing" referred to by Commodore Perry, but young Speiden somehow got it for his own (contraband) journal.

Chew, and sometimes, though very rarely, they are seen when in the shops sitting cross-legged, tailor fashion.

Japanese Costumes and Collations

The costumes of the various classes are as unchangeable in fashion, cut, and color as are unchangeable their laws and customs, and the rank and condition of the wearer are known by their dress. None but those of the higher rank are allowed to wear white as a sort of under shirt or vest, the upper part of which is shown over the chest, and inside the outer robe. I noticed that only the three princes composing the commission had this white vest and my attention was called to this peculiarity by the interpreters.

The daily dress of the higher classes is an undergarment, something similar to an old-fashioned doublet, and a pair of very wide trousers of figured silk, reaching nearly to the ankles, with cotton or woolen socks, laced above the ankle bone. These socks are made to allow the great toe to be separated from the other four, for the convenience of securing sandals upon the feet. Over the doublet and trousers is worn a sort of gown secured to the waist by a strong sash or girdle, between which and the gown the two swords are thrust. The sleeves of the gown are made short and very large with pockets, into which the hands are put in cold weather. Everyone carries in another large pocket in the left and inner side of the gown over the breast, a large wallet filled with square pieces of white paper with writing materials. The paper is used indifferently for making notes, or for the same purpose for which we use a pocket handkerchief. And each person wears upon one or more parts of the dress the armorial badge of his own family, or that of the person of whom he is a vassal or retainer.

But the numerous drawings which will be appended to this journal will furnish a much better idea of the costumes of the country than I can possibly describe in writing. No very great praise can be given to the fare of these people. However sumptuous they may be in outward show and pomp, their kitchens do not furnish anything remarkable if we are to judge from what we have seen; or if the dinner given by the commissioners on the occasion of the signing of the treaty can as it certainly ought to be taken as a test of their gastronomic propensities and tastes.

It is true that apologies were made, and causes assigned for the meagreness of the dinner, for reason principally of the difficulty of obtaining the best things at Kanagawa, but this was a shallow excuse as Edo was close at hand, and the cooks of the prince of Tsushima were in attendance. The dinner given by me on board *Powhatan* to the commissioners and their several escorts would have made twenty such as theirs.

The dishes if so they may be called were prepared in a manner similar to the Chinese and Lew Chew mode of cookery; they were chiefly thick soups or rather thin stews, in most of which fresh fish was a component. These were served in succession, in small bowls, accompanied by soy and other

Meeting Hall business session, 8 March 1854. Portman sketch from journal of William Speiden, Jr.
(Courtesy Naval Historical Foundation)

Meeting hall collation, 8 March 1854. Sketch by Japanese artist. Setting order of Americans is (nearest) O. H. Perry,
Commander Adams, A. L. C. Portman, S. Wells Williams, and Commodore Perry. (Courtesy Shiryo Hensanjo)

188 condiments. Confectionary and cakes were also a universal accompaniment, saying nothing of the *saké,* strong and weak, which was served hot or cold.

The different courses were brought to the table on small lacquered stands, probably 14 inches square, and 10 high, and one for each guest. The dining tables were nothing more than wide benches such as we sat on and of the same height; these were covered with colored crepe, and the stands containing each one's portion placed in front of the·respective guests.

Near the close of the dinner, a plate containing a boiled crawfish, a piece of fried fish, two or three boiled shrimp and a small square pudding,[21] something of the consistency of blanc mange was placed before each one with a hint that it was to follow us on board ship, and accordingly they were sent after us.

If this entertainment were to be taken as a criterion of their mode of living we might reasonably have doubted whether its scantiness and want of elegance were not accidental. Yet on several other occasions tables were arranged for us, not as plentiful to be sure, but very much of the same character of dishes and of cookery. On the whole, I give the Lew Chewans decidedly the palm in gastronomy over the Japanese and the Chinese.

Reception on Board Powhatan
27 MARCH 1854

Two days before this display of the commissioners, I had entertained them on board *Powhatan,* and learned from the chief interpreter that they could not sit at table with any of their followers or escorts, in number about seventy, exclusive of the menials and boatmen.

I spared no pains in providing most bountifully for this numerous party, being desirous of giving them some idea of American hospitality in comparison with their portions of fish soup. My Paris cook labored for a week, night and day, in getting up a variety of ornamental dishes which would have done credit to Delmonico of New York. I had always intended to have given this dinner if the negotiations had taken a favorable turn, and had therefore retained alive a bullock, sheep and many kinds of poultry. These with hams, tongues, and numerous preserved fish, vegetables, and fruit furnished an abundant feast, not only for the Japanese, but for all the officers of the squadron, who were invited to join the party, the better to entertain the Japanese guests. Of course there was plenty of champagne and other wines with a good supply of punch for the upper table, and in the cabin almost every description of delicate wines for the commissioners with liqueurs, which they seemed to prefer, especially maraschino.

The chief commissioner Hayashi ate and drank sparingly though tasting of almost everything, but the others proved themselves good trenchermen, Matsuzaki getting gloriously drunk, and the other three quite mellow.

Besides the five commissioners, I had at my table Captains Abbot, Walker, Adams, and Lee, and Messrs. Williams and Perry. As a special condescen-

21. This was probably *tofu,* a bean-curd cake.

sion the chief commissioner permitted Moriyama to take some dinner at a side table.

The party on deck was very uproarious, the Japanese taking the lead in proposing toasts and cheering "à l'Anglaise" at the top of their lungs whilst two bands stationed nearby added to the din.

Notwithstanding the quantity and variety of viands placed upon the table, they all disappeared as if by magic. What they could not eat, the Japanese took away in their capacious pockets, wrapped in paper, which everyone always, in accordance with their custom, carries with him, neatly folded in a large wallet in abundant supply—as well for the nose as to make notes—and to contain the remains of whatever of eatables may be left when enjoying the hospitality of their friends. On every occasion of our partaking of their meals they brought each one of us papers to wrap anything we desired to take on board ship. They frequently selected confectionary and cakes, put them in paper themselves, and thrust them into our hands.

It was curious to notice their indifference to the description or quality of the dishes from which they made their selections to take away. They mingled meats, stews, and preserves altogether regardless of gravies or syrups.

Previous to the dinner hour the commissioners with their attendants visited the *Macedonian* and saw the crew of that ship at general exercise and also witnessed the movements of the engines of *Powhatan,* put in motion purposely for their examination. They were saluted by *Macedonian, Mississippi,* and *Saratoga,* and after retiring from the table were entertained on deck with the performances of the very excellent corps of Ethiopians belonging to *Powhatan.* Even the gravity of Hayashi could not withstand the hilarity which this most amusing exhibition excited. He and his coadjutors laughed as merrily as ever the spectators at Christy's have done.[22] At sunset they all left the ship with quite as much wine as they could well bear. Matsuzaki threw his arms about my neck and repeated in Japanese as interpreted into English: "Nippon and America, all the same heart," and in his drunken embrace crushed my new epaulettes.

The following day when we met at the Treaty House to conclude the business of the treaty preparatory to its being signed, the old gentleman looked quite grave, his gravity doubtless proceeding from the effects of the debauch on board ship.

Entertainment Ashore

31 MARCH 1854

I have already presented a brief description of the dinner given by the commissioners on 31 March in commemoration of the signing of the treaty, and it remains for me to mention the show gotten up on the occasion.

On proceeding to the large audience hall after landing, I was met by the five commissioners who pointed out to me various presents which were

22. Christy's Minstrels toured the United States and England receiving popular acclaim and being widely imitated. Edwin P. Christy (1815–1862), as interlocutor and singer, popularized Stephen Foster songs, which were first published under Christy's name. Perry crewmen provided entertainment in emulation of Christy's Minstrels, billed as The Ethiopians.

190 arranged on benches. The commissioners stood in a line at the head of the hall, whilst the chief interpreter called off from written lists the several presents, by whom presented, and for whom intended. These consisted of lacquered ware, silks, and other articles the production of Japan, of no very great value, the reason of which they explained by remarking that they had not had time to prepare more suitable gifts; that before my departure from Shimoda, a collection better corresponding with those I had given would be provided. Every individual composing what in the Army language would be considered the staff—and in Naval lingo any term you might choose to give it—was remembered, and the interpreter announced the names of each as the presents were pointed out.

This matter being over, I was ushered into the small retiring room already described and in a few moments the documents embodying the treaty in the English and Japanese languages were brought out and signed, and in a manner already described in the notes which I have forwarded to the government. After this great object of my mission was accomplished, I felt myself relieved of an immense weight of responsibility, made more so by previous representations, and acts of my own which led to the organization of the Japan expedition.

I was now told that one of the articles intended to be presented to the President had not yet been exhibited, and was requested to walk out of the building. The commissioners leading the way, we went to the nearby beach, where we saw some two hundred bales of rice piled up ready for being sent on board the ships. The interpreter remarked that with the Japanese, on all occasions of making presents, a certain quantity of rice was always included.

After we were seated near to these bales some twenty-five or thirty huge men, naked with the exception of a narrow girdle around the loins, were paraded before us. Never have I seen grouped together so many brawny men, giving a better idea of an equal number of stall-fed bulls than human beings. These men were professional wrestlers, most of them belonging to the retinues of the commissioners, though there were one or two of the highest reputation in Edo, the Tom Cribbs and Tom Hyers[23] of the country. One of them was especially brought to me that I might examine his massive form; massive because his frame was covered with a mass of flesh, which to our ideas of athletic qualities would seem to incapacitate him from any violent exercise.

He was richly dressed, and seemed to have attendants of his own, who very carefully and respectfully unrobed him in the open air, leaving him entirely naked, excepting the invariable strip of cloth round the loins. I was requested to feel the hardness of his immense arms, and his double bull neck. When he observed that I manifested much surprise, he exhibited his gratification by a self-satisfied grunt. See drawing, copied from a Japanese print.[24]

23. Hall of Fame heavyweight boxer Cribb (1781–1848) of England, and Hyer (1819–1864), America's first heavyweight champion.
24. No drawing in original Journal, but photograph is from a contemporary Japanese print.

Dinner given by the Japanese Commissioners at Yokohama, 31 March 1854. Rough sketch by artist Hideki
(Courtesy Shiryo Hensanjo)

Finished Hideki painting of Japanese dinner at Yokohama. (Courtesy Shiryo Hensanjo)

192   After this scene had passed, the whole troop of naked giants commenced transporting, for our edification and amusement, the bales of rice from the spot upon which they had been at first deposited, to a convenient place near the shore in readiness for shipping. These bales weighed each 135 pounds, and each man with two exceptions carried two on his right shoulder, the first being lifted from the ground and placed by himself, but in shouldering the other he was assisted. One man carried a bale suspended by his teeth, and another held one in his arms and repeatedly turned a somerset upon the ground, retaining the bale in the same embrace.

During this exhibition the bands of the squadron played some of their best airs. When they terminated, Captain Tansill, commanding the guard of Marines, at the request of the commissioners, put his men through several evolutions. By this time arrangements had been made for the wrestling match and we were escorted back to the audience hall in the portico of which seats were arranged for the commissioners and myself and other officers, and the wrestlers.

Those "Daniel Lamberts"[25] were paraded before us in two opposing parties, naked and prepared for the contest. On passing behind screens they were covered with robes which they retained until brought into the ring. This was a circular space of about twelve feet diameter, carefully prepared with the earth broken up and smoothed, and every hard substance removed.

On a signal being given by a person who seemed to be a sort of herald, two whose names were called stepped into the ring and began to eye each other with threatening looks, rather dramatic to be sure, stamping the soft ground with their naked feet, stooping down and grasping handfuls of the earth with which they rubbed themselves under the arm pits, and seemed to besmear the palms of their hands. Whether this was to imitate the action of the bull, who paws the earth when preparing for an attack, or for what purpose, I am ignorant, but it seemed to be very foolish.

At last they placed themselves opposite to each other crouched upon their hams, each warily watching the eye and movements of his antagonist. Quick as lightning they sprang upon each other, and writhing their arms about the upper parts of the bodies of their opponents commenced a contest which was neither wrestling nor boxing. Each occasionally was whirled about by some extraordinary effort of the arms and thrown violently upon the ground. One of their modes of attack was to strike their foreheads and breasts together with the greatest apparent wrath, the blood flowing from the forehead and the flesh covering the breast bones. Some were so severely wounded as to cause large indurated excresences to be formed.

One of the contestants invariably exhibited the greatest rage, constantly howling and screeching at the top of his lungs, making a noise similar to that of dogs in combat. This was evidently to show that he was the attacking party, as his opponent seemed to be occupied only in defending himself from

25. Professional English fat man (1770–1809) who at death weighed 739 pounds; other statistics: height 5'11", waist 9'4", leg girth 3'1".

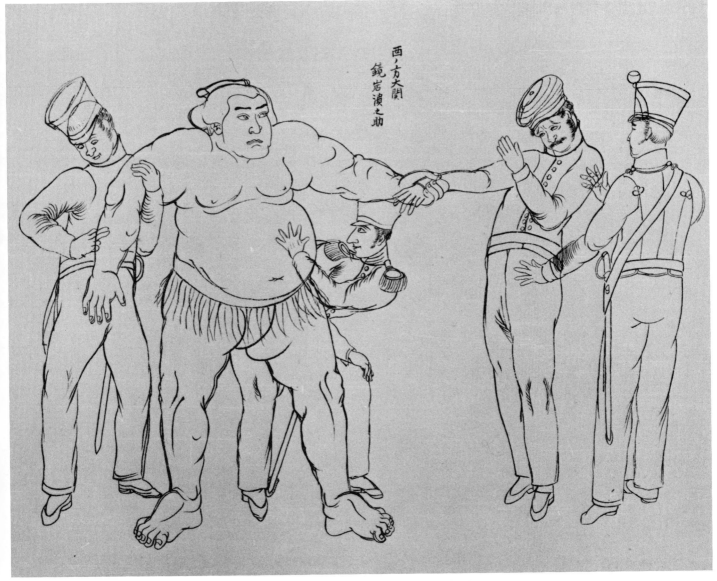

西ノ方大関
鏡岩濱之助

Marines examine *sumo* wrestler, 24 March 1854

the attacks of his enraged assailant. It was noticed by all the officers that the one who made the noise was in every instance overcome.

This farce continued until all had taken a bout, not excepting Koyanagi the reputed bully of the capital, who seemed to labor like a Chinese junk in chow-chow water, but as a matter of course he was triumphant and remained master of the field.

Gifts

This being over, we now proceeded to examine the presents sent by the President to the Emperor, and particularly to witness the operations of the magnetic telegraph and the movements of the locomotive engine around its circumscribed track, preparatory to these and other articles being formally presented and received. The Japanese being equally formal in the presentation and receiving of presents, the ceremony was yet to come off.

Steam had been raised in the little furnace, the car attached, and the secretary of one of the commissioners, not a little alarmed, was placed upon the roof of the car whilst Mr. Danby sat upon the tender feeding the fire with one hand and managing the engine with the other. The beautiful little machine whirled round the circle filling the air with its shrill steam whistle, to the astonishment and delight of the immense crowd collected. After this the telegraph was for the last time put in operation, and the commissioners having also seen the numerous agricultural implements and their various uses being briefly explained to them, the prince of Mimasaka was deputed on the part of the commissioners to go through the form of accepting the President's gifts. Captain Adams received the same authority from me to present them, which was done by a half dozen formal bows on both sides.

The bales of rice were sent to the *Supply* and the miscellaneous presents to *Powhatan,* and on the following day were examined and compared with the lists furnished, and a few articles were found to be missing, abstracted probably by the Japanese servants.[26]

All were put in suitable packages and carefully marked with the names of the persons for whom they were intended, and the whole packed in strong boxes, addressed to the Navy Department and sent to the *Supply* to be shipped to the United States, subject to the decision of the government, whether to forward them to the persons to whom they were given, or deposit them in the State Department, or sell them at auction for the benefit of the Treasury.

They were of little value as will be perceived by reference to the list on the following page. [See Appendix D for list of American gifts.]

List of presents received from the Emperor of Japan and his high ministers for the government of the United States and others.

26. Commodore Perry also inserted "somebody" and another word or two which are illegible.

1st. From the Emperor.

   1 lacquered writing table.

   1 gold   "   book case.

   1   "   "   paper box.

   1   "   "   writing apparatus.

   1 bronze censer on stand, shaped like an ox with silver flower on his back.

   1 set of two lacquered trays.

   1 bamboo bouquet holder and stand.

   2 braziers or censers with silver tops.

   10 pieces fine red pongee.

   10   "   fine white pongee.

   5   "   each figured and dyed flower crape.

   2 swords and 3 matchlocks.

2nd. From Abe, prince of Ise.

   15 pieces striped and figured pongee or taffeta.

3rd to 7th. From Matsudaira and each of the other four imperial councilors.

   10 pieces striped and figured pongee or taffeta silk, 50 pieces in all.

8th. From Hayashi, 1st commissioner.

   1 lacquered writing apparatus.

   1 lacquered paper box.

   1 box flowered paper.

   5   "   stamped note paper.

   1   "   flowered note paper.

   1   "   branch of coral and silver feather of "byssus."

   1 lacquered chow chow box.

   8 boxes cups and spoons of conch shell and shell cup.

   100 kinds sea shells in 4 boxes.

   1 box 3 lacquered cups.

9th. From Ido, 2d commissioner.

   2 boxes lacquered waiters, 2 in each.

   2   "   20 umbrellas each.

   1   "   30 coir brooms.

10th. From Izawa, 3d commissioner.

   2 pieces red and white pongee.

   8 boxes of 13 dolls.

   1   "   bamboo ware.

   2   "   bamboo low tables.

11th. From Udono, 4th commissioner.

   3 pieces striped crape.

   2 boxes 20 porcelain cups.

   1   "   soy, 10 jars.

12th. From Michitaro Matsuzaki.

   3 boxes porcelain cups.

   1   "   figured matting.

   35 bundles oak charcoal.

13th. For Commodore Perry from the Emperor.

   1 lacquered writing apparatus.

   1   "   paper box.

   3 pieces red and 2 pieces white pongee.

   3   "   dyed and 2 pieces flowered crape.

14th. From the commissioners, for Captain Adams.

    3 pieces plain red pongee.

    2   "   red dyed figured crape.

    20 lacquered cups and covers.

15th to 17th. For Messrs. S. W. Williams, O. H. Perry, and A. C. Portman.

    2 pieces red pongee.

    2   "   red dyed figured crape.   }—to each.

    10 lacquered cups and covers.

18th to 22d. For Messrs. J. Gay, R. Danby, J. Williams, J. Morrow, W. B. Draper.

    1 piece dyed figured crape.

    10 lacquered cups and covers.   }—to each.

23d. For the squadron from the Emperor.

    300 fowls.

    200 bales rice, each 135 pounds.

24th. For United States of America from the prefect and interpreters.

    5 pieces figured crape.

This may be a very proper law, but it bears very hard upon the officers, who in their intercourse with the Asiatic and other eastern nations must necessarily conform to the practices which govern such intercourse. They consequently are put to inconvenient expense in gratuities to attendants upon those whom the public duties require them to visit, and in presents and entertainments to functionaries visiting the ships.

The presents which they receive in return though rarely of any intrinsic value would be prized by them as memorials of interesting events in their lives. But the government becomes the recipient of these trifles, and makes no compensation to the officer for his outlay.

The government of the United States is the only one in the world that expects of its naval officers serving abroad to reciprocate, even under instructions, the civilities of foreign officers without making the slightest provision for the expenses which must be the consequence of such civilities, i.e., entertainments.

A commanding officer returning from a responsible and laborious cruise, during which he deems it necessary to effect certain objects, stated to be important by the instructions of his government, ventures into expenses in which he can have no private interest, presents on arrival at Washington his accounts to the department, and is told that the law forbids any allowances for such extra expenses, however necessary and proper they may have been. He is coolly advised to apply to Congress for justice, an alternative by no means agreeable to a man of independent feelings. Unless he resorts to the disgraceful practice of employing agents at an exorbitant contingent fee to prosecute his claims, he stands very little chance of obtaining justice.

These remarks were made before my return to the U.S. The action of Congress in my case modifies these remarks.[27]

With all other nations and governments—including the most insignificant in political consequence—suitable allowances are made to defray the reasonable contingent expenses of those entrusted with specific duties, and

27. By an appropriations act of 3 March 1855, Congress voted $20,000 to Commodore Perry for extraordinary expenses incurred on his Japanese expedition. *U.S. Statutes At Large*, volume 10, page 659.

Sumo wrestlers carrying rice bales at Yokohama, 24 March 1854. (Courtesy Mariner's Museum)

Norris Locomotive, ¼-scale model, with tender and passenger car. (Courtesy Shiryo Hensanjo)

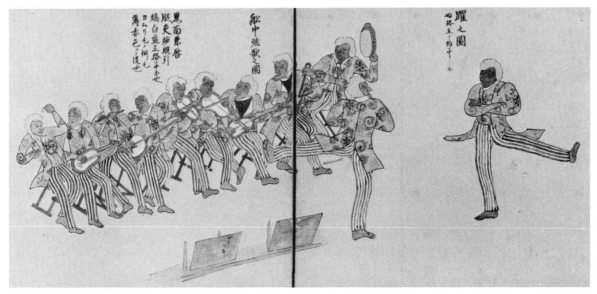

Japanese sketch of the *Powhatan* minstrels. (Courtesy Shiryo Hensanjo.)

of those also who may by their position be called upon to incur extra expenses. In order to secure proper economy in these matters, fixed allowances are established by most European governments, as well for table money as for extraordinary expenses. Upon us the most responsible duties are imposed with exacting expectations of their faithful fulfillment, without the slightest consideration of the personal inconvenience and expense to which the officer is subjected. It is not unusual for the government to offer passages in our ships of war, and to recommend to the civilities of naval officers persons of rank and consideration, regardless of the circumscribed accommodations of the officer, and his equally narrow purse.

Approach to Edo

From the day of the signing of the treaty, up to the departure of the *Saratoga* for home, via California, on 4 April (with Commander Adams on board, in charge of that important document, under instructions to land at the most convenient point, whether in California or Mexico, for intercepting either of the mail steamers), I was busily engaged in preparing my despatches and private letters to be sent by her. From that time to the 10th I was occupied in completing my business at Yokohama. On the 9th, notwithstanding the urgent remonstrances of the commissioners, I informed the chief interpreter, that I should on the following day approach with the steamers as near to Edo as the depth of water would allow. Accordingly on the 10th the whole squadron got under way and the *Powhatan* and *Mississippi* doubled the point near to Shinagawa, the southern suburb, and we came in full view of this far-famed capital, but unfortunately a mist or haze, so common upon this coast, prevented our seeing objects very distinctly.

We could distinguish, however, the outline of the city and the description and character of the buildings as similar to those of Uraga and other places visited by us. Several "dungaree" forts[28] were visible, and what seemed to be fortified places commanding the city, but we may have mistaken Buddhist temples for what in the distance seemed to be forts; as these buildings are more conspicuous, and are usually higher than the ordinary dwelling houses.

We observed along the whole sea front of the city, a row of high palisades, some distance from the margin of the shore, with occasional openings for the admission inside of boats or small junks. Whether this was intended to defend the city from an attack of boats, or to protect the landing places from the effects of the sea, is of course a matter of uncertainty. Possibly they may have been put up before our arrival to prevent the approach of our armed boats in the supposition that we might attempt to land by force. One thing is quite certain, the city of Edo can be destroyed by a few steamers of very light draft, and carrying guns of the heaviest caliber.

In consequence of the strong ebb tide, the boats that were pulling ahead

28. A name applied by Perry and his men to Tokyo Bay forts and hastily erected earthworks which were partially concealed by canvas screens.

sounding the channel toward the city, which is formed by sand banks, could 199 make but little headway—owing in a measure to the exhaustion of the men —and the steamers also stemming the tide, could not be kept under safe steerage. The sail ships had already anchored some distance astern, as I had promised, in order to allay the apprehensions of the commissioners not to anchor the steamers near to the city, but merely to take a look at it.

The fears of the commissioners were founded upon the supposition that if the squadron were to anchor near to and in full view of the city, the populace would become so much affrighted as to produce the greatest disorder, resulting in disastrous consequences. Although they did not particularly name the Emperor and his household, I am satisfied that they were deeply concerned with respect to him and the court.

As the law forbids the Emperor to leave the capital, excepting on certain state occasions, which do not now occur more than two or three times in a reign for reason of the expense of such pageants,* he could not leave his palace without a violation of such law.

*Our departure from Jedo was fixed for the 25th of May [1776] and was to take place inevitably, as the 13th of Siguats, or the 30th of May, was appointed by Kubo, the reigning secular emperor, for his setting out on a journey to the temple of Niko [Nikko], which is very large, stands thirty-six leagues to the east of Jedo, and was the place where a great festival was to be kept. This journey had been in agitation three years, and a great many preparations made for it, although it had been continually put off from year to year.

As both the monarch himself, and all the princes of the country are clothed, and their hair dressed, in the same manner as the rest of the inhabitants, and consequently, being destitute of thrones, jewels, and the rest of their paraphernalia, cannot be distinguished from others, they have adopted the expedient of exhibiting themselves on journies and festive occasions according to their condition in life, and the dignity of their respective offices, with a great number of people, officers, and attendants hovering about them. It was therefore necessary that extraordinary preparations should be made for the supreme ruler of the country. On the roads, new houses were to be built to bait at, as well at night as in the daytime. Every convenience that could be thought of was to be in abundance, and previously in proper order at each place. All the domestics, both before and during the journey, were to be in the highest degree vigilant, every one in his station. During Kubo's absence, the imperial citadel was to be in charge with the prince of the province of Mito, and the government with some of the privy counsellors. Orders had already been issued out that a careful watch should be kept everywhere to prevent fires, popular commotions, and other untoward accidents. The money ordered to defray the expenses of the journey amounted to 280,000 kobangs, or 1,680,000 rixdollars. Of this money distributions were made to the privy counsellors, princes of the country, and others who were to be in the emperor's suite. The journey was to be performed to the temple of Nikko in three days, and the day after their arrival was to be a day of rest. On the 17th of Siguats, or the third of July,[29] the festival was to be celebrated, and the day following they were to set out on their return home. At our departure on the 25th of May from Jedo, we already saw several large companies, which were to go before; but three days before the emperor set out, such companies as these began to follow very close

29. Thunberg meant June.

upon each other. On the day before the emperor's departure, toward the evening, they crowded so close on each other, that there was only an interval of half an hour between the appearance of each company; and this continued till five o'clock in the morning, when the emperor himself set out with the hereditary prince. In the train of this innumerable multitude, followed, as the interpreters informed us, several very old men, beggars, executioners, and even coffins, that nothing might be wanting to complete the procession.

Thunberg, Vol. III, pages 207–9

Therefore, in consideration of the very kind and friendly manner in which I had been received by the princes, and placing some reliance in their repeated assurances that they would be held personally accountable for any catastrophe that might result from anchoring the steamers off the city and saluting the palace as I at first intended—though somewhat incredulous as to the necessity of their performing the *hari-kari* [*harakiri*][30] upon themselves—I thought it the better policy not to proceed so far in my previous determination as to bring about an issue that would endanger the very friendly position which we already held with these people. It would have been a source of never-ending regret for which I could not have forgiven myself if, to gratify a profitless curiosity, misfortune should have been brought upon our good friends the commissioners. Therefore the squadron was ordered to the American Anchorage from whence *Macedonian* was despatched the next day for Peel Island. The remainder of the squadron proceeded on different days of sailing for Shimoda.*

Shimoda

18 APRIL–13 MAY 1854

I purposely sent them in succession in order to enable the first that arrived time for examining the harbor, and selecting convenient anchoring places for those that were to follow. And it was fortunate that I took this precaution, as the *Southampton* in warping into the inner port, came upon a rock lying directly in the middle of the channel, on which there is but twelve feet of water at low tide; a danger which had escaped the hasty examination of Lieutenant Bent.

It is quite probable that if it had not been for this timely discovery, one or both of the steamers would have struck upon it, as it is not more than 35 feet in diameter, and made the more dangerous for being cone shaped. Lieutenant Commander Boyle had very prudently placed a buoy upon it, which enabled the steamers to pass in without inconvenience, though the channel is at this point only 600 yards wide.

Both steamers had sufficient room to moor without interfering with the *Southampton* and *Supply*, already in the inner harbor. The *Lexington* also

* *Southampton* and *Supply* left the American Anchorage for Shimoda on the 14th; *Vandalia* and *Lexington* on the 16th; and *Powhatan* and *Mississippi* on the 18th of April.

30. The scrivener made the mistake of many foreigners who pronounce this particular kind of suicide as if it were Harry Carey. The word consists of *hara* (stomach) and *kiri* (cut).

came in and anchored but Captain Pope in *Vandalia* preferred a position farther out.

The ports of Shimoda and Hakodate—being those assigned by treaty for the admission of vessels of the United States under certain rights and privileges never before granted to the people of any foreign nation—possessed an uncommon interest. We may except Nagasaki where the Dutch and Chinese are admitted to limited privileges, but upon an entirely different footing compared to our treaty rights.

There can be no better harbor than this for a limited number of vessels, and when its contiguity to the sea, its easy and safe approach, and its convenience of ingress and egress are taken into consideration, I do not see how a more desirable port could have been selected to answer all the purposes for which it is wanted.

Enlarge at the next visit upon a description of Shimoda.

Having remained at anchor in the inner harbor since the 18th of the preceding month (April), wearing away the time until the near approach of the day appointed for my being at Hakodate (19 May) I sailed for that port on the 13th in company with *Mississippi*—the other ships of the squadron having been despatched a week before.

On leaving the outer harbor O Shima and others of the cluster of islands lying at the entrance of the gulf of Edo were in full sight. The ships were steered to pass near to the southern end of O Shima, as well to examine the island as to have a near view of the volcano, at the time in active eruption. There seemed to be either a number of craters, or one of great extent, as we could see the vapor and smoke rising at short intervals and at different places along the crest of a ridge of mountains extending four or five miles.

After passing O Shima, we hauled up for Cape King, in view of establishing the position of that important headland by our meridian observations. Up to the southern end of O Shima I could discover but little current, but after we reached the channel between that island and Cape King it ran with considerable rapidity in a direction nearly east, and on approaching and doubling the cape, its velocity increased.

In running along the coast between Capes Susaki,[31] Serofama [Shirahama][32] and Firatatsi [Erachi],[33] the last being usually called Cape King, the three forming the principal southern headlands of the promontory of Awa [the southern half of Chiba Prefecture], we had opportunities of noticing the extraordinary extent and perfection of cultivation of the land. Every little nook, up to the very summits of the mountains was terraced and planted with grain. Upon the hillsides and in the valleys, towns and villages were seen in every direction. After passing Cape King the same scenery presented itself as far as the eye could reach.

Northward Bound

31. Latitude 34°58′ N, longitude 139°45′ E.
32. Latitude 34°54′ N, longitude 139°54′ E.
33. Latitude 34°57′ N, longitude 139°58′ E.

During the entire day we were within the influence of the stream, called by the Japanese Kuroshio,[34] which never ceases to run in a northeasterly direction, and which will be fully described in the appendix[35] of this journal.

Cape King, the southeastern extremity of the great island of Nippon and as before observed also of the promontory of Awa, is in latitude 34°53′15″ north, and longitude 140°18′50″ east,[36] as deduced from observations taken on board the *Powhatan* and *Mississippi*. This headland runs off in an easterly direction to a low point rising gradually inland, and at about two miles from the extremity of the point is a cone-shaped elevation crowned by a tuft of trees.

A little more than halfway between Cape King and Cape Shirahama and near to the shore, is another conical hill also crowned with trees, which makes a good landmark.

Vessels from the eastward bound to Shimoda should endeavor to make Cape King and after getting it to bear north, distant six miles, should steer for the southern end of O Shima, which from this position can be seen in clear weather. After passing the southern end of O Shima, steer west for the harbor, observing the following sailing directions. I make no allowance for currents which are rapid and irregular throughout the Gulf of Edo; therefore the only sure guides are the charts, the cross bearings of the most prominent islands, and last of all, a good lookout.

The marks for approaching Shimoda from all directions are so numerous and so conspicuous that there can be no possibility of mistake. The only real dangers are Redfield Rocks,[37] already described, which bear from Rock Island[38] S by W westerly 41 miles and lie in latitude 33°56′13″ north, and longitude 138°48′31″ east.

Returning to my remarks upon our passage to Hakodate. At 2 P.M. whilst steering along the shore to the northward and being off Isomura[39] with a good many fishing boats around us, the steamers being about six miles from the land, we noticed a discoloration of the water with an unusual drift of gulf weed. Sounded with the deep-sea lead and got 74 and shortly after 80 fathoms, the lead bringing up fine black sand.

Still continuing to run along the shore within five or six miles, and having made Dai ho Saki [Taito Zaki][40] (White Cape) we noticed a cluster of fishing boats under sail, apparently trailing for fish, and about them broken and discolored water. On approaching them within a mile, stopped the engines and obtained soundings in 30 fathoms, coral bottom, and though on the eastern edge of this broken water and the ship's course being changed from

34. Blank space in manuscript, but Perry refers to this Kuroshio (lit., "black current") in a Hawks *Narrative* appendix (pp. 363–72), comparing it with the Gulf Stream of the Atlantic.
35. Words "the appendix," in Perry's hand, replace the scrivener's "another part."
36. These coordinates are a few minutes off, as may be seen by comparing them with footnote 33 above.
37. Called Zeni Su in Japan, in latitude 33°56′ N, longitude 138°48′ E.
38. Miyake Jima.
39. Now part of Kamogawa-machi, latitude 35°06′ N, longitude 140°06′ E.
40. Latitude 35°18′ N, longitude 140°25′ E.

NE by E to southeast, and moving very slowly, we suddenly fell into 21 fathoms, coral bottom, from the appearance of the discolored water being such as are called overfalls. I am satisfied that this is a dangerous ledge lying directly in the fairway along the coast, and at a distance at which such danger would not be looked for. I should have anchored and examined this ledge, were it not that night was approaching and my engagements made it necessary that I should reach Hakodate by the 19th. Although in good weather this might be easily accomplished a day or two before the time appointed, I was aware of the prevalence of fogs about the Strait of Sangar, and experience had taught me that in latitudes subject to these annoying visitations, no calculation could be made as to length of passage.

The southern and eastern coast of Japan from Cape Shirahama, as far as I have observed, is not so high as that on the western side of the Gulf of Edo. It is, however, of sufficient height to be seen from 40 miles in tolerably clear weather.

We continued along the coast during the day and at night hauling a little off. On the 15th we were in sight of Cape Kurosaki, the elevated peaks in the interior being covered with snow. The atmosphere was fresh and invigorating. The mean temperature of the air was 59° Fahrenheit, and that of the water 55°. Great numbers of whales of different kinds were seen today, also some porpoises. The water was perfectly smooth and partaking of an oily appearance, the surface being covered with a substance supposed to be the excrement of whales.

At daylight of the 16th we shaped our course at an angle approaching the coast and, after again making the land, traced it along until we reached the northeastern extremity of Nippon, called by the Japanese Shiriya Saki.[41] On getting abreast of this cape, the Strait of Sangar was fully open to our view, with the high land of Hokkaido also in sight. We steered a direct course for Hakodate, but on getting into the middle of the strait we encountered a current or tide, probably one accelerating the velocity of the other running to the east at the rate of at least six knots, which prevented our reaching port that night, and made it prudent to put the heads of the steamers to seaward. This would not have been necessary if any dependence could have been placed upon the continuance of clear weather. Here as in thousands of other instances of my professional life I practiced a well known, and, to me, favorite adage, "An ounce of prevention is worth a pound of cure."

The engines were so managed as to expend little coal and to retain our position. At daylight on taking the cross bearings it was found that, notwithstanding the current, the ships were not a mile from their positions when night shut in. Scarcely had we at 3:30 A.M. stood again for our destined port, than a dense fog shut every object from our sight, and again were we compelled to head toward the east. The sun, however, on approaching the zenith, cleared it away and we were so fortunate as again and more successfully to distinguish bearings which guided us to the port. As we approached

41. Latitude 41°26′ N, longitude 141°28′ E.

204 the cape called by the Japanese Shirokubi[42]—which I have named in our newly made chart Cape Blunt, in honor of my good friends Edmund and George W. Blunt[43] of New York—we could discern, over the neck of land which connects the promontory of Treaty Point* with the interior, the three ships which I had sent in advance safely at anchor. From each of them, in accordance with my previous orders, boats were sent with officers to pilot us to this unfrequented anchorage.

Here, as well as at Shimoda, a dangerous obstruction was timely discovered and buoyed out, consisting of a long spit of shoal water, making out from the center of the town to an extent of about 1200 yards. Though this spit would be a danger to a stranger entering the harbor of Hakodate, it in fact makes the anchorage the more safe by its forming a natural breakwater; sheltering vessels at anchor inside of it from all inconvenient swells.

The navigation of the Strait of Sangar as far as it has been examined by us, is safe and convenient, and the entrance to the port of Hakodate as accessible as that of Shimoda, which is saying everything in its favor. Like Shimoda, Hakodate has an outer and inner harbor. The outer being formed by the bay which is somewhat of a horseshoe shape, and the inner as being sheltered by the spit of sand already mentioned. As to expansiveness and entire safety from all winds it has not its superior in the world, with anchorage in the inner harbor of five to seven fathoms, good holding ground and clear bottom, and room to moor a hundred sail. What more could be desired?

Hakodate and Its People

17 May–3 June 1854

The town lies in latitude 41°45′ north, and longitude 140°43′ east.

Hakodate is the largest city in the island of Hokkaido, next to Matsumae, the capital and the residence of the prince. It is situated on the western slope or rather at the bottom of a high promontory, very much resembling in appearance that of Gibraltar, being connected with the main shore by a low neck of land like the neutral ground which separates the fortress from the Spanish territory. The receding country and capacious bay in front with other peculiarities of appearance are constantly reminding one of that celebrated fortress and its neighborhood.

The similarity is the more striking from the fact of its being situated in a narrow strait, like that which connects the Atlantic with the Mediterranean, and at the same distance from the former, having Nippon to the south to correspond with the coast of Africa, and the towns of Say [Sai][44] and Mimaja [Mimaya][45] to answer for Tangier and Ceuta. The city may contain 6000 or 8000 inhabitants, and appears more flourishing than Shimoda. The people

* So named by us.

42. Shirokubi Misaki is at latitude 41°42′ N, longitude 140°58′ E.
43. Hydrographer sons of hydrographer E. M. Blunt. Both brothers shared Commodore Perry's views about American lighthouses.
44. Latitude 41°26′ N, longitude 140°52′ E.
45. Latitude 41°12′ N, longitude 140°26′ E.

seem to possess in a greater degree the comforts and even the luxuries of
life, having larger and more convenient dwellings. The entire means of the
people are derived from extensive and profitable fisheries in the vicinities of
the islands. The fish are preserved in various ways and shipped to all parts of
the empire.

As with all people who gain their livelihood by taking fish, they pay but
little attention to agricultural pursuits, although the soil as we had opportunities of observing is excellent for farming purposes. They probably find it
more profitable or at least more congenial to their habits to employ themselves in the fisheries. Their chief supplies being drawn from the islands of
Kyushu and Sikok [Shikoku], an active coasting trade is prosecuted. The
junks take from Hakodate cargos of dried fish, prepared kelp, and several
descriptions of preserved sea weed, and bring back in return rice and other
grains, sweet potatoes, tobacco, tea, sugar, cloths, silks, cutlery, lacquered
ware, porcelain, and whatever else they need. More than a hundred of these
vessels sailed for different southern ports of the empire during our short stay
at Hakodate, with cargos entirely made up of the productions of the sea.

They generally traverse the western coast as being less boisterous and
offering a greater number of safe anchoring places. These junks are all
nearly of the same dimensions, and in construction, rig, and equipment are
precisely alike, and in burden corresponding to about a hundred tons of our
measurement. We were told that more than a thousand of these singular
vessels are seen at one time at anchor in this noble port.

There is so much sameness in the appearance of Japanese towns, that the
description of one will answer for the description of all others. They are
generally pleasantly and conveniently located, most of the houses are of one
story, some few are reared to what we call a story and a half. What is wanted
in height is made up in the extent of ground which they usually cover,
exclusive of the gardens and out buildings. The interior has no permanent
partitions, but the apartments are made large or small, as convenience may
require, by movable panels which are fixed in grooves, and slide to and fro
in the same manner that scenes are shifted at theaters. Light is admitted
through windows framed similar to those in the cottages of our country,
though with smaller panes, and instead of glass, oiled paper is used. These
also slide horizontally.

The panels or sliding doors, as they may as correctly be called, are about
the height and width of ordinary doors, but are quite light. They are
framed, and either made entirely of wood, beautifully finished, or of thick
oiled paper, ornamented with various drawings, mostly of landscapes and
birds, but in a style and art nothing superior to similar drawings in China.
A description of stork, a bird held sacred by the Japanese, is always seen
figured upon these panels. Besides these panels, the sides of the rooms are
frequently decorated with paper hangings, which are on rollers, and are
hung up or taken down at pleasure, in the same manner that we suspend our
maps.

The carvings in wood with which many of the dwellings and all the temples are ornamented are well executed. Of furniture they have little or none beyond a few small vessels used at their meals. The floors of the principal apartments are covered with mats, made soft and thick by being lined at the bottom with straw. These mats according to a law of the empire are of uniform dimensions, three feet by six, and are placed in rows upon the floor with so much nicety as to give them the appearance of being sewed together. Upon these mats they sit to take their meals, to smoke and to converse, and upon them they sleep at night without disrobing themselves.

I will endeavor to enumerate the few articles of furniture which have come under my notice at the different entertainments given by the Japanese, and on ordinary occasions of interviews on business, specimens of all of which I shall take home with me.

The ordinary crouching posture of the Japanese has already been described, and as they sit as we do only when in company with strangers, probably out of respect for them, chairs or benches are rarely used. Indeed I have never seen in Japan more than one at a time which has been provided for me, the other officers being seated on benches covered usually with red cloth.

In all my interviews with the imperial commissioners, they and those with me have been seated on these sort of benches. Directly in front parallel benches were placed, covered with colored crape, upon which the dishes containing the refreshments they gave us were arranged.

The various preparations are served in lacquered cups placed upon small tables or waiters about 14 inches square and 12 high, each person having a table to himself. On each of these tables are usually placed a lacquered bowl with a saucer cover containing fish soup; another with some cold preparation of fish intermixed with grated radish or some other vegetable; and another containing hard-boiled eggs cut in halves, mingled with other preparations of fish, dried kelp, and shrimps. Accompanying these bowls are always to be seen two small porcelain cups, one containing soy, into which most of the preparations are dipped before being swallowed; the other is used as a drinking cup, *saké* being the only beverage drunk, excepting tea, which is served before and after meals. The tea is made very weak and is drunk without sugar, as in China and Lew Chew, but I noticed that in Hokkaido they used a good deal of sugar in this their constant beverage.

It is brought from the kitchen in porcelain cups with a lacquered cover, and each cup is placed upon a lacquered stand. The *saké* cups are filled and replenished from small tea kettles, some of which are silver and others bronze or of fireproof China. Chop sticks are invariably used, and occasionally China spoons as in Lew Chew and China. The Japanese drink the soup directly from the bowl, and seize with their chop sticks the small pieces of fish which are floating in the liquid.

They do not seem to have any other means of warming their houses than by braziers, similar to those used in the south of Europe and Asia Minor. These are moved from one room to the other as needed. In the center of their ordinary sitting room is a square hole filled with sand, upon which a charcoal fire is constantly burning by day, and suspended over this fire upon a tripod is always to be seen a tea kettle of hot water, so that the moment a visitor enters tea is handed to him. At this fire they cook sundry small dishes, and heat their *saké*. For the general cooking of the family, they have in another room a sort of stove, not unlike a French cooking stove, in which wood is most generally used, of which article they are very economical.

Each boat has a cooking apparatus, and the messes which I have seen them prepare are incredibly meager for 15 or 16 men—a few small fish, some greens, rice and soy—hardly enough to keep alive a hard-working American.

The streets of Hakodate are of tolerable width, and most of them cross each other at right angles; the principal one running parallel with the water-front of the city, with which it communicates by alleys at the end of which are convenient landing places.

The leading men have their residences with ornamental gardens upon elevated situations a little back of the town. The same municipal regulations are enforced here as in every city and town in Japan. At the end of each street are gates which are closed at night, and the inhabitants of the several streets form so many separate communities, each governed by an officer called *otona*,[46] who is held responsible for the good order of all people under his especial charge, and these are also made responsible for the conduct of each other. In almost every street is a watch house, and there night watchmen are stationed to give the alarm in case of fire, the *otona* on such occasions always taking the command. To guard as much as possible against the consequences of these frequent fires, tubs filled with water are placed upon the roofs of the houses, and others along the streets; they have also numerous fire engines.

And the better to protect their more valuable goods and merchandise, a number of fireproof warehouses have been provided in which to store them. Whether these buildings belong to the government or to individuals I could not learn.

The roofs of the houses here are of the same form as those at Shimoda, but instead of being covered with tiles or thatch, are shingled, and to prevent them from being blown off they are covered with cobblestones.

Of temples there are but seven; three belong to the Shinto, and four to those professing the more modern doctrine of Buddha. One of the latter is of comparative recent construction, and its elegant appearance, and costliness of interior decoration give evidence of the wealth and munificence of the people. As to the arrangement and decorations of the altar, it would be difficult to distinguish it from one in a Roman Catholic church.

It might appear to strangers visiting the ports of Hakodate and Shimoda, who did not move much about, that neither of these cities had any means of defense, but some of the officers in their rambles, found at both places a few guns concealed from observation, and so on the passing of the squadron beyond Uraga, every appearance of military defense was studiously concealed.

46. Literally, "big man."

The guns in the works at Uraga, with which they made such display on our visit in July last, were removed from sight, and the work on the fortifications discontinued.

This it may be presumed was done to avoid every possibility of collision at arms with us, knowing as they must have known that their works could not stand an hour before the heavy batteries of our ships—thus wisely deciding that "discretion is the better part of valor."

Doubtless Hakodate will in future be frequently visited by our whaling ships as it offers many advantages. It is true that supplies of meats and vegetables are scarce, and for reason that the people of this island are chiefly employed in the fisheries, exchanging the produce of the sea for such grain and the few esculents they need. Fish is the common food of the people of the whole empire, high or low. It seems to be a component of almost every dish prepared for the table, and is justly called by them the staff of life. Hence when they send presents to each other, a piece of dried fish wrapped in paper invariably accompanies the gift. Cattle are reared only for the plough; and for inland transportation pack horses are employed, of which we noticed great numbers constantly passing in and out of the city.

One or two ships could always obtain tolerable supplies of poultry, eggs, and vegetables such as Irish and sweet potatoes, peas, beans, lettuce, and onions. The harbor abounds with excellent fish, of which the seines of the squadron provided abundance of salmon, salmon trout, groupers, white fish, porgies, perch, flounders, herrings, and various other kinds.

The salmon are not more than half the size of those of our eastern rivers, but are quite equal to them in delicacy of flavor. Crabs, clams, and the large blue muscle are found in any quantities. The clams are of the Venus genera, and the shells of some of them are beautifully marked. The crabs are large and surpass in flavor those of the Chesapeake.

Wild geese, ducks, and various descriptions of game and other birds are abundant at their respective seasons, but the pheasant is rarely or never seen in Hokkaido. The only quadrupeds hunted by the people are the fox, the wild boar, and the bear. Our sportsmen obtained but few specimens either of birds or quadrupeds, drawings of most of which are in this journal.

The fox is looked upon by the Japanese as possessing an evil spirit, and is represented in all their allegories as a willing agent of the devil. For this reason they are hunted and destroyed, thus giving evidence that these people do not attempt to deprecate the wrath of his satanic majesty as in some countries, but hold him in defiance. A male and female were shot and their skins preserved, as was also that of an animal somewhat resembling the fox in appearance and habits, and probably belonging to the same species.

Of birds, the curlew, plover, snipe, and quail were found, as also the dove; all of the kinds common to our country. The other varieties differ considerably from those known to us.

Having thus given a brief description of this very interesting town and harbor, I must refer to the proceedings of the squadron during the short time we remained in port. Anchoring on 17 May, I lost no time in commencing upon business with the authorities. Captain Abbot, as senior officer preceding me, had already opened communication with the governor, but nothing, of course, had been arranged. I therefore despatched on the following morning the flag lieutenant Mr. Bent, accompanied by Messrs. Williams and Portman, to the governor, and the following is a condensed account of the transactions which passed between myself and officers, and the authorities of the place.

We found as the principal people of the place several high officers named Yendo Matazaimon [Matazaemon Endo], Ishuka Kongo [Kanzo Ishuzuka], Kudo Moyoro [Mogoro Kudo], Tudinaro Sumei [Shume Fujiwara], Sheke Natabe [Nakaba Seki], Daishamar Gohei [Gohei Daishima], and Yebeko Jiro [Jiro Ebiko]. These were soon after joined by Matsmai Kaneager [Kageyu Matsumae] a relative of the prince of Matsumae, and sent by that personage as his delegate, and though all matters of business were referred to him, and he was apparently treated as the superior by all the others, he had little to say. Matazaemon Endo appeared to be the leading and most practical man amongst them, and certainly we found him the most sensible and the easiest with whom to transact business of any we have yet met in Japan.

The Dutch interpreter and other officials despatched from Edo had not yet arrived and, according to their statement, the arrival of *Macedonian* and the other ships of the advanced detachment of the squadron with a letter from the high commissioner gave them the first intelligence of our negotiations at Kanagawa, and they knew nothing of the treaty, until I showed it to them in the Japanese language, and presented them a copy in Chinese. And after some little demur a suite of rooms were assigned for my accommodation when I visited the shore, another for the other officers of the squadron, and another for the convenience of the artists. The shops were thrown open and such articles of supply as they had to furnish were sent on board. But it was here as at Shimoda, they had little to spare, living—as the people did as before mentioned—almost entirely upon the produce of the sea. The seines, however, furnished us with an abundance of fine fish of which the best were excellent salmon and salmon trout. The wood and water was excellent, and we obtained also some lumber.

Finding that many mistakes occurred in conducting purchases at the shops, I proposed that the authorities should establish a bazaar where articles should be exposed for sale, with the prices affixed to them. This they agreed to and during the remainder of our stay all the purchases were made in this way.

It would be tiresome as well as unprofitable to detail all the incidents that occurred during our short stay at this place. The authorities were invariably kind and civil to myself and officers, and I entertained them on board

Mississippi at supper and delighted them with an exhibition of the corps of Ethiopian minstrels, belonging to *Powhatan*.

I made an attempt to have the limits established within which Americans might freely go and come, but they declined to enter upon the subject for reason that they had no authority to act in the premises.

Having completed the survey of the harbor and transacted all necessary business with the authorities I despatched *Vandalia* to Shanghai to relieve *Plymouth* at that place, and sent *Macedonian* back to Shimoda, retaining only *Powhatan* and *Mississippi*. Singular enough the day before our intended departure, two delegates from Edo,[47] Amma-Zhuim no Shin [Junnosuke Amma] and Hirayama Kenzhiro [Kenjiro Hirayama] accompanied by a Dutch interpreter arrived, but I had little to say to them, and left the port on the morning of 3 June for Shimoda.

I may here remark that I had directed Commander Pope in the *Vandalia* to take the western passage to Shanghai, by passing through the Strait of Sangar, the Japan Sea, and China Gulf. I also sent *Southampton* (Lieutenant Commander Boyle) to survey Volcano Bay and the harbor of Endermo, with instructions for him to proceed thence to join the squadron at Shimoda.

During our stay at Hakodate, two of *Vandalia*'s crewmen, who had been long sick, died and were buried with the full consent of the authorities near one of the temples in the outskirts of the city. Head boards were put up and the Japanese enclosed the graves and planted within the enclosure various flowering plants.

We left Hakodate a little after sunrise [3 June 1854], *Powhatan* and *Mississippi* together, and had scarcely passed beyond the mouth of the harbor when both steamers were suddenly enveloped in a dense fog. Fortunately we had time to secure sure bearings which enabled us to obtain a safe anchorage. The fog, however, cleared away by 10 o'clock and we again weighed and got clear of the straits before night.

Shimoda Revisited

7–28 June 1854

Nothing of interest occurred during our passage to Shimoda. We saw a good many whales of different descriptions, and experienced the same easterly current. On reaching the vicinity of the islands in the Gulf of Edo a thick fog delayed us for a day but we arrived on 7 June at Shimoda, a day before the expiration of the time appointed by me in my letter to the chief commissioner.

Lieutenant Commander Sinclair who had been left in the *Supply* in port during our absence immediately reported that all had gone well, that the commissioners had arrived with two others who had been added to their number. As I was desirous of completing my final business with these great functionaries, who as I well knew from experience would be provokingly

47. Not from Edo, but from Moheji, these were retainers of the lord, or prince, of Matsumae.

slow in their movements, I proposed an interview for the following day.

Accordingly, I landed with an escort of 300 officers, seamen and Marines and marched to the temple occupied by me during my former visit. Here I found the seven commissioners in waiting to receive me. After introducing the two new ones by name and title—Tzudsuki [Minoshige Tsuzuki], Suruga *no kami*, prince of Suruga, and Takenouchisetaro [Seitaro Takenouchi], comptroller of the revenue—and enquiring after my health, the commissioners informed me that Shimoda had been made an imperial city, and that Izawa, prince of Mimasaka, and Tsuzuki, prince of Suruga, had been appointed governors of the city, and Kahei Kurokawa, and Ise sin toheiro [Shinjiro Isa], lieutenant governors, besides these, a number of under officers had been appointed. I was also told that the jurisdiction of the imperial city did not extend as far as the limits of seven Japanese miles, and that gates had been put up upon the roads leading from the city. They desired that I would agree to a regulation making it imperative on the part of all Americans intending to pass these gates, first to obtain permission from the proper officer on duty. This I positively refused to consent to, and I soon found that the great object of the commissioners was to induce me to agree to certain regulations which should govern Americans visiting the port, and would in a measure modify and weaken the stipulations of the treaty. I determined to hold out against all propositions that would have such construction or bearing. I intimated my willingness to agree to some regulations which were unquestionably necessary for the government of the authorities as well as Americans. After an immense deal of discussion and various turnings and twistings of the commissioners they agreed to all that is set forth in the following paper. The greatest struggle was in reference to the limits with which Americans should be free to go where they pleased in the vicinity of Hakodate. At first they wished to confine the limits to one street, then to the town, then to the projecting promontory extending toward the sea, then to 3 Japanese miles, again to 3½. My proposition was to give us the same limits here as at Shimoda, 7 Japanese *ri,* about 16 English miles. I held out for two or three days but at last thought it advisable to compromise for 5 Japanese miles, equal to 12 of ours.

Besides the foregoing, a few port regulations were agreed upon and at my suggestion a harbor master and three pilots were appointed, the latter being brought to me to have my confirmation of their appointment. To the harbor master I presented on the part of the United States a spyglass, always to be kept at the lookout place, and to pass to his successor in office. To each of the pilots I gave a comfortable overcoat.

It would be useless and uninteresting to detail in full all the particulars of these tiresome discussions; a record has however been preserved and can at any time be referred to. Japanese diplomatists are certainly very pertinacious in holding out. They fall back from their advanced positions step by step, preserving their equanimity, nor do they take offence at any hasty expression of their opponents.

212   One of the objects of appointing two additional commissioners was to make some arrangement with respect to the currency or exchange. I was, at the beginning of the discussions, requested to appoint a board of officers to meet a certain number of Japanese officers to arrange this important matter. I told them that I would have no objections to do so, and asked what number would compose the Japanese board, and was informed that nine had been appointed. I told them that I had intended to have employed one but would increase the number to two; accordingly I issued the following order to pursers Speiden[48] and Eldridge, being determined to agree to nothing with respect to the currency that could in the slightest degree affect any transactions beyond those of the squadron now in port. Having long before discovered the deceitful character of the Japanese officials, I was not disposed to become their dupe.

The following are copies of my order to the pursers and their report.

United States Flag Ship *Powhatan*
Shimoda, 12 June 1854.

Gentlemen,

You are hereby appointed to the duty of holding communication with certain Japanese officials delegated by the imperial government in conformity with the treaty of Kanagawa, to arrange with officers alike delegated by me, the rate of currency and exchange which shall for the present govern the payments to be made by the several ships of the squadron for articles that *have* been and *are* to be obtained, also to establish as far as can be the price at which coal, per picul or ton, can be delivered on board at this port of Shimoda.

It is not to be understood that the rate of currency or exchange which may be agreed upon at this time is to be permanent; on the contrary, it is intended only to answer immediate purposes. Neither you nor myself are sufficiently acquainted with the purity and value of the Japanese coins to establish a fixed rate of exchange, even if I had the power to recognize such arrangement.

It will, however, be very desirable for you to make yourselves acquainted with all the peculiarities of the Japanese currency, and also, if practicable, with the laws appertaining thereto; as the information will be valuable in facilitating all future negotiations upon the subject.

You will of course before entering into any agreement which may be considered binding, refer to me.

Very respectfully,
Your obedient servant,
(signed) M. C. Perry
Commander-in-chief United States Naval Forces
East India, China, and Japan Seas.

To Purser William Speiden
"   "   J. C. Eldridge
United States Navy.

United States Steam Frigate *Powhatan*
Shimoda, 15 June 1854.

Sir,

The committee appointed by you in your letter of the 12th instant to confer with a committee from the Japanese commissioners in reference to the rate of ex-

48. His son (18) and namesake, who was assistant purser, kept a personal journal which provided the Portman sketch facing page 186 above.

settle the price of coal to be delivered at this port, beg leave to report.

The Japanese committee it was soon seen came to the conference with their minds made up to adhere to the valuation they had already set upon our coins, even if the alternative was the immediate cessation of trade. The basis upon which they made their calculations was the nominal rate at which the government sells bullion when it is purchased from the mint, and which seems also to be that by which the metal is received from the mines. The Japanese have a decimal system of weights, like the Chinese, of catty, tael, mace, candareen, and cash, by which articles in general are weighed, but gold and silver are not reckoned above taels. In China, a tael of silver in weight and one in currency are the same, for the Chinese have no silver coin; but in Japan as in European countries, the standard of value weight, and that of currency weight differ. We were told that a tael weight of silver has now come to be reckoned, when it is bullion, as equal to 225 candareens, or 2 taels, 2 mace, 5 candareens; but when coined the same amount in weight is held to be worth 6 taels, 4 mace. It is at the bullion value that the government has decided to receive our dollar, the same at which they take the silver from the mines, asserting that, as its present die and assays give it no additional value, it is worth no more to them. In proportion to a tael a dollar weighs 7 mace, 1⅕ candareens, which at the rates of bullion value, makes it worth 1 tael, 6 mace, or 1600 cash. Thus the Japanese government will make a profit of 66⅔ per cent on every dollar paid them of full weight with the trifling deduction of the expense of recoining it. The injustice of this arrangement was shown, and the propriety of paying to the seller himself the coin we gave at this depreciated rate urged, but in vain.

For gold the rate is more, as the disparity between the value of bullion and that of coin among the Japanese is not so great. A tael of gold is valued at 19 taels in currency, and a mace at 1 tael, 9 mace; the gold dollar weighs almost 5 candareens, but the Japanese have reckoned it as the 20th part of a $20 piece to be worth 16,720 cash or 16 taels, 7 mace, 2 candareens. This, when converted into a silver value makes a gold dollar worth 52¼ cents when reckoned at 836 cash; its assessed value by the Japanese government suffers the same depreciation as our silver; and its real value, when compared with the inflated currency in use among the people, is only about 17¼ cents. Consequently, by this estimate, gold becomes 50 per cent worse for us to pay in than silver. The currency value of a gold dollar, taking the *ichibu* as of equal purity and comparing them weight for weight, is only 1045 cash, or nearly 22 cents in silver; so that the actual depreciation on the part of the Japanese is not so great as in silver, being for the two metals when weighed with each other, for silver as 100 to 33⅓, and for gold as 22 to 17. The elements of this comparison are not quite certain, and therefore its results are somewhat doubtful, but the extraordinary discrepancy of both metals compared with our coins, and with their own copper coins shows how the government has inflated the whole monetary system in order to benefit itself.

The parties could come to no agreement as we declined to consent to the proposals of the Japanese who were decided to adhere to their valuation of a silver dollar at 1 tael, 6 mace, or 1600 cash. Neither would they consent to do justly by us in relation to the moneys paid them at this place before our departure for Hakodate, at the rate of only 1 tael, 2 mace, or 1200 cash to the dollar, stating that the money paid them at this rate had passed out of their hands, and moreover that the prices placed upon the articles furnished had been charged at reduced prices with reference to the low value placed upon the dollar.

For the amount due and unsettled for supplies received at Yokohama, and on account of which purser Eldridge paid Einosuke Moriyama, imperial interpreter, $350 in gold and silver that they might be assayed and tested at Edo; they consent to receive the dollar at the valuation now placed on them, that is, at the rate of 1600 cash for the silver dollar.

We carefully investigated the price of the coal to be delivered to vessels in this port. We learn that 10,000 catties, or 100 piculs have arrived, and this at the rate of 1680 catties to a ton of 2240 pounds or 16⅘ piculs, costs 262 taels, 6 mace, 5 candareens, 3 cash or $164.14 making the rate to be $27.91 per ton. The Japanese state that the price of coal would be considerably reduced, as the demand for it increased and their facilities for mining became more perfect.

In conclusion we take pleasure in expressing our thanks to Messrs. Williams and Portman, whose services as interpreters were indispensable, and from whom we received important aid in our investigations.

> We have the honor to be,
> your obedient servants,
> (signed) William Speiden
> (signed) J. C. Eldridge
> Pursers, United States Navy.

To Commodore M. C. Perry
Commander-in-chief United States Naval Forces
East India, China, and Japan Seas.

Before leaving Shimoda I again entertained the imperial commissioners and their numerous retinues, at this time on board *Mississippi*,[49] and amused them as before with the performance of the Ethiopian minstrels, dancing, etc. On my taking final leave they really exhibited much friendly feeling, notwithstanding the expressions made use of by me in the following note sent to them the day before. [This note is missing from the Journal.]

A Japanese, however, never takes offence at being charged with disingenuousness or even with duplicity. One would suppose that they consider it a compliment to be thought tricky and deceitful.

Friday, 23 June 1854. Having completed all business with the commissioners and taken final leave of them I directed the accounts of the squadron to be settled preparatory to sailing, intending to leave on the following morning, and knowing the difficulty of winding the steamers, owing to their great length, in the inner harbor, I caused them to be moved into the outer road, as also the *Supply. Macedonian* and *Southampton* remained at their anchorage.[50]

The wind came in strong from the sea, and neither of the sail vessels could be moved with safety. On Saturday and the next morning *Macedonian* and *Supply* both failed to get to sea owing to light and unfavorable winds. As I was pressed for time and having steam on *Mississippi* and *Powhatan*, I was not satisfied with the unnecessary consumption of coal caused by waiting for these ships, bound as they were in another direction to the steamers. Consequently I sent the flag lieutenant with a written memorandum to Captain Abbot, and immediately left the port [28 June] in company with *Powhatan* and *Southampton*, the latter in tow of *Powhatan*.

49. While at Shimoda, on 19 June, Commodore Perry transferred his broad pennant back to *Mississippi* and returned to that ship with his retinue.

50. In the evening of 24 June a number of birds and dogs were brought to the flagship as a gift for Commodore Perry. The dogs were named Master Sam Spooner, Madame Shimoda, and Monsieur Edo. The first two died on board *Mississippi* before reaching the United States.

Say to Captain Abbot, if he has not a good berth, to warp into a safe one, and sail with the *Supply* when the wind and weather permit. I ish the two ships to keep company to Killon [Keelung, Formosa], if possible.

In passing out beyond Rock Island we encountered a high sea which gave me additional proof that the outer as well as the inner harbor of Shimoda is perfectly safe. The violence of the sea was in a considerable degree broken by the ledge of rocks extending, though not continuously, from Rock Island to Cape Izu. There are doubtless two good channels, one between Rock Island and the next rock to the westward, and the other between the western extremity of the ledge and Cape Izu, but these channels were not sufficiently explored by us. I should not like myself to venture through either of them, and would not recommend others to do so. It is more prudent to go outside of Rock Island, by which ships will not be so much endangered by the influence of the rapid current seemingly setting at all times to the eastward.

There can be no better harbor for a limited number of vessels than the inner port of Shimoda, and when its contiguity to the sea, its easy and safe approach, its convenience of ingress and egress are taken into consideration, I do not see how a better or more desirable port could have been selected to answer all the purposes for which it is wanted. Like that of Hakodate, it would always appear to have been located to suit the convenience of our whaling and other ships; and as resorts in the sickly seasons for the vessels of the China Squadron. These two ports offer every advantage for the refitment of whaling ships, provided they do not stand much in need of supplies, which, however, will doubtless be more abundant as the demand increases; the Japanese giving sufficient evidence of their fondness for profit, and indeed for outwitting those who bargain with them, but these things usually regulate themselves.

The following is a copy of a very interesting report of the fleet surgeon,[51] prepared in conformity with the order which precedes it.

> United States Flagship *Powhatan*
> Hakodate, 1 June 1854.

Sir,

You will be pleased to prepare and communicate to me for the information of the government, a report upon the character of the climate of the ports of Shimoda and Hakodate, as to salubrity, and especially with reference to the advantages they may offer as places of resort to our ships of war on the China Station.

Also report upon the medicinal properties of the mineral spring water near our present anchorage.

> Respectfully
> Your Obedient Servant, (signed) M. C. Perry
> Commander-in-chief United States Naval Forces
> East India, China, and Japan Seas.

To Fleet Surgeon D. S. Green
United States Steam Frigate *Mississippi*.

51. Fleet Surgeon Daniel S. Green's report concerning Hakodate water is noted in Hawks *Narrative*, p. 447.

During our last visit to Shimoda the surveying officers were constantly employed in finishing up their work preparatory to the construction of an accurate chart of the harbor. They, with others for which we have abundant materials, will be completed in time to be taken home with me.

The sailing directions which follow will I trust be easily understood, indeed there can be no possible mistake if a sight of Rock Island is secured, and it be brought to bear west one or two miles distant. The harbor will be in full view, though the town may not be seen, as it will be screened by the projecting headlands and islands which form the inner harbor.

This town is situated at the northwestern termination of the harbor, its front extending along the margin of a shallow stream which empties itself at this point. In appearance and apparent trade and wealth it is inferior to Hakodate, but the people seem happy and contented, and were it not here as in every part of Japan, that the middle and lower classes were kept in the most servile state of obedience to the will of the princes and their satellites, they would be well disposed toward strangers. They seem to be prone to gaiety and kind hospitality, but it is only by stealth that they exhibit these traits of character.

Southward from Shimoda

After leaving Shimoda, I directed the squadron to be steered to the south in view of again seeing the cluster of very dangerous rocks discovered by us on our passage up in February last. We found their positions very correctly established by former notes, but took care to verify these notes by new observations.

As we were the first of modern navigators who discovered and marked the position of these rocks, I claim the right of naming them, and consequently have given them the name of a man to whom every sailor, in truth every man, woman, or child who may embark upon the ocean, ever will be immeasurably indebted. I allude to a most esteemed friend William C. Redfield, and trust that when the government of the United States shall have entered into a closer commercial intercourse with Japan that the position of Redfield Rocks will be as familiar to our navigators as that of every other danger to be avoided in their passage to and fro.

From these rocks a course was made for the northeast end of O Shima, the island claimed to have been discovered by Commander Glynn. It will be recollected that in our last passage up I was particular in making observations of the western shore of this and the adjacent islands; that I made a report to the Navy Department upon the subject. In my passage down I determined to examine very closely the eastern side of the coast of the same island, and consequently on the morning of 29 June we made the northern point of O Shima bearing N 82° W, and which is erroneously placed on the chart. Passing between O Shima and Kikai Shima, or Bungalow Island, we traversed the eastern coast of this island so closely that we could mark with much accuracy all its sinuosities, bays, and inlets, and having at meridian obtained excellent observations of latitude and longitude, the result of the notes of the three ships, we had it in our power to determine the positions of the most prominent headlands by a series of angles deduced from those observations.

Before the visit to these seas by the United States Squadron, a French chart constructed by Capitaine de Vaisseau, Monsieur N. Guerin, and published at Paris in 1848, was the most approved guide. This, however, has been greatly improved by the observations and notes of the officers under my command, and though there are doubtless many dangers not yet discovered and laid down I feel justified in saying that we have contributed very much in improving the hydrography of this part of the world, and more especially in the waters of the gulf and bay of Edo, where the ground has been almost entirely new to strangers.

After our meridian observations had been calculated, I despatched two of the boats of *Mississippi* in charge of Lieutenants Maury and Webb to a little bay abreast the ships and about two miles distant, being determined to communicate with this terra incognito. The officers landed and found only a small hamlet, and a squad of miserably armed natives drawn up to meet them, but they were very civil and gave in exchange for bread and pork some fowls and vegetables. The party also brought off a few botanical specimens.

I regretted that I had not time, and what was still more valuable any coal to spare, to remain longer and to explore further these interesting islands. They will deserve more complete examination, and I hope that the government of the United States will ere long send suitable vessels for such purpose. One small steamer, and a schooner of about 120 tons, with a storeship for carrying coals and provisions, would be adequate for the work.

Keeping as near as safety would permit to the chain of islands lying between O Shima and Lew Chew, we continued to steer southward and westward through the night, and at daylight made the northern end of great Lew Chew and the islands in the vicinity. At 10 A.M. of 30 June, the *Southampton,* until this time in tow of *Powhatan,* was cast off and ordered to part company.

Thus ended the personal journal
kept by Commodore Matthew C. Perry
on his Japan Expedition.

Steamers *Mississippi* and *Powhatan* entered Naha Harbor for their final visit to Okinawa on 1 July 1854. Perry there had to investigate the 10 June death of an American sailor from *Lexington*. The victim had attempted while drunk to attack a young girl. Her neighbors chased and stoned the offender, who fell into the harbor and drowned. When the Commodore declined to take jurisdiction over the case, the local authorities banished the sailor's principal attacker. It must have been trying for Perry to learn of the incident, but it is a tribute to his discipline that this was the only action of violence against a native by any member of the Japan Expedition.

On 11 July Perry succeeded in negotiating a Lew Chew agreement similar to his Kanagawa Treaty with the Japanese. From the regent he received a stone for the Washington Monument, and a large gong which he presented to the Naval Academy.

After a farewell dinner and entertainment for Okinawan officials Perry sailed from Naha for the last time on 17 July, first arranging for the Bettelheim family to be removed to Hong Kong in *Powhatan*. Flagship *Mississippi* reached Hong Kong in the early morning of 22 July.

There Commodore Perry settled the affairs of his squadron command. Worn down by long-continued anxiety and ill health he began to look toward the rest of home, which he so much needed. He had written to the Secretary of the Navy some time before, asking leave, when his work was done, to turn over the command to the officer next in rank, and return to the United States. At Hong Kong he received dispatches conveying the leave he sought. He chose to return by the overland route from India and delivered command of the squadron to Captain Abbot. His countrymen living in China gave him a kind farewell and he embarked, in company with his flag lieutenant, in the English mail steamer *Ganges*. They arrived Pointe de Galle, Ceylon, 29 September and departed the same day in steamer *Hindostan*, which reached Suez 17 October. Thence overland to Alexandria and again by ship to arrive 20 November at The Hague where he met his family and they were guests—until 7 December—of his son-in-law August Belmont, the American minister to the Netherlands. Thence by way of England, where he inspected some Royal Navy steamers, Commodore Perry arrived in New York on 12 January 1855, after an absence from the United States of two years and two months.

U.S.S. *Mississippi* reached the navy yard at Brooklyn on 23 April 1855. The next day Commodore Perry repaired on board and formally hauled down his flag, the final act in the story of the United States Expedition to Japan.

APPENDIX A

Letter of the President of the United States
to the Emperor of Japan

Great and Good Friend!

I send you this public letter by Commodore Matthew C. Perry, an officer of highest rank in the Navy of the United States, and commander of the squadron now visiting Your Imperial Majesty's dominions.

I have directed Commodore Perry to assure Your Imperial Majesty that I entertain the kindest feelings toward Your Majesty's person and government, and that I have no other object in sending him to Japan but to propose to Your Imperial Majesty that the United States and Japan should live in friendship and have commercial intercourse with each other.

The constitution and laws of the United States forbid all interference with the religious or political concerns of other nations. I have particularly charged Commodore Perry to abstain from every act which could possibly disturb the tranquility of Your Imperial Majesty's dominions.

The United States of America reach from ocean to ocean, and our territory of Oregon and state of California lie directly opposite to the dominions of Your Imperial Majesty. Our steamships can go from California to Japan in eighteen days.

Our great state of California produces about sixty millions of dollars in gold every year, besides silver, quicksilver, precious stones, and many other valuable articles. Japan is also a rich and fertile country and produces many very valuable articles. Your Imperial Majesty's subjects are skilled in many of the arts. I am desirous that our two countries should trade with each other for the benefit both of Japan and the United States.

We know that the ancient laws of Your Imperial Majesty's government do not allow of foreign trade except with the Dutch. But as the state of the world changes, and new governments are formed, it seems to be wise from time to time to make new laws. There was a time when the ancient laws of Your Imperial Majesty's government were first made.

About the same time America, which is sometimes called the New World, was first discovered and settled by the Europeans. For a long time there were but a few people, and they were poor. They have now become quite numerous; their commerce is very extensive; and they think that if Your Imperial Majesty were so far to change the ancient laws as to allow a free trade between the two countries, it would be extremely beneficial to both.

If Your Imperial Majesty is not satisfied that it would be safe, altogether, to abrogate the ancient laws which forbid foreign trade, they might be suspended for five or ten years, so as to try the experiment. If it does not prove as beneficial as was hoped, the ancient laws can be restored. The

United States often limits its treaties with foreign states to a few years, and then renew them or not, as they please.

I have directed Commodore Perry to mention another thing to Your Imperial Majesty. Many of our ships pass every year from California to China, and great numbers of our people pursue the whale fishery near the shores of Japan. It sometimes happens in stormy weather that one of our ships is wrecked on Your Imperial Majesty's shores. In all such cases we ask and expect that our unfortunate people should be treated with kindness, and that their property should be protected till we can send a vessel and bring them away. We are very much in earnest in this.

Commodore Perry is also directed by me to represent to Your Imperial Majesty that we understand that there is a great abundance of coal and provisions in the empire of Japan. Our steam ships, in crossing the great ocean, burn a great deal of coal, and it is not convenient to bring it all the way from America. We wish that our steam ships and other vessels should be allowed to stop in Japan and supply themselves with coal, provisions, and water. They will pay for them in money, or anything else Your Imperial Majesty's subjects may prefer, and we request Your Imperial Majesty to appoint a convenient port in the southern part of the empire where our vessels may stop for this purpose. We are very desirous of this.

These are the only objects for which I have sent Commodore Perry with a powerful squadron to pay a visit to Your Imperial Majesty's renowned city of Edo: friendship, commerce, a supply of coal, and provisions and protection for our shipwrecked people.

We have directed Commodore Perry to beg Your Imperial Majesty's acceptance of a few presents. They are of no great value in themselves, but some of them may serve as specimens of the articles manufactured in the United States, and they are intended as tokens of our sincere and respectful friendship.

May the Almighty have Your Imperial Majesty in his great and holy keeping!

In witness whereof I have caused the great seal of the United States to be hereunto affixed, and have subscribed the same with my name, at the city of Washington in America, the seal of my government, on the thirteenth day of the month of November, in the year one thousand eight hundred and fifty-two.

Your good friend,
Millard Fillmore

By the President
Edward Everett
Secretary of State

(E)

Translation of answer to the President's letter to the Emperor of Japan.

The return of Your Excellency as Ambassador of the United States to this Empire has been expected according to the letter of his majesty the President, which your excellency delivered last year to his majesty the Emperor of this nation. It is quite impossible to give satisfactory answers at once to all the proposals of your government.

Although a change is most positively forbidden by the laws of our imperial ancestors, for us to continue attached to ancient laws seems to misunderstand the spirit of the age. Nevertheless we are governed now by imperative necessity. At the visit of your excellency to this Empire last year, his majesty the former Emperor was sick and is now dead. Subsequently his majesty the present Emperor ascended the throne. The many occupations in consequence thereof are not yet finished and there is no time to settle other business thoroughly. Moreover his majesty the new Emperor at his succession to the throne promised the princes and high officers of the empire to observe the laws; it is therefore evident that he cannot now bring about any alterations in the ancient laws.

Last autumn at the departure of the Dutch ship, the superintendent of the Dutch trade in Japan was requested to inform your government of this event, and we have been informed in writing that he did so.

The Russian Ambassador arrived recently at Nagasaki to communicate a wish of his government. He has since left the said place because no answer would be given to whatever nation that might communicate similar wishes. We recognize necessity, however, and shall entirely comply with the proposals of your government concerning coal, wood, water, provisions, and the saving of ships and their crews in distress. After being informed which harbor your excellency selects, that harbor shall be prepared, which preparation it is estimated will take about five years. Meanwhile commencement can be made with the coal at Nagasaki, by the first month of the next Japanese year (16 February 1855).

Having no precedent with respect to coal, we request your excellency to furnish us with an estimate, and upon due consideration this will be complied with if not in opposition to our laws. What do you mean by provisions, and how much coal will be required?

Finally, anything ships may be in want of that can be furnished from the production of this Empire shall be supplied; the prices of merchandise and articles of barter to be fixed by Kahei Kurokawa and Einosuke Moriyama. After settling the points beforementioned, the treaty can be concluded and signed at the next interview.

Seals attached by order
of the high Gentleman,
(signed) Einosuke Moriyama

(F)

United States Flag Ship *Powhatan*
At anchor off the Town of Yokohama.
Edo Bay, 10 March 1854.

To His Highness,
Hayashi, *Daigaku-no-kami*
etc.   etc.   etc.

Your Highness,

In reply to the communication of your highness which was brought to me yesterday by Kahei Kurokawa, and the chief interpreter Einosuke Moriyama, I hasten to remark that it has given me the greatest satisfaction to learn from its contents that the imperial government of Japan has at last awakened to a conviction of the necessity of so altering its policy with respect to foreign nations as to consent to an interchange of friendly intercourse with the United States.

Though the propositions set forth in the communication of your highness furnish strong evidence of the enlightened spirit with which the imperial commissioners are disposed to meet the suggestions which I have had the honor to submit, they fall far short of my anticipations, and I do not hesitate to say that they would not satisfy the views of the President.

I cheerfully accede to those of the propositions of your highness which offer to guarantee kind treatment to such vessels of the United States as may hereafter visit the parts of Japan or be wrecked upon its coasts, with protection and suitable hospitality to the people who may belong to them.

Also that provisions and other supplies shall be furnished to them and payment received for the same.

Also that American steamers shall be supplied with reasonable quantities of coal and at fair and equitable prices.

These are all very well so far as they go and can be incorporated in the treaty which I shall expect to make, but my instructions require me to look for an intercourse of a more enlarged and liberal character, and I feel assured that the imperial government, in consideration of the spirit of the age and with full knowledge of my strong desire to conduct my mission in peace and friendship, will no longer hesitate to enter with cordiality into a treaty that will be mutually honorable and advantageous to both nations.

The convenience of the immense and growing commerce of the United States in these seas will require certainly as many ports of resort in Japan as are specified in the treaty with China, and these must be free from any restrictions not recognized, by the usages of free and independent nations.

In a word I again earnestly urge upon your highness the policy of fixing upon some written compact, that will be binding as well upon the citizens of the United States as the subjects of Japan.

It would be needless in me again to express the sincerest desire of my heart to bring these negotiations to an amicable and satisfactory termination, nor will I again allude to the importance of such an issue, important as well to save time as to prevent the necessity of sending from America more ships and men and possibly with instructions of more stringent import.

I have the power and the wish to meet the imperial commissioners in all good faith, believing that there can be no more favorable time than the present to settle all the questions under consideration in such manner as will bring about a good understanding between two nations whose geographical positions lying in comparative proximity would seem to enjoin as a measure of wise foresight a mutual interchange of those acts of kindness and good will which will serve to cement the friendship happily commenced and to endure I trust for many years.

With the most profound respect
(signed) M. C. Perry
Commander-in-chief United States Naval Forces
East India, China, and Japan Seas.
And Special Ambassador to Japan.

APPENDIX B

Ships of the United States Far East Squadron, 1853–1854*
Commodore Matthew C. Perry, commanding

Ship	Class	Built (Rebuilt)	Length in feet	Tons	Crew	Guns Shell	Other	Commander	Remarks and Disposition
SUSQUEHANNA	frigate	1850 Philadelphia	257	2450	300	6	3	Cdr. F. Buchanan	Two 31-foot diam. paddle-wheels. Two inclined direct-acting condensing engines, built in Balto. Sold 1863.
POWHATAN	frigate	1852 Norfolk	253	2415	300	6	3	Capt. W. J. McCluney	Same as Susquehanna, but built at Gosport, Va. Sold 1887.
MISSISSIPPI	frigate	1839 Philadelphia	225	1692	268	12	0	Cdr. S. S. Lee	Two side-lever engines built in Philadelphia. Sunk in Mississippi River, 1863 at Port Hudson.
MACEDONIAN	sloop	1832 Norfolk (1853)	164	1341 (1726)	380	6	16	Capt. Joel Abbott	Laid up at Norfolk in 1874; sold 1875.
PLYMOUTH	sloop	1843 Boston	147	989	210	4	18	Cdr. John Kelly	Burned and scuttled at Norfolk, 20 April 1861, to prevent capture.
SARATOGA	sloop	1842 Portsmouth	150	882	210	4	18	Cdr. W. S. Walter	Sold 1907.
VANDALIA	sloop	1828 Philadelphia (1848)	127 (140)	770	190	8	16	Cdr. John Pope	Receiving and guard ship at Portsmouth in 1863.
SOUTHAMPTON	store-ship	1842 Norfolk	156	567	45	0	2	Lieut. J. J. Boyle	Sold before Civil War.
LEXINGTON	store-ship	1826 New York (1843)	127	691	45	0	2	Lieut. J. J. Glasson	Decommissioned 1855.
SUPPLY	store-ship	1846	141	547	37	0	4	Lieut. A. Sinclair	Sold 1884.

The first three vessels were steamers; the others, three-masted, square-rigged ships.

Crew is full complement for each ship; probably not achieved in any case during the Japan Expedition. *Susquehanna, Mississippi, Plymouth*, and *Saratoga* made it to Japan in 1853. *Plymouth* did not go to Japan in 1854, but the squadron arrived 13 February, followed by *Saratoga* on 4 March, and *Supply* on the 15th. *Saratoga* departed 4 April carrying Commander Adams with the Kanagawa Treaty.

The Smithsonian Institution, Division of Naval History, has excellent models of *Mississippi* and *Powhatan*, a half model of *Saratoga*, and a painting of storeship *Supply*.

*Based on Morison "*Old Bruin*", page 356, with additions from Frank M. Bennett *The Steam Navy of the United States*. Pittsburgh, 1896, and Ships History Branch, Division of Naval History, Department of the Navy.

APPENDIX C

Officers and Chief Petty Officers of the Japan Expedition, 1852–1855
Prepared by Antha Eunice Card

Based on the list printed in the official *Narrative* II 410–14,
augmented by information from other sources.

Abbreviations

Act. Mast.: Acting Master; Act. Mast. M.: Acting Master's Mate.

C.S.N.: Confederate States Navy.

D.A.B.: *Dictionary of American Biography* has sketch of this officer.

Eng.: Engineer.

Flagship: This officer went with Commodore Perry on his successive flagships: *Mississippi, Susquehanna,* and *Powhatan.*

Lt. Comdg.: Lieutenant Commanding, equivalent to Lieutenant Commander.

Morison: See S. E. Morison, "*Old Bruin": the Biography of Commodore Matthew C. Perry USN.*

Narrative: The official *Narrative of the Expedition* (3 vols., Washington: 1856) contains reports by this officer in Vol. II.

P. Mid.: Passed Midshipman.

Name	Rank	Ship	Remarks
Abbot, Charles W.	Captain's Clerk	*Macedonian*	Son of Capt. Joel Abbot; sent home for misconduct; pay director 1871, ret. 1891.
Abbot, Joel	Captain	*Macedonian*	D.A.B.; Morison; Narrative, reports on Formosa, Manila, west coast of Japan; d. 14 Dec. 1855, at Hong Kong.
Adams, Henry A.	Commander	Flagship	Captain of the Fleet; Morison; Narrative; exchanged ratifications of Treaty; ret. as Commodore 1862; d. 1869.
Adams, Joseph H.	Lieutenant	*Powhatan*	Died at Macao 1853.
Adams, N. B.	Captain's Clerk	Flagship	Son of Cdr. H. A. Adams.
Alexander, George W.	2nd Asst. Eng.	*Mississippi*	Resigned 1861.
Allison, Richard T.	Purser	*Macedonian*	Dismissed 1861; Major in Confederate Marine Corps.
Allmand, Albert	P. Mid.	*Saratoga*	
Archbold, Samuel	Chief Eng.	*Susquehanna*	Engineer-in-chief 1857; resigned 1861.
Armstrong, William McN.	Midshipman	*Mississippi*	Went home in charge of sick, 1853; resigned 1854.
Arnold, Henry N. T.	P. Mid. & Act. Mast.	*Plymouth*	Commander 1865; ret. 1871; d. 1881.
Arnold, Le Roy	3rd Asst. Eng.	*Powhatan*	Resigned 1856.
Ashbury, ————	Act. Mast. M.	*Vandalia*	Probably asst. to Dr. Morrow.

Name	Rank	Ship	Remarks
Avery, Latham B.	Lieutenant	*Macedonian*	Dropped from rolls 1855.
Babbitt, Charles W.	Carpenter	*Plymouth*	Died 23 Sept. 1865.
Balch, George B.	Lieutenant	*Plymouth*	D.A.B.; Narrative, report on Bonin Is.; Rear Adm. 1878; sup't. Naval Academy 1879–81; C.inC. Pacific Sta., 1881–82; ret. 1883, d. 1908.
Barbot, Alphonse	Lieutenant	*Vandalia*	Surveyor; Lieut. C.S.N.
Barrand, John T.	Act. Mast.	S.S. *Queen*	Lieut. 1855, d. 1860.
Barry, Garrett R.	Purser	*Susquehanna*	Pay Director, ret. 1871, d. 1876.
Beardslee, Lester A.	Midshipman	*Plymouth*	Commodore 1894, Rear Adm. 1895, ret. 1898; visited Japan in 1900–01, d. 1903.
Bell, Edward B.	Boatswain	*Vandalia*	Died 1875.
Bell, Hamilton	Gunner	*Macedonian*	Deserted 1854.
Bennett, John W.	P. M. & Act. Mast.	*Susquehanna*	Lieutenant 1855; dismissed 1861·
Bent, Silas	Flag Lieutenant	Flagship	Morison; Narrative has journal and reports; letters in Rutgers Univ. Lib. Dismissed 1861.
Bibby, _____	Captain's Clerk	*Powhatan*	
Bierbower, J. H.	Act. Mast. M.	*Lexington*	
Bittinger, Edmund C.	Chaplain	*Susquehanna*	Morison; ret. 1881, d. 1889.
Blackford, George T.	Sailmaker	*Plymouth*	Dismissed 1861.
Boardman, Frederick A.	Midshipman	*Susquehanna*	Resigned 1856.
Boudinot, William E.	Lieutenant	*Powhatan*	Resigned 1858.
Boyle, Junius J.	Lt. Comdg.	*Southampton*	Morison; Narrative has report on Volcano Bay; d. 1870.
Brayton, W. S. L.	Sailmaker	*Vandalia*	Taken prisoner in Civil War, d. at Charleston 1864.
Breese, K. Randolph	P. Mid.	*Mississippi*	Captain 1874, d. 1881.
Brown, Eliphalet, Jr.	Act. Mast. M.	Flagship	Artist; Morison; Narrative. Acting Master, 1864; Admiral's Sec. Med. Squadron; ret. 1875, d. 1886.
Brown, John Hogan	Lieutenant	*Susquehanna*	Died 1861.
Buchanan, Franklin	Commander	*Susquehanna*	D.A.B.; Morison; Captain 1855; Rear Adm. C.S.N.; d. 1874.
Butler, John O.	Carpenter	*Powhatan*	Died 1862.
Butt, Thomas V.	Carpenter	*Vandalia*	Died 1857.
Caulk, John	Gunner	*Mississippi*	Died 1873.
City, Samuel G.	Gunner	*Powhatan*	Died 1860.
Clitz, John M. B.	Lieutenant	*Mississippi*	Rear Adm. 1880; ret. 1883, d. 1897.
Collins, John	Act. Boatswain	*Macedonian*	Dismissed 1859.
Colson, Amos	Boatswain	*Mississippi*	Died 1858.
Conover, Francis S.	P. Mid. & Act. Mast.	*Supply*	Act. Lieut. 1862; resigned 1863.
Contee, John	Flag Lieutenant	Flagship	Morison; Narrative, journal used.
Cooper, George H.	Lieutenant	*Susquehanna*	Rear Adm. 1881; ret. 1884, d. 1891.
Crosby, Eli	2nd Asst. Eng.	*Susquehanna*	Died at·Okinawa 1854.
Danby, Robert	1st Asst. Eng.	*Mississippi*	Chief Engineer 1856; ret. 1883, d. 1886.

Name	Rank	Ship	Remarks
Doran, Edward C.	Purser	*Plymouth*	Pay Director 1871; ret. 1882, d. 1883.
Draper, William B.	Act. Mast. M.	*Mississippi*	Mate 1852; resigned 1863.
Duer, John K.	Lieutenant	*Susquehanna*	Morison; d. 1859.
Eldredge, Joseph C.	Purser	*Powhatan*	Pay Director 1871, ret. 1880, d. 1881.
Enniston, Garrit V.	P. Mid. and Act. Mast.	*Vandalia*	Lieutenant 1855, d. 1858.
Fahs, Charles T.	Asst. Surgeon	*Susquehanna*	Morison; Narrative has reports on botany of Okinawa and exploration of Chichi Jima. Surgeon C.S.N.
Faron, John	2nd Asst. Eng.	*Powhatan*	Chief Engineer 1859; lost on *Tecumseh* 1864.
Fauth, Henry	3rd Asst. Eng.	*Powhatan*	2nd Asst. 1855; resigned 1856.
Fithian, Edwin	2nd Asst. Eng.	*Susquehanna*	Chief Engineer 1859; ret. 1882.
Fitzgerald, William B.	Lieutenant	*Supply*	Returned home sick 1853; Lieut. C.S.N.; d. 1862.
Frost, Charles T.	Sailmaker	*Macedonian*	Warranted 1851; lost in U.S.S. *Levant* 1860.
Fry, Joseph	P. Midshipman	*Supply*	Lieutenant 1855; Lieut. C.S.N.
Gambril, Amos G.	Surgeon	*Plymouth*	Died at Hong Kong 12 April 1854.
Gay, Jesse	Chief Engineer	*Mississippi*	Resigned 1859.
Gideon, George, Jr.	2nd Asst. Eng.	*Powhatan*	Chief Engineer 1859; d. 1863.
Gilliam, James S.	P. Asst. Surgeon	*Macedonian*	Lost in U.S.S. *Levant* 1860.
Gillis, John P.	Lieutenant	*Plymouth*	Captain 1862, ret. 1864, d. 1873.
Glasson, John J.	Lt. Comdg.	*Lexington*	Morison; ret. as Commodore 1867, d. 1882.
Glisson, Oliver S.	Lieutenant	*Powhatan*	Rear Adm. 1870, ret. 1870, d. 1890.
Goldsborough, John R.	Lieutenant	*Saratoga*	Commodore 1867, ret. 1870, d. 1877.
Gray, Charles	P. Midshipman	*Southampton*	Dropped from rolls 1855.
Gray, Edwin F.	P. Midshipman	*Plymouth*	Lieutenant 1855, resigned 1857.
Green, Daniel S.	Fleet Surgeon	*Mississippi*	Morison; report in Narrative on mineral spring, Hakodate; Surgeon C.S.N., d. 1864.
Green, John	Carpenter	*Susquehanna*	Died 1864.
Guest, John	Lieutenant	*Plymouth*	Morison; Commodore 1872, d. 1879.
Gwathmey, Washington	Lieutenant	*Macedonian*	Lieutenant C.S.N.
Haggerty, Francis S.	Lieutenant	*Powhatan*	Commander 1861, ret. as Captain 1867, d. 1899.
Hamilton, William H.	Gunner	*Saratoga*	Died 1865.
Harcourt, William	Gunner	*Plymouth*	Act. Master 1864; hon. discharged 1865.
Harris, Reuben	P. Mid. and Act. Mast.	*Susquehanna*	Morison; Lieut. 1855, d. 1857.
Harrison, Napoleon B.	Lieutenant	*Supply*	Captain 1868, d. 1870.
Harwood, James K.	Purser	*Vandalia*	Paymaster C.S.N.
Hawley, Charles E.	Midshipman	*Susquehanna*	Lieutenant 1856, ret. as Lt. Cdr. 1867, d. 1898.
Hayden, John C.	Boatswain	*Macedonian*	Dismissed 1857.

Name	Rank	Ship	Remarks
Hebard, George F.	1st Asst. Eng.	*Susquehanna*	Act. Chief Eng. 1864; hon. discharged 1866.
Heine, William	Act. Mast. M.	Flagship	Principal artist of the Expedition; Morison and Narrative; see Introduction to this volume.
Hibbert, Stephen D.	3rd Asst. Eng.	*Susquehanna*	Chief Eng. 1861, ret. 1889, d. 1897.
Holland, William	1st Asst. Eng.	*Mississippi*	Died 1856.
Houston, Thomas T.	P. Midshipman	*Southampton*	Lieutenant 1855; d. 1860.
Hunter, Thomas T.	Lieutenant	*Susquehanna*	Commander 1856; Commander C.S.N., captured 1865.
Jones, Daniel	Carpenter	*Macedonian*	Ret. 1869, d. 1877.
Jones, George	Chaplain	*Mississippi*	D.A.B.; Morison; journal and reports in Narrative, of which Vol. III is devoted to his study of zodiacal lights; d. 1870.
Jones, James H.	1st Lieut. USMC	*Macedonian*	Colonel 1879; d. 1880.
Jones, Walter F.	P. Midshipman	*Mississippi*	Died 1855.
Kell, John M.	Acting Master	*Mississippi*	Lieutenant 1855; Commander C.S.N.; in *Alabama* during fight with *Kearsarge*.
Kellogg, Mortimer	3rd Asst. Eng.	*Powhatan*	Chief Engineer 1851, d. 1870.
Kelly, John	Commander	*Plymouth*	Morison; ret. as Commodore 1862, d. 1863.
King, William H.	2nd Asst. Eng.	*Powhatan*	1st. Asst. Engineer 1853; d. 1859.
Lanier, Edmund	Lieutenant	*Mississippi*	Commander 1861, ret. as Captain 1867, d. 1872.
Lawrence, John C. E.	2nd Asst. Eng.	*Susquehanna*	Resigned 1856.
Lee, Sidney S.	Commander	*Mississippi*	Morison; Captain C.S.N.
Lewis, John R. C.	Act. Mast. Mate	*Vandalia*	Morison; diary in H. F. Graff ed., *Bluejackets with Perry in Japan*.
Lewis, Lawrence	Act. Mast. Mate	*Vandalia*	John's twin.
Logan, George T. W.	2nd Asst. Eng.	*Mississippi*	Dropped 1856.
Lowry, Henry M.	Carpenter	*Mississippi*	Died 1868.
Lowry, Reigart B.	Act. Master	*Powhatan*	Commodore 1880, d. 1880.
Lynah, Arthur M.	Asst. Surgeon	*Mississippi*	Morison; member of party that explored Okinawa.
Madigan, John	P. Mid. & Act. Mast.	*Saratoga*	Commander 1865, d. 1870.
March, J. Howard	Act. Master	*Mississippi*	Lieutenant 1855, d. 1858.
Mason, John T.	Surgeon	*Vandalia*	Surgeon C.S.N. 1861.
Matthews, John	Lieutenant	*Plymouth*	Morison; drowned in typhoon at Chichi Jima 1853.
Maury, William L.	Lt. Comdg.	Barque *Caprice* & *Mississippi*	Morison; surveys in *Mississippi*; Narrative; Commander C.S.N. 1861.
Maxwell, Charles D.	Surgeon	*Powhatan*	Medical Director 1871, d. 1890.
May, Robert L.	Midshipman	*Southampton*	Lieutenant Commander 1862, ret. 1866.
McCauley, Edward Y.	Act. Master	*Powhatan*	Morison; Rear Adm. 1885, ret. 1887, d. 1894; his *Diary* was published (1942).
McClenahan, _____	Captain's Clerk	*Southampton*	
McCluney, William J.	Captain	*Powhatan*	Morison; ret. 1861 as Commodore, d. 1864.

Name	Rank	Ship	Remarks
Mercer, John D.	3rd Asst. Engineer	*Mississippi*	Resigned 1856.
Messersmith, John S.	P. Asst. Surgeon	*Southampton*	Medical Director 1871, ret. 1872, d. 1891.
Minor, Robert D.	P. Midshipman	*Lexington*	Lieutenant 1855, 1st Lieut. C.S.N.; ms. journal of Expedition in Va. Hist. Soc.
Mish, Simon C.	Midshipman	*Mississippi*	Resigned 1856, Act. Lieut. 1861; dismissed 1861.
Morris, Charles M.	Lieutenant	*Mississippi*	1st. Lieut. C.S.N.; commanded C.S.S. *Florida* 1864–65.
Morrison, George F.	Midshipman	*Plymouth*	Master 1855; ret. as Lt. Cdr. 1867.
Morrow, James	Act. Mast. M.	*Vandalia* & Flagship	Morison; report on agriculture of Okinawa in Narrative; Surgeon C.S.A., d. 1865. A. B. Cole ed. his Diary as *A Scientist with Perry in Japan* (1947).
Moses, Leonard	Carpenter	*Saratoga*	Died 1857.
Nelson, William A.	P. Asst. Surgeon	*Lexington*	Surgeon 1854; resigned 1858.
Nicholson, James W. A.	Lieutenant	*Vandalia*	Commodore 1873; C.O. New York Navy Yard 1876–80; Rear Adm. 1881; ret. 1883, d. 1887.
Nicholson, Somerville	Lieutenant	*Powhatan*	Commodore 1880, ret. 1881.
Norris, Joseph P.	Captain's Clerk	*Plymouth*	
Ochiltree, David	Act. Mast.	*Mississippi*	Master 1855; dropped 1855.
Oliver, Charles B.	Gunner	*Susquehanna*	Gunner and Lieutenant C.S.N.
Otis, Jenks H.	Asst. Surgeon	*Plymouth*	Surgeon 1861, d. 1864.
Parker, George	Sailmaker	*Powhatan*	Died 1857.
Pegram, Robert B.	Lieutenant	*Powhatan*	Lieutenant C.S.N.
Perry, Matthew C.	Commodore	Flagship	D.A.B.; Morison; Narrative; d. 1858.
Perry, Oliver H. II	Secretary	Flagship	Morison; U.S. Consul Hong Kong 1855, d. 1870.
Pope, John S.	Commander	*Vandalia*	Morison; Captain 1855, ret. as Commodore 1862, d. 1876.
Portman, Antón L. C.	Commodore's Clerk	Flagship	Morison; Dutch interpreter hired in Shanghai.
Preble, George H.	Lieutenant	*Macedonian*	Morison; survey and sailing directions for Kelung in Narrative; Rear Adm. 1876, ret. 1878, d. 1885. B. Szczesniak ed. his diary of Expedition (1962); wrote *Our Flag* (1872) and other books and articles.
Randall, _____	Act. Mast. Mate	*Vandalia*	Probably an asst. to Dr. Morrow.
Randolph, John B.	Lieutenant	*Susquehanna*	Returned home sick 1854, and died.
Read, Jacob	1st. Lieut. USMC	*Vandalia*	Captain Confed. Marine Corps; dismissed 1863.
Robie, Edward D.	3rd Asst. Eng.	*Mississippi*	Chief Engineer 1861; ret. 1893.
Rochelle, James H.	P. Midshipman	*Southampton*	Lieutenant 1855; dismissed 1861; 1st Lieut. C.S.N. 1861.
Rootes, Thomas R.	Lieutenant	*Vandalia*	Commander 1855; dismissed 1861; Commander C.S.N., surrendered 1865.

Name	Rank	Ship	Remarks
Rutherford, William H.	2nd Asst. Engineer	*Mississippi*	Morison; letters in Lib. Congress; Chief Engineer 1861; ret. 1874, d. 1898.
Scott, Robert W.	P. Midshipman	*Saratoga*	Lt. Comdr. 1862; d. 1866.
Sewall, John S.	Captain's Clerk	*Saratoga*	Morison; became Congregational minister; pub. *Logbook of the Captain's Clerk* (1906), d. 1911.
Sewell, George	Chief Engineer	*Powhatan*	Retired 1885, d. 1895.
Shirk, James W.	Midshipman	*Mississippi*	Commander 1866, d. 1873.
Shock, Thomas A.	3rd Asst. Eng.	*Susquehanna*	Chief Engineer 1860, d. 1873.
Shriver, Albert	Asst. Surgeon	*Powhatan*	Surgeon 1861, ret. 1868, d. 1873.
Sinclair, Arthur	Lt. Comdg.	*Supply*	Morison; Commander 1855; Commander C.S.N.; drowned in foundering of blockade runner *Leila* 1865.
Sinclair, Arthur Jr.	Captain's Clerk	*Supply*	Lieutenant C.S.N., in *Alabama.*
Slack, William B.	Captain USMC	*Mississippi*	Major 1860, ret. 1885, d. 1895.
Sloane, ————	Act. Master's Mate	*Vandalia*	See Randall.
Smith, Charles.	Boatswain	*Saratoga*	Dismissed 1853.
Smith, Thomas L.	Fleet Surgeon	*Susquehanna*	Medical Director 1871; d. 1891.
Smith, William	Boatswain	*Plymouth*	Boatswain C.S.N. 1861; in 1862 asked to be reinstated in U.S.N.
Spalding, J. W.	Captain's Clerk	*Mississippi*	Morison; wrote *My Voyage Around the World* (1855).
Speiden, William	Purser	*Mississippi*	Died 1861.
Sproston, John G.	P. Midshipman	*Macedonian*	Morison; Lieutenant 1855, d. 1862. *Private Journal* ed. by Shio Sakanishi (Tokyo: 1940).
Stamm, William S.	3rd Asst. Eng.	*Powhatan*	Chief Engineer 1861; retired 1887, d. 1897.
Stanton, Oscar F.	Midshipman	*Plymouth*	Commodore 1891; commanded N. Atlantic Squadron 1894, Rear Adm. 1894; retired 1894, d. 1924.
Steele, Thomas B.	Asst. Surgeon	*Saratoga*	Surgeon 1860; resigned 1861.
Stevens, George A.	P. Mid. and Act. Mast.	*Southampton*	Captain 1882, ret. 1883, d. 1892.
Stevens, Jacob	Sailmaker	*Mississippi*	
Stewart, Henry H.	1st Asst. Eng.	*Susquehanna*	Chief Engineer 1858, retired 1885, d. 1893.
Stocker, Henry T.	Sailmaker	*Saratoga*	Retired 1884, d. 1897.
Stockton, Edward C.	Midshipman	*Plymouth*	Lieutenant 1857; dismissed 1858. 1st. Lieut. Confed. Marine Corps.
Tansill, Robert	Captain USMC	*Powhatan*	Capt. Confed. Marine Corps 1862 and later C.S.A.; taken prisoner and exchanged.
Taylor, Alfred	Lt. Comdg.	S.S. *Queen*	Ret. as Rear Adm. 1872, d. 1891.
Taylor, Bayard	Civilian, joined at Hong Kong.	Flagship	D.A.B.; Morison; report on Peel I. in Narrative; wrote *Visit to India, China and Japan* (1855) and many other works; d. 1878.
Upshur, John H.	P. Midshipman	*Supply*	D.A.B.; Morison; Rear Adm. 1884, retired 1885, d. 1917.
Vreeland, Benjamin	Asst. Surgeon	*Vandalia*	Surgeon 1861; d. 1866.
Wager, Peter	P. Midshipman	*Lexington*	Master 1855; dropped from rolls 1855.

Name	Rank	Ship	Remarks
Walcutt, John	P. Mid & Act. Mast.	*Macedonian*	Master 1855; dropped from rolls 1855.
Walker, William S.	Commander	*Saratoga*	Captain 1855, Commodore retired 1862, d. 1863.
Watters, John	P. Midshipman	*Macedonian*	Commander 1866; d. 1874.
Wayne, William A.	Lieutenant	*Saratoga*	1st Lieutenant C.S.N.; d. 1863.
Webb, William A.	Lieutenant	*Mississippi*	Commander C.S.N.; captured and paroled, 1864.
Wheeler, _____	Act. Mast. M.	*Vandalia*	See Randall.
Wheelwright, Charles W.	P. Asst. Surgeon	*Powhatan*	Morison; Surgeon 1853, returned home in *Plymouth*, d. 1862. Hildegard B. Forbes ed. his *Correspondence* (privately printed 1958).
Whipple, John P.	1st. Asst. Eng.	S.S. *Queen*	Chief Engineer 1855; d. 1864.
Whiting, William	Boatswain	*Powhatan*	Died 1855.
Whiting, William B.	Lieutenant	*Vandalia*	Surveyor; nautical remarks in Narrative; Commo. Retired 1872, d. 1883.
Whittlesey, _____	Captain's Clerk	*Vandalia*	See Randall.
Wilkins, John	Gunner	*Vandalia*	Dismissed 1853.
Williams, John	Act. Mast. Mate	*Powhatan*	Morison; telegrapher; d. at Hong Kong, buried at Macao.
Williams, Lewis J.	P. Asst. Surgeon	*Mississippi*	Medical Director 1871; ret. 1881, d. 1888.
Williams, Samuel Wells	Chief Interpreter	*Susquehanna* or Flagship	D.A.B.; Morison; reports in Narrative; Prof. Chinese at Yale; d. 1884. *Journal* pub. in *Transactions* Asiatic Soc. of Japan (1910).
Winder, Edward L.	Lieutenant	*Macedonian*	Returned home sick, 1854; 1st Lieut. C.S.N.
Woodworth, Robert	Surgeon	*Macedonian*	Retired 1857, d. 1870.
Zeilin, Jacob	Major USMC	*Mississippi*	D.A.B.; Morison; Brig. Gen. Comdt. 1867, ret. 1876, d. 1880.

APPENDIX D

List of American Presents brought ashore in Japan, 13 March 1854[1]

For the Emperor:

Miniature steam engine, ¼ size, with track, tender, and car.
2 telegraph sets, with batteries, three miles of wire, gutta percha wire, and insulators.
1 Francis' copper lifeboat.
1 surfboat of copper.
Collection of agricultural implements.
Audubon's Birds, in nine vols.
Natural History of the State of New York, 16 vols.
Annals of Congress, 4 vols.
Laws and Documents of the State of New York.
Journal of the Senate and Assembly of New York.
Lighthouse Reports, 2 vols.
Bancroft's History of the United States, 4 vols.
Farmers' Guide, 2 vols.
1 series of United States Coast Survey Charts.
Morris *Engineering*.
Silver-topped dressing case.
8 yards scarlet broadcloth, and scarlet velvet.
Series of United States standard yard, gallon, bushel, balances and weights.
Quarter cask of Madeira.
Barrel of whiskey.
Box of champagne and cherry cordial and maraschino.
3 boxes of fine tea.
Maps of several states and four large lithographs.
Telescope and stand, in box.
Sheet-iron stove.
An assortment of fine perfumery.
5 Hall rifles.
3 Maynard muskets.
12 cavalry swords.
6 artillery swords.
1 carbine.
20 Army pistols in a box.
Catalogue of New York State Library and of Postoffices.
2 mail bags with padlocks.

For the Empress:

Flowered silk embroidered dress.   Toilet dressing-box gilded.   6 dozen assorted perfumery.

For Commissioner Hayashi:

Audubon's *Quadrupeds*.
4 yards scarlet broadcloth.
Clock.
Stove.
Rifle.
Set of Chinaware.
Teaset.
Revolver and powder.
2 dozen assorted perfumery.
20 gallons of whiskey.
1 sword.
3 boxes fine tea.
1 box of champagne.
1 box of finer tea.

For Abe, prince of Ise, first councilor:

1 copper lifeboat.
Kendall *War in Mexico* and Ripley *History of the War in Mexico*.
1 box of champagne.
3 boxes fine tea.
20 gallons whiskey.
1 clock.
1 stove.
1 rifle.
1 sword.
1 revolver and powder.
2 dozen assorted perfumery.
4 yards scarlet broadcloth.

For each of the other five councilors:

1 book.[2]
10 gallons of whiskey.
1 lithograph.
1 clock.
1 revolver.
1 rifle.
1 sword.
12 assorted perfumery.

1. Derived from *Powhatan* log and S. Wells Williams "A Journal of the Perry Expedition to Japan," Asiatic Society of Japan *Transactions*, XXXVII (1910), pages 131–34.
2. The books thus distributed were Lossing *Field Book of Revolution*, Owen *Architecture*, *Documentary History of New York*, Downing *Country Houses*, and Owen *Geology of Minnesota*.

For Ido, prince of Tsushima, second commissioner:

Appleton's *Dictionary*
9 assorted perfumery.
Lithograph of New Orleans.
5 gallons whiskey.

1 box of tea.
1 clock.
1 revolver.

1 rifle.
1 sword.
1 box of cherry cordial.

For Izawa, prince of Mimasaki, third commissioner:

Model of lifeboat.
View of steamer *Atlantic*.
5 gallons whiskey.
1 rifle.

1 revolver.
1 clock.
1 sword.
9 assorted perfumery.

Box of cherry cordial.
Small box of tea.
Brass howitzer and carriages.

For Udono, fourth commissioner:

List of post-offices.
Box of tea.
Lithograph of elephant.

9 assorted perfumery.
1 rifle.
1 revolver.
1 clock.

5 gallons whiskey.
1 sword.
Box of cherry cordial.

For Michitaro Matsuzaki, fifth commissioner:

Lithograph of a steamer.
1 revolver.
6 assorted perfumery.

1 clock.
1 sword.
5 gallons whiskey.

Box of tea.
Box of cherry cordial.

*In addition there was a quantity of tools, agricultural equipment,
and seeds for general distribution.*

Appleton's *Cyclopaedia of American Biography*. New York City. 1887–89.

Bakumatsu Gaikoku Kankei Monjo. Volume 1.

Beechey, Capt. (RN) Sir Frederick William. *Voyage to the Pacific*. London, 1831.

Beirne, F. F. *War of 1812*. New York: E. P. Dutton, 1949.

Belcher, Sir Captain Edward. *Voyage of the* Samarang. London, 1848.

Broughton, Captain W. R. *Voyage to the North Pacific Ocean*. London, 1804.

Brydone, Patrick. *A Tour Through Sicily and Malta*. 1774.

Bukan, Kaei 7 (Samurai Directory, 1854).

The Chinese Repository. 20 volumes, May 1832–December 1851. Canton, etc.

Cholmondeley, L. B. *History of the Bonin Islands*. London, 1915.

Davis, Sir John Francis. *China, During the War and Since the Peace*. London: Longman, Brown, Green, and Longmans, 1852.

Findlay, Alexander G. *Directory of the Pacific Ocean*. London: R. H. Laurie, 1851.

Golovnin, Vasili M. *Memoirs of a Captivity in Japan*. London, 1824.

Hakluyt, Richard. *Collection of Voyages*. London, 1811.

Hall, Captain Basil. *Voyage of Discovery to the West Coast of Korea and the Great Loo-Choo Island*. Philadelphia, 1818.

Heine, William. *Graphic Scenes of the Japan Expedition*. New York: G. P. Putnam & Company, 1856.

Higa, Shuncho. *Okinawa no Rekishi* [History of Okinawa]. Naha, Okinawa: Taimusu Sha, 1960.

Hokama, Seisho (editor). *Commodore Perry's Visit to Okinawa*. Tokyo: Kenkyusha Publishing K.K., 1962.

Horsburgh, James. *Memoirs: Comprising the Navigation to and from China . . . etc.* London, 1805.

Hummel, Arthur W. *Eminent Chinese of the Ch'ing Period (1644–1912)*. Volume 2. Government Printing Office, 1944.

Kaempfer, Engelbertus. *The History of Japan*. 2 volumes. London, 1727.

Kanda, Seiki (translator). *Peruri Teitoku Ryukyu Homon Ki* [Record of Commodore Perry's Visit to the Ryukyus]. Kitsuki-machi, Oita-ken, 1926.

Klaproth, J. *San Kokf Tsou Ran To Sets* [Sankoku Tsuran Tosetsu]; *Ou Apercu Général des Trois Royaumes* [A General View of the Three Kingdoms]. [Accompanying plates and maps separately bound.] Paris, 1832.

Kojima, Matajiro. *Commodore Perry's Expedition to Hakodate*. Hakodate: The Hakodate Kyodo Bunkai, 1953.

Krusenstern, Adam Johann von. *Voyage Around the World*. London, 1813.

Lettres édifiantes et curieuses concernant l'Asie l'Afrique et l'Amérique . . . (Publiées sous la direction de M. L. Aimé-Martin.) 4 volumes. Paris: A. Desrez, etc., 1838–43.

Logs of ships in United States East India Squadron. National Archives.

MacLeod, Dr. J. *Voyage in His Majesty's Ship* Alceste. London, 1817.

Majikina, Yasuoki, and Shimakura, Ryuji. *Okinawa issen-nenshi* [1000-year History of Okinawa]. Fukuoka: Okinawa Shin Mimpo Sha, 1952.

Martin, R. Montgomery. "China: Political, Commercial, and Social." *In An Official Report to Her Majesty's Government*. London: J. Madden, 1847.

Mitchell, James L. *COLT*. Harrisburg, Pennsylvania: The Stackpol Company, 1959.

Morison, Samuel Eliot. *"Old Bruin," Commodore Matthew C. Perry, 1794–1858*. Boston, Toronto: Little, Brown and Company, 1967.

National Cyclopedia of American Biography. New York: James P. White, 1892–

Perry, M. C. *Narrative of the Expedition of an American Squadron to the China Seas and Japan, performed in the years 1852, 1853, and 1854, under the Command of Commodore M. C. Perry, United States Navy, by Order of the Government of the United States. Compiled from the Original Notes and Journals of Commodore Perry and his Officers, at his request, and under his supervision, by Francis L. Hawks, D.D., L.L.D.* (Published by Order of the Congress of the United States.) 3 quarto volumes. Washington, D.C.: Beverly Tucker, Senate Printer, 1856. [Volumes II and III actually appeared in 1857–58.]

Piddington, Henry. *The Horn-Book of Storms for the India and China Seas.* 2nd edition. London: Bishop's College Press, 1845.

Preble, Rear Admiral George Henry. *The Opening of Japan.* Edited by Boleslaw Szczesniak. Norman: University of Oklahoma Press, 1962.

Raffles, Sophia (Hull), Lady. *Memoir of the Life and Public Services of Sir Thomas Stamford Raffles, F.R.S. etc.* London: John Murray, 1830.

Ruschenberger, William Samuel Waithman. *A Voyage Round the World; Including an Embassy to Muscat and Siam in 1835, 1836, and 1837.* Philadelphia: Carey, Lea & Blanchard, 1838.

Sansom, Sir George B. *The Western World and Japan.* New York: Alfred A. Knopf, 1950.

Shimabukuro, Gen'ichro. *Densetsu hoi Okinawa rekishi* [History of Okinawa based on Tradition and Additional Supplements]. Naha, Okinawa: Shoseki K.K., 1952.

Shimakura, Ryuji. See Majikina, Yasuoki.

Smith, The Reverend George A. *Narrative of an Exploratory Visit to Each of the Consular Cities of China . . . in Behalf of the Church Missionary Society, in the years 1844, 1845, 1846.* London: Seeley, Burnside & Seeley, etc., 1847.

Speiden, William, Jr. *Journal of a Cruise in the U.S. Steam Frigate* Mississippi [9 March 1852–16 January 1855]. Unpublished manuscript, Naval Historical Foundation, Washington, D.C. [A manuscript journal in two volumes by a young clerk to the purser in Commodore Perry's flagship on the Japan Expedition.]

Szczesniak, Boleslaw, *see* Preble.

Tamaki, Hajime. See: Tsuchiya, Takao.

Thunberg, Charles Peter. *Travels in Europe, Africa, and Asia.* Volume III: Containing a Voyage to Japan and Travel in Different Parts of that Empire in the years 1775 and 1776. 3rd edition. London, 1795.

Tiffany, Osmond. *The Canton Chinese; or The American Sojourn in the Celestial Empire.* Boston and Cambridge: J. Munroe and Company, 1849.

Tsuchiya, Takao and Hajime Tamaki (joint translators). *Peruri Teitoku Nihon ensei ki* [Commodore Perry's Expedition to Japan]. Tokyo: Iwanami Shoten, 1948.

Valentiun, François. *Oud en nieuw Oost-Indien . . .* Amsterdam, 1724–26.

Von Siebold, Dr. P. F. *Nippon.* London, 1817.

Wildes, Harry Emerson. *Aliens in the East.* Philadelphia: University of Pennsylvania Press, 1937.

William, Samuel Wells. *The Middle Kingdom; A Survey of the . . . Chinese Empire and Its Inhabitants.* New York & London: Wiley & Putnam, 1848.

———. "A Journal of the Perry Expedition to Japan," Asiatic Society of Japan *Transactions,* XXXVII (1910), pages 1–261.